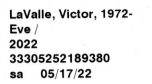

VICTOR LaVALLE

eve
™

JO MI-GYEONG   BRITTANY PEER

Published by

BOOM!™
S T U D I O S

LOGO DESIGNER
SCOTT NEWMAN

SERIES DESIGNER
MADISON GOYETTE

COLLECTION DESIGNER
MICHELLE ANKLEY

SPECIAL THANKS
AMANDA LAFRANCO

ASSISTANT EDITOR
RAMIRO PORTNOY

EDITOR
ELIZABETH BREI

SENIOR EDITOR
ERIC HARBURN

BOOM! Studios, 5670 Wilshire Boulevard, Suite 450, Los Angeles, CA 90036-5679.

Printed in China. First Printing.

ISBN: 978-1-68415-808-9, eISBN: 978-1-64668-441-0

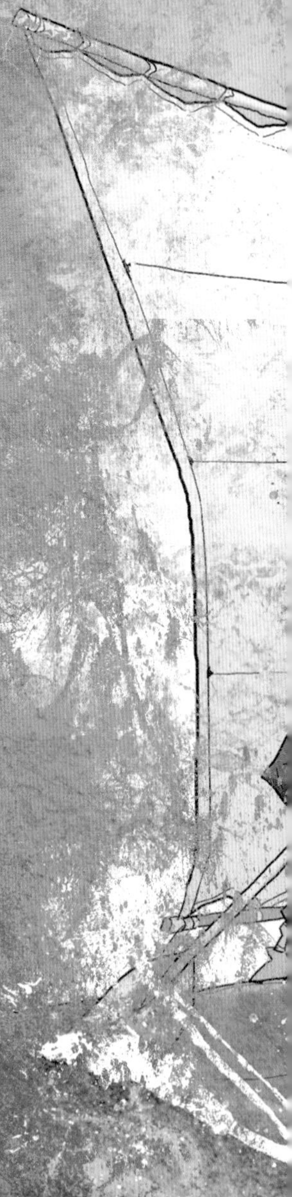

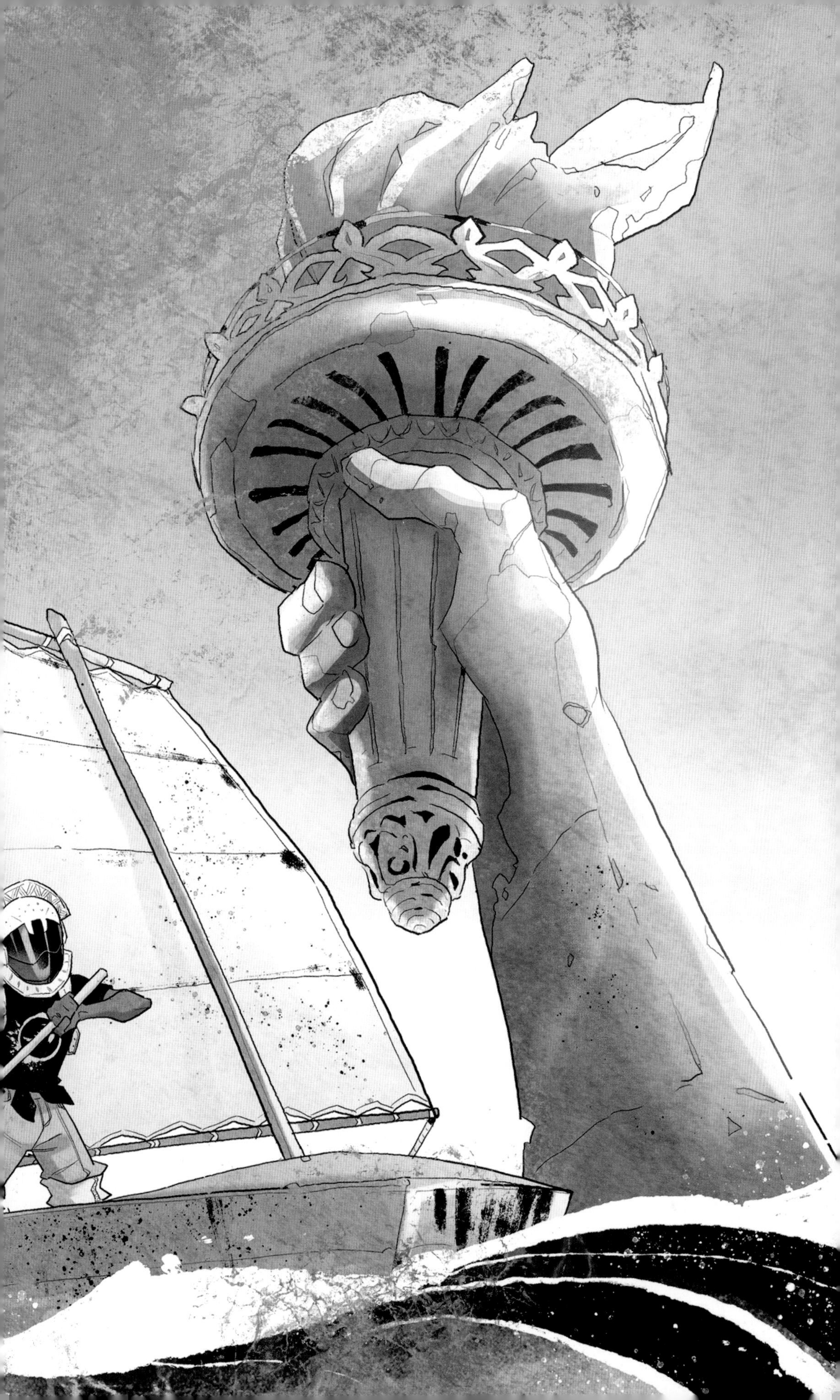

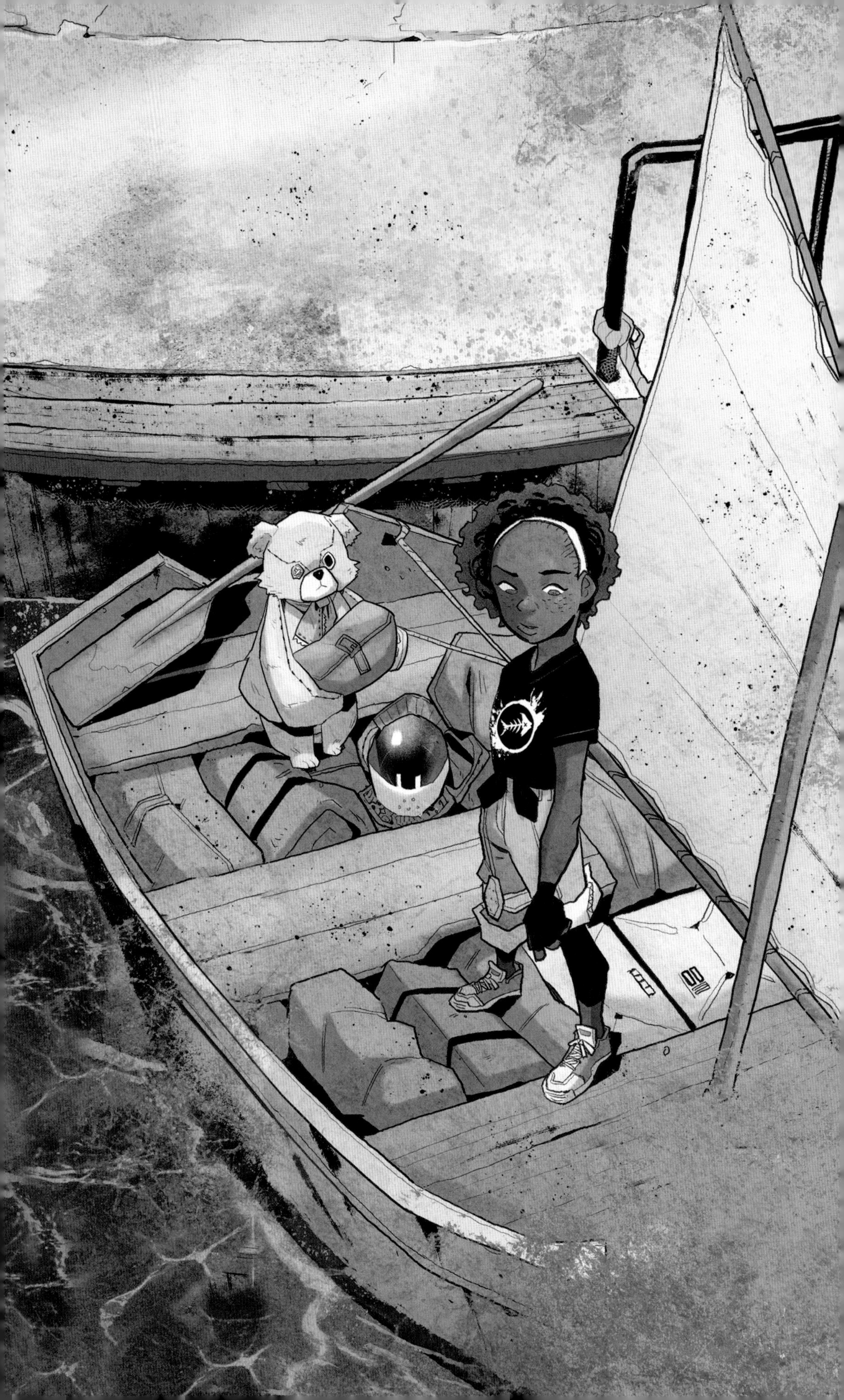

WRITTEN BY

VICTOR LaVALLE

ILLUSTRATED BY

JO MI-GYEONG

COLORED BY

BRITTANY PEER

LETTERED BY

ANDWORLD DESIGN

COVER BY

ARIO ANINDITO
WITH COLORS BY **PIERLUIGI CASOLINO**

eve™

CREATED BY

VICTOR LaVALLE & JO MI-GYEONG

CHAPTER
ONE

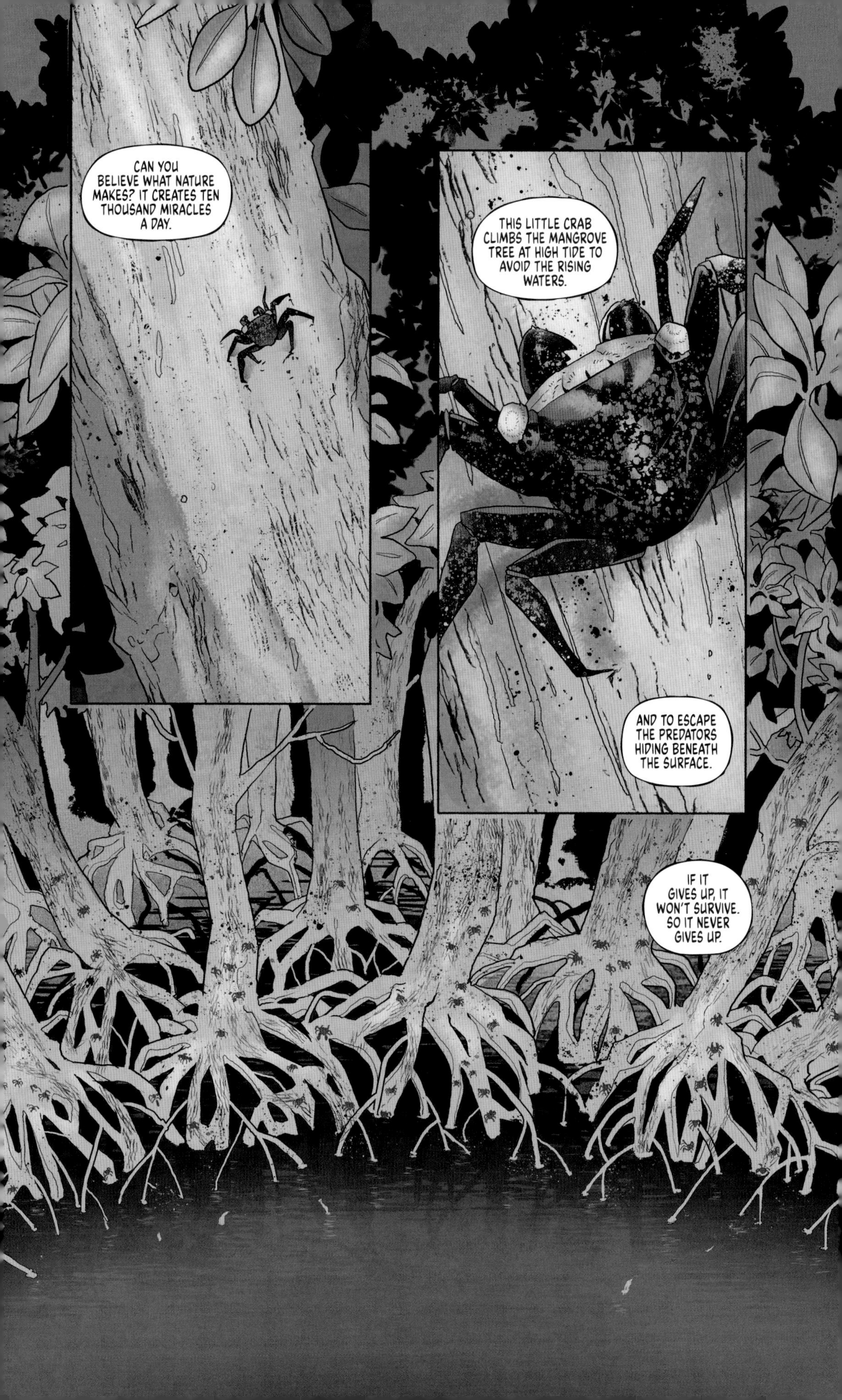
CAN YOU BELIEVE WHAT NATURE MAKES? IT CREATES TEN THOUSAND MIRACLES A DAY.
THIS LITTLE CRAB CLIMBS THE MANGROVE TREE AT HIGH TIDE TO AVOID THE RISING WATERS.
AND TO ESCAPE THE PREDATORS HIDING BENEATH THE SURFACE.
IF IT GIVES UP, IT WON'T SURVIVE. SO IT NEVER GIVES UP.

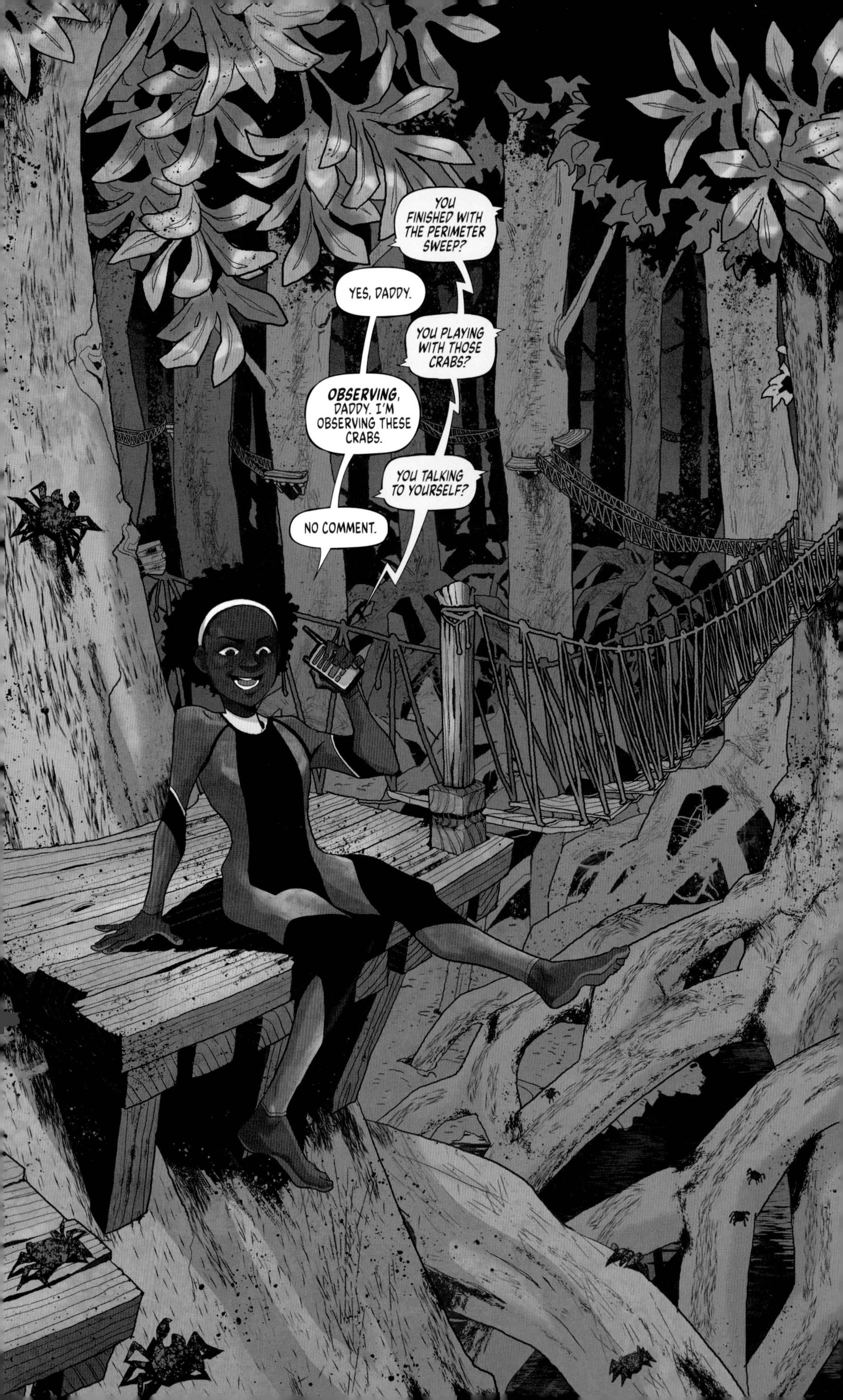
YOU FINISHED WITH THE PERIMETER SWEEP?
YES, DADDY.
YOU PLAYING WITH THOSE CRABS?
OBSERVING, DADDY. I'M OBSERVING THESE CRABS.
YOU TALKING TO YOURSELF?
NO COMMENT.

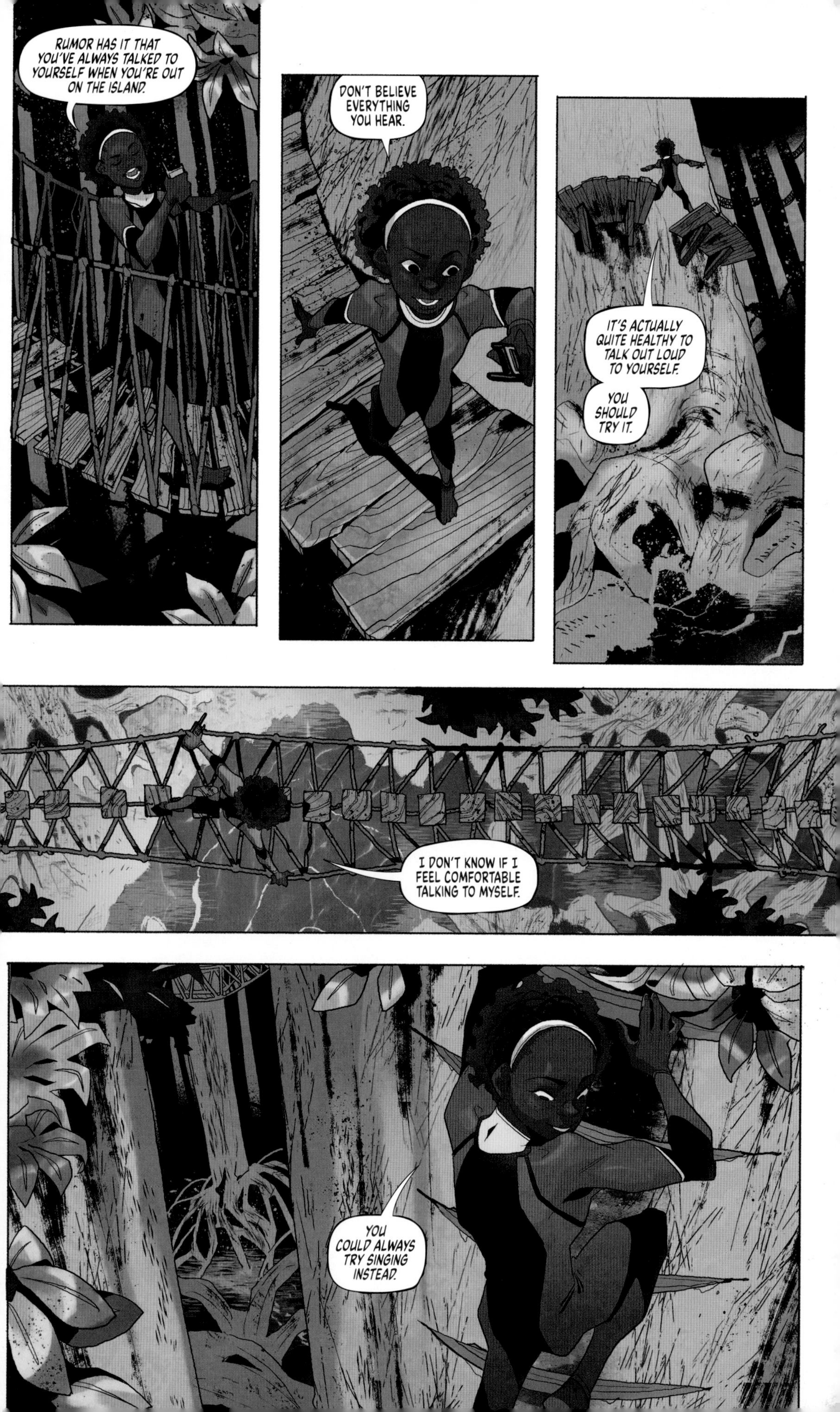
RUMOR HAS IT THAT YOU'VE ALWAYS TALKED TO YOURSELF WHEN YOU'RE OUT ON THE ISLAND.
DON'T BELIEVE EVERYTHING YOU HEAR.
IT'S ACTUALLY QUITE HEALTHY TO TALK OUT LOUD TO YOURSELF.
YOU SHOULD TRY IT.
I DON'T KNOW IF I FEEL COMFORTABLE TALKING TO MYSELF.
YOU COULD ALWAYS TRY SINGING INSTEAD.

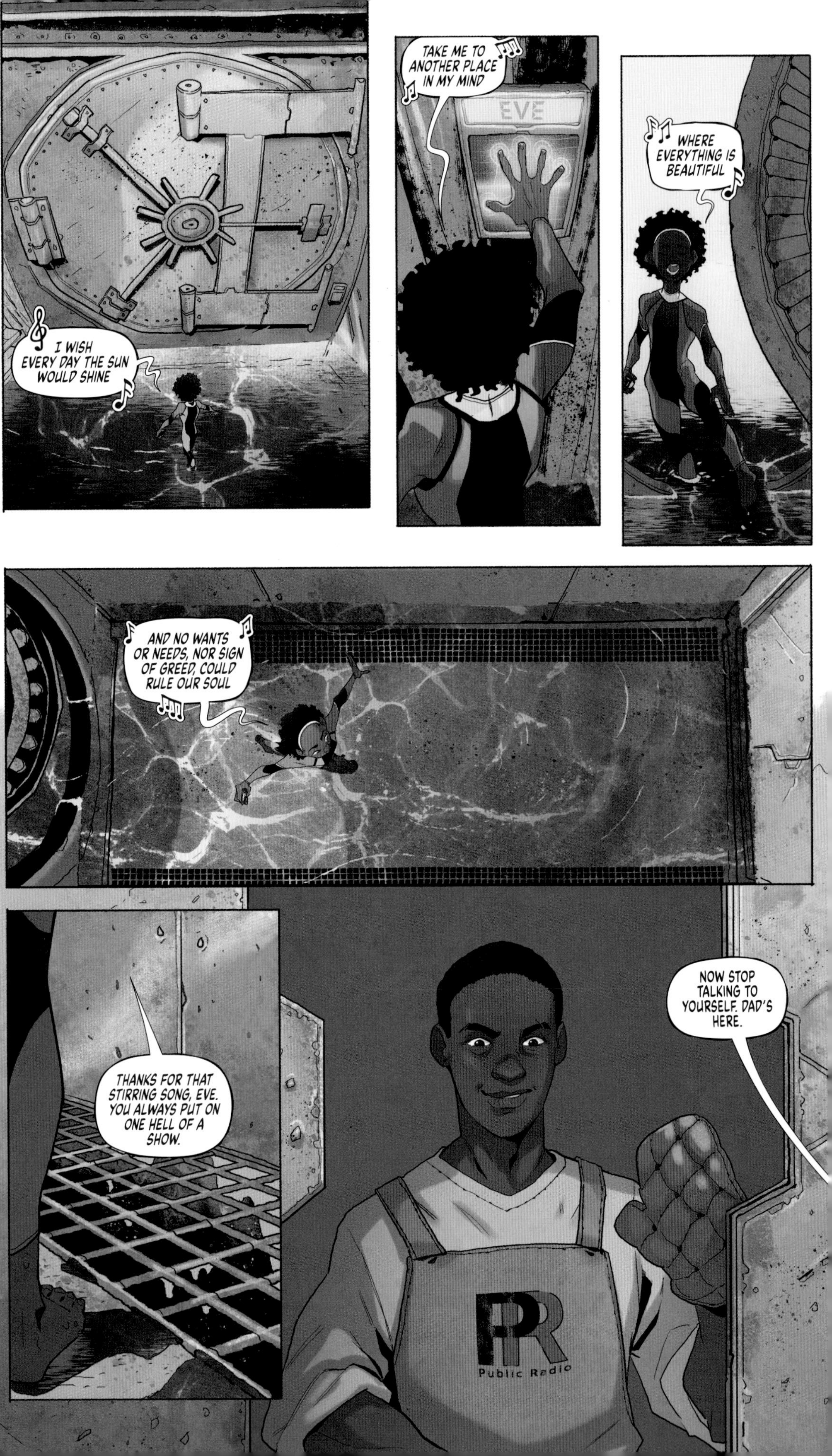
I WISH EVERY DAY THE SUN WOULD SHINE
TAKE ME TO ANOTHER PLACE IN MY MIND
EVE
WHERE EVERYTHING IS BEAUTIFUL
AND NO WANTS OR NEEDS, NOR SIGN OF GREED, COULD RULE OUR SOUL
THANKS FOR THAT STIRRING SONG, EVE. YOU ALWAYS PUT ON ONE HELL OF A SHOW.
NOW STOP TALKING TO YOURSELF. DAD'S HERE.
PR
Public Radio

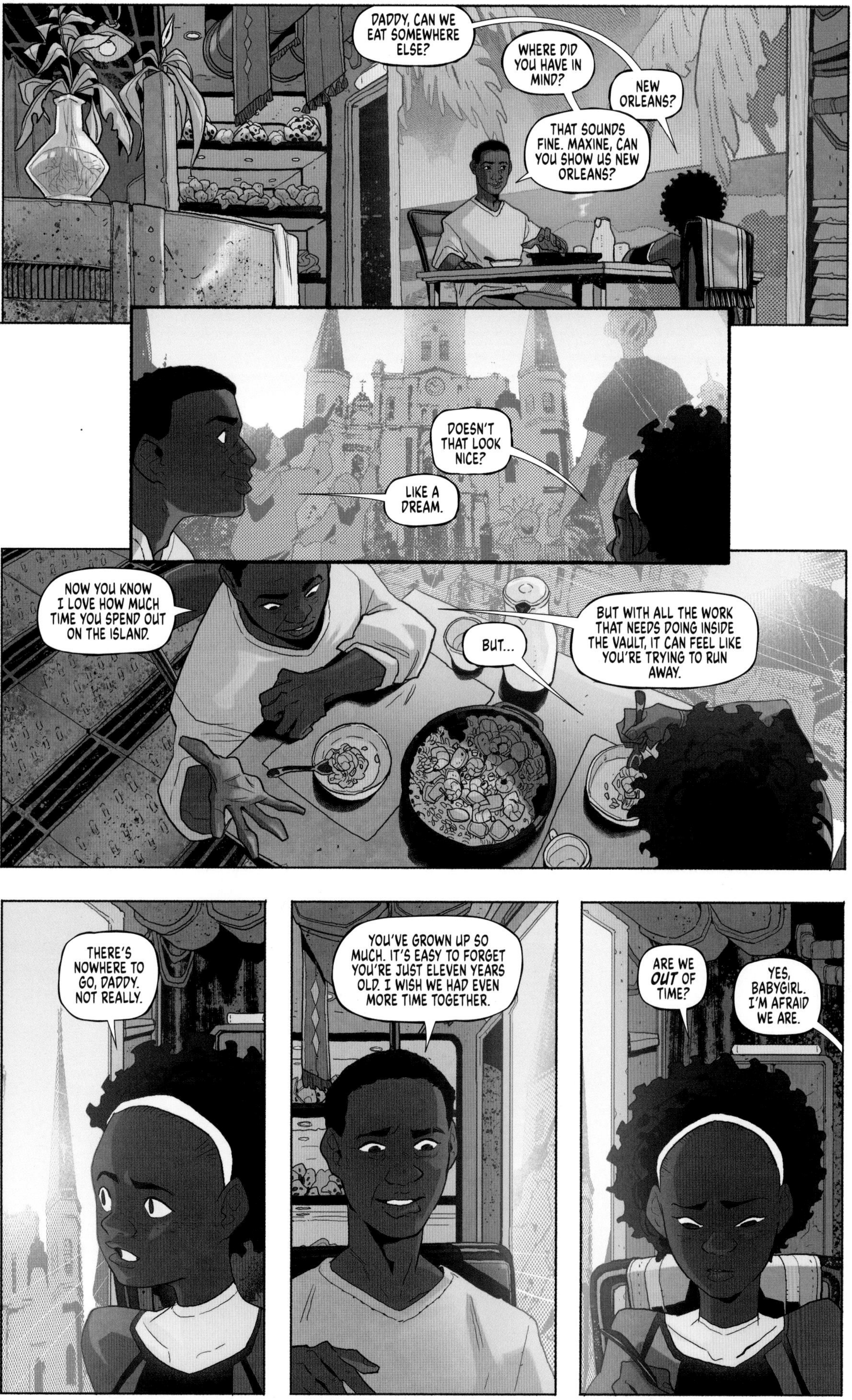
DADDY, CAN WE EAT SOMEWHERE ELSE?
WHERE DID YOU HAVE IN MIND?
NEW ORLEANS?
THAT SOUNDS FINE. MAXINE, CAN YOU SHOW US NEW ORLEANS?
DOESN'T THAT LOOK NICE?
LIKE A DREAM.
NOW YOU KNOW I LOVE HOW MUCH TIME YOU SPEND OUT ON THE ISLAND.
BUT...
BUT WITH ALL THE WORK THAT NEEDS DOING INSIDE THE VAULT, IT CAN FEEL LIKE YOU'RE TRYING TO RUN AWAY.
THERE'S NOWHERE TO GO, DADDY. NOT REALLY.
YOU'VE GROWN UP SO MUCH. IT'S EASY TO FORGET YOU'RE JUST ELEVEN YEARS OLD. I WISH WE HAD EVEN MORE TIME TOGETHER.
ARE WE *OUT* OF TIME?
YES, BABYGIRL. I'M AFRAID WE ARE.

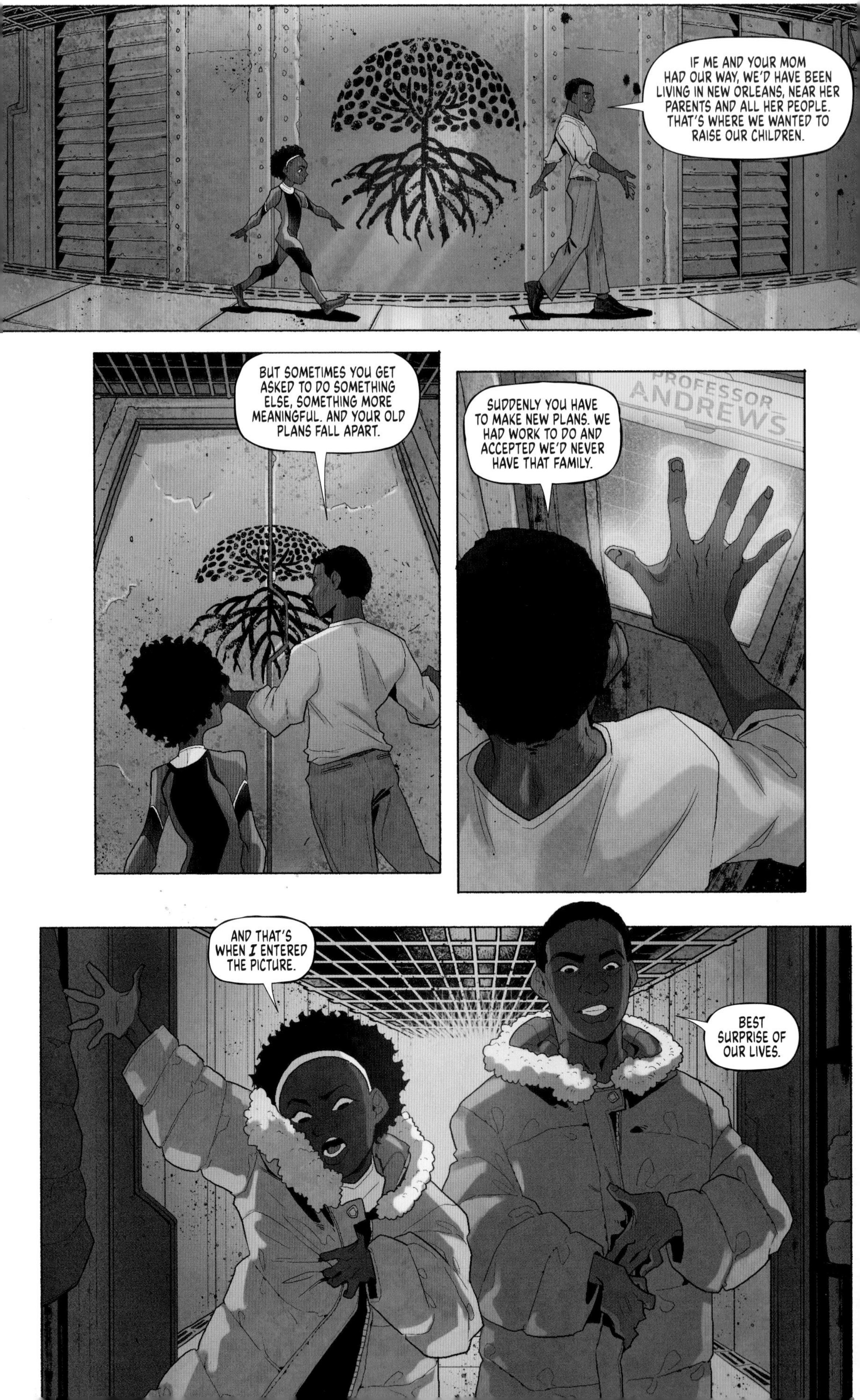
IF ME AND YOUR MOM HAD OUR WAY, WE'D HAVE BEEN LIVING IN NEW ORLEANS, NEAR HER PARENTS AND ALL HER PEOPLE. THAT'S WHERE WE WANTED TO RAISE OUR CHILDREN.
BUT SOMETIMES YOU GET ASKED TO DO SOMETHING ELSE, SOMETHING MORE MEANINGFUL. AND YOUR OLD PLANS FALL APART.
PROFESSOR ANDREWS
SUDDENLY YOU HAVE TO MAKE NEW PLANS. WE HAD WORK TO DO AND ACCEPTED WE'D NEVER HAVE THAT FAMILY.
AND THAT'S WHEN I ENTERED THE PICTURE.
BEST SURPRISE OF OUR LIVES.

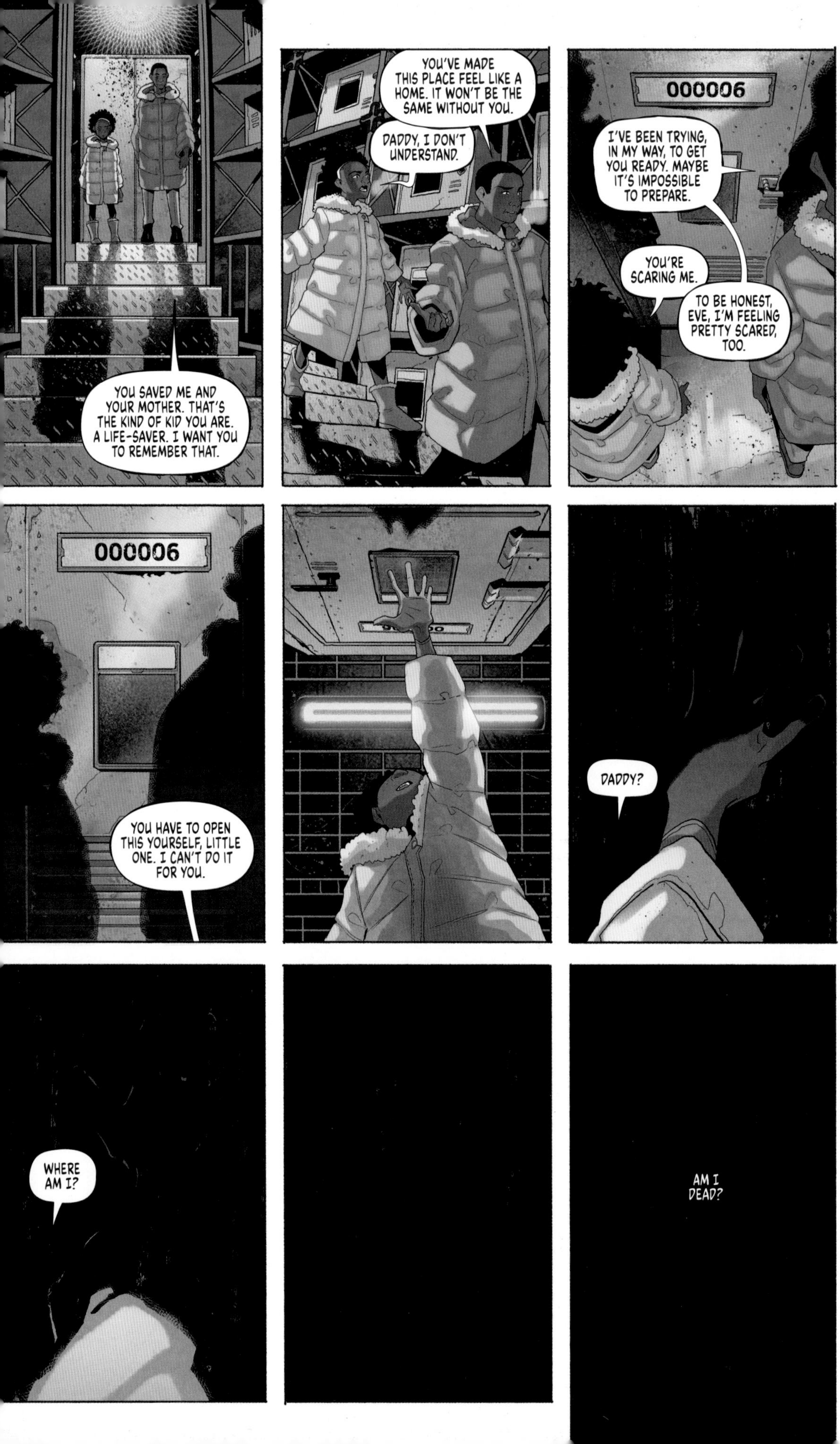
YOU SAVED ME AND YOUR MOTHER. THAT'S THE KIND OF KID YOU ARE. A LIFE-SAVER. I WANT YOU TO REMEMBER THAT.
YOU'VE MADE THIS PLACE FEEL LIKE A HOME. IT WON'T BE THE SAME WITHOUT YOU.
DADDY, I DON'T UNDERSTAND.
000006
I'VE BEEN TRYING, IN MY WAY, TO GET YOU READY. MAYBE IT'S IMPOSSIBLE TO PREPARE.
YOU'RE SCARING ME.
TO BE HONEST, EVE, I'M FEELING PRETTY SCARED, TOO.
000006
YOU HAVE TO OPEN THIS YOURSELF, LITTLE ONE. I CAN'T DO IT FOR YOU.
DADDY?
WHERE AM I?
AM I DEAD?

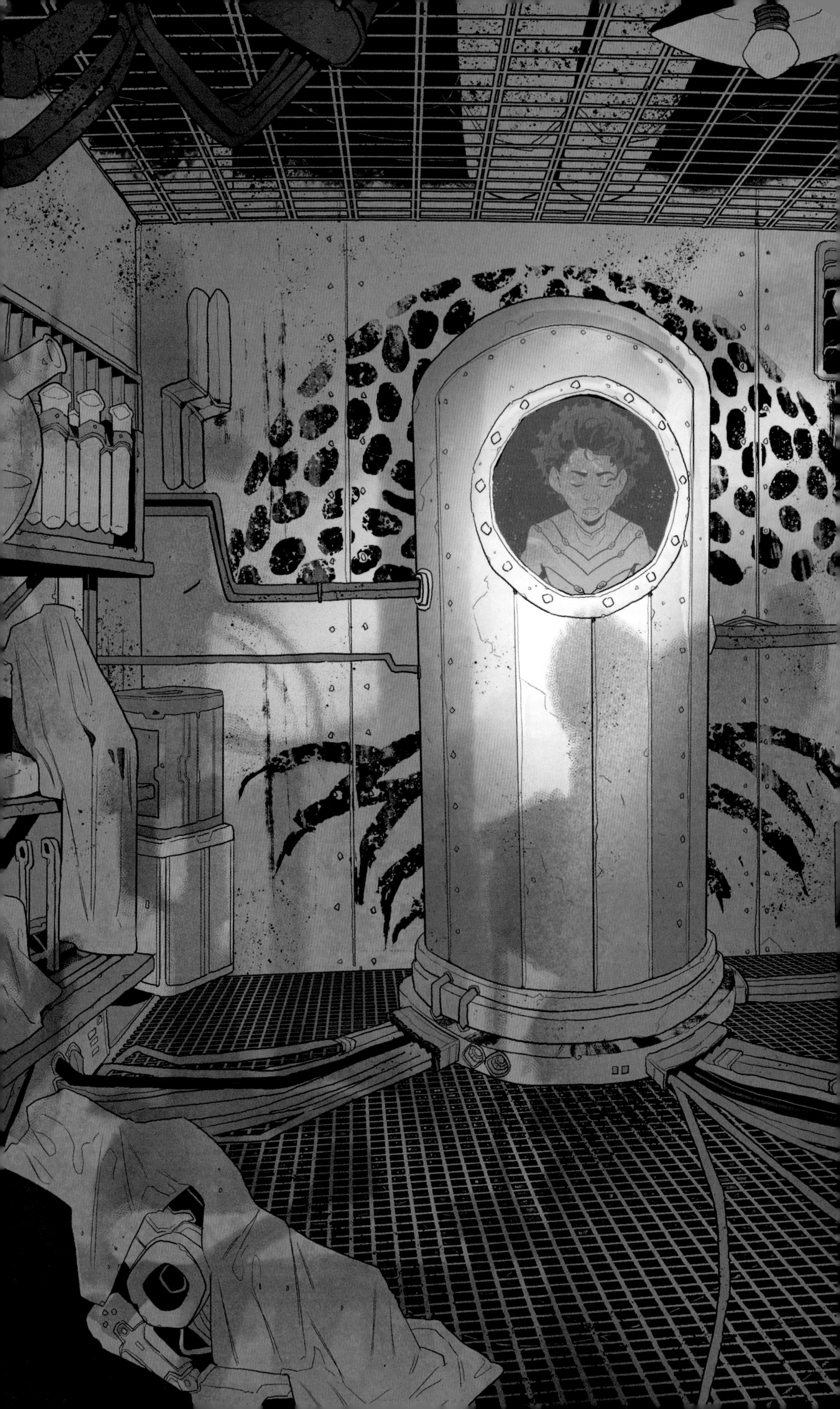

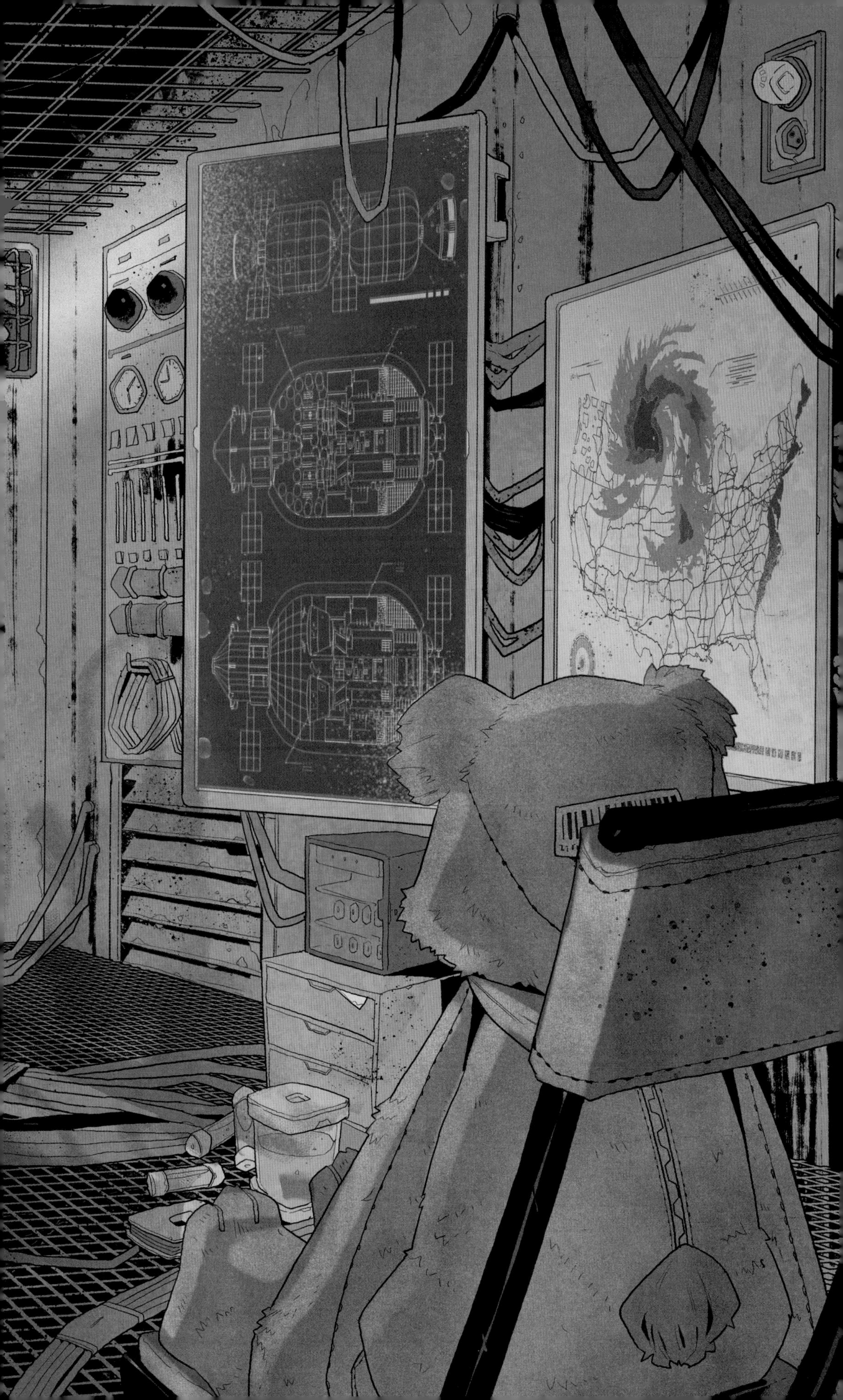

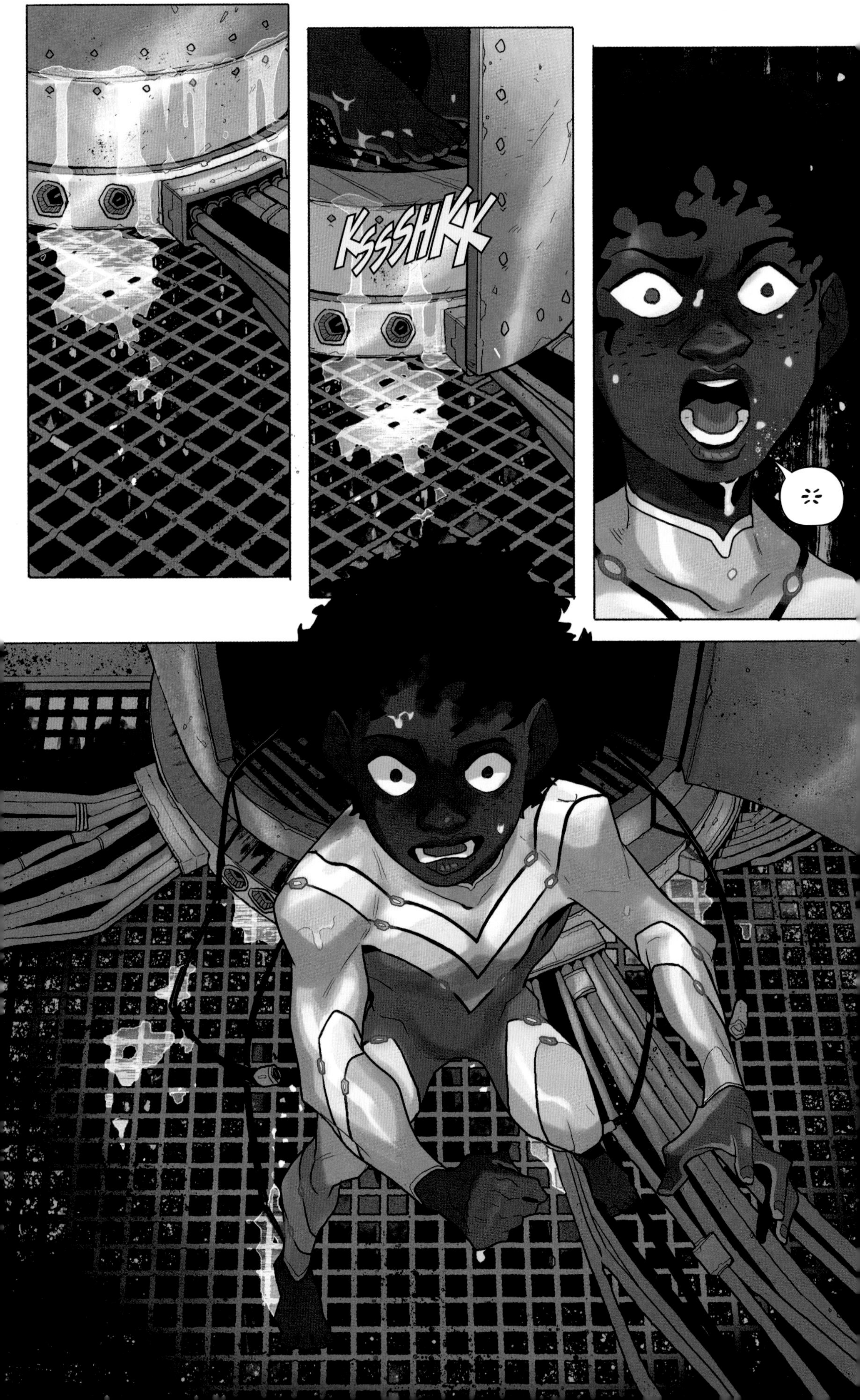
KSSSHKK

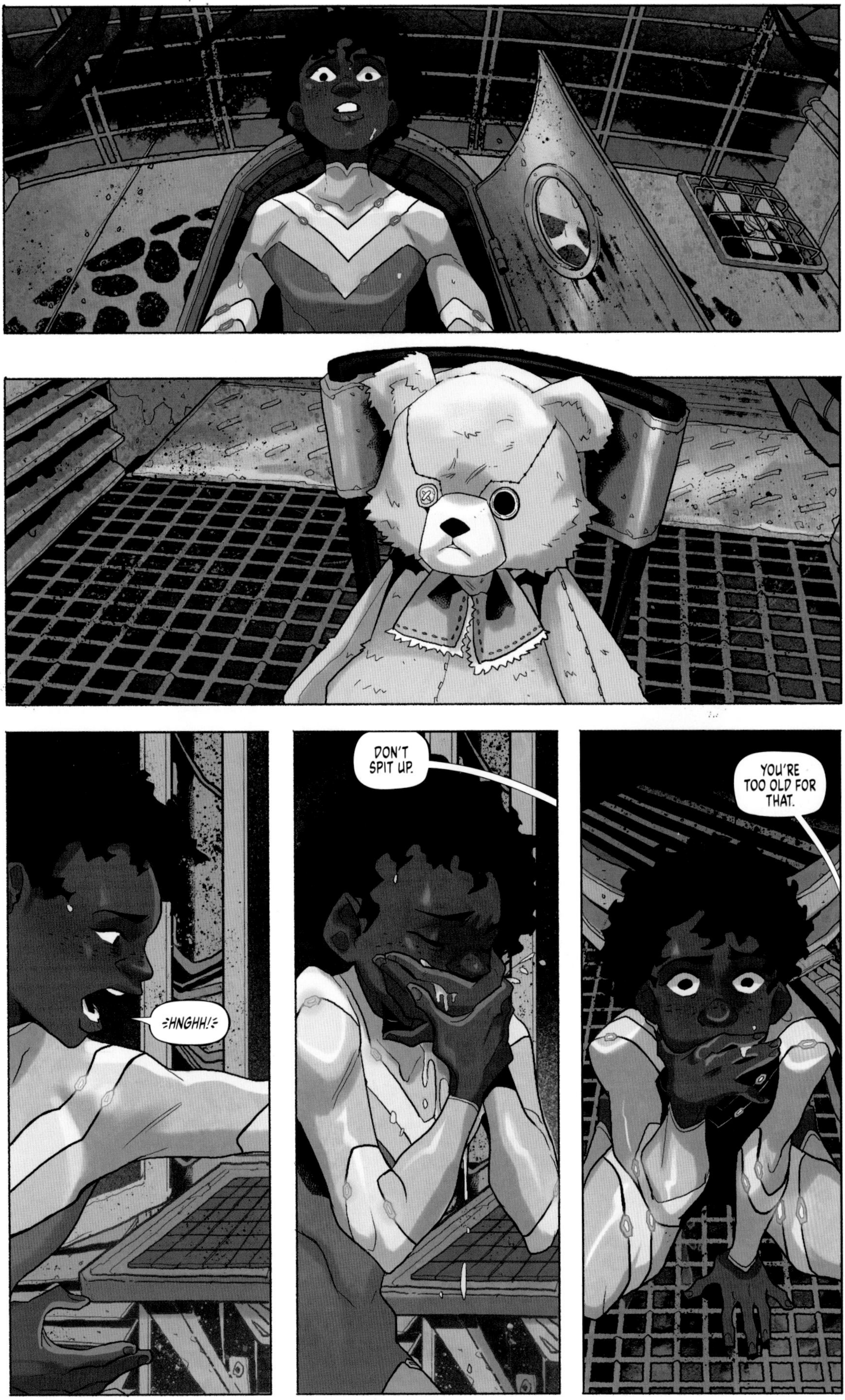

HNGHH!
DON'T SPIT UP.
YOU'RE TOO OLD FOR THAT.

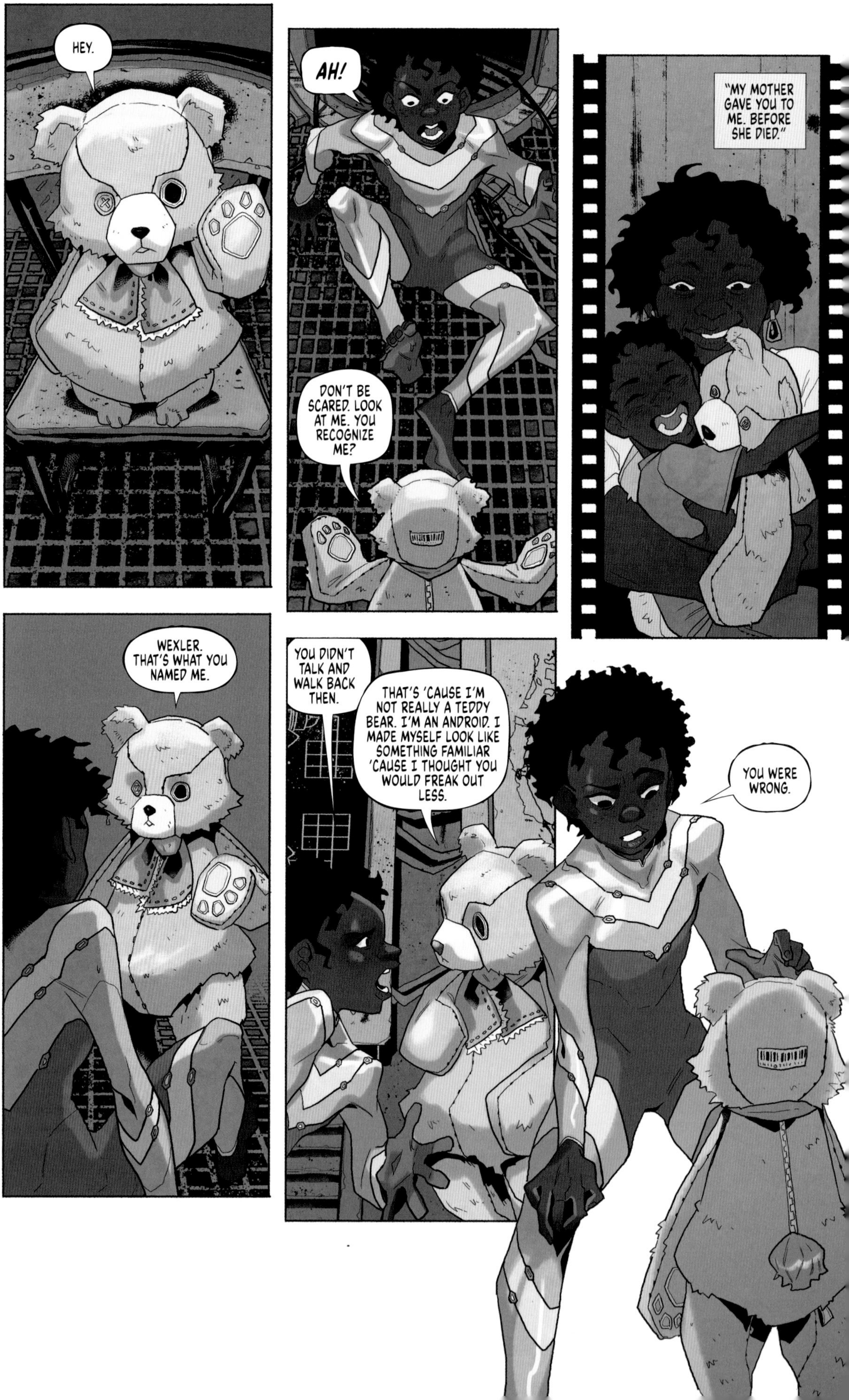
HEY.
AH!
DON'T BE SCARED. LOOK AT ME. YOU RECOGNIZE ME?
"MY MOTHER GAVE YOU TO ME. BEFORE SHE DIED."
WEXLER. THAT'S WHAT YOU NAMED ME.
YOU DIDN'T TALK AND WALK BACK THEN.
THAT'S 'CAUSE I'M NOT REALLY A TEDDY BEAR. I'M AN ANDROID. I MADE MYSELF LOOK LIKE SOMETHING FAMILIAR 'CAUSE I THOUGHT YOU WOULD FREAK OUT LESS.
YOU WERE WRONG.

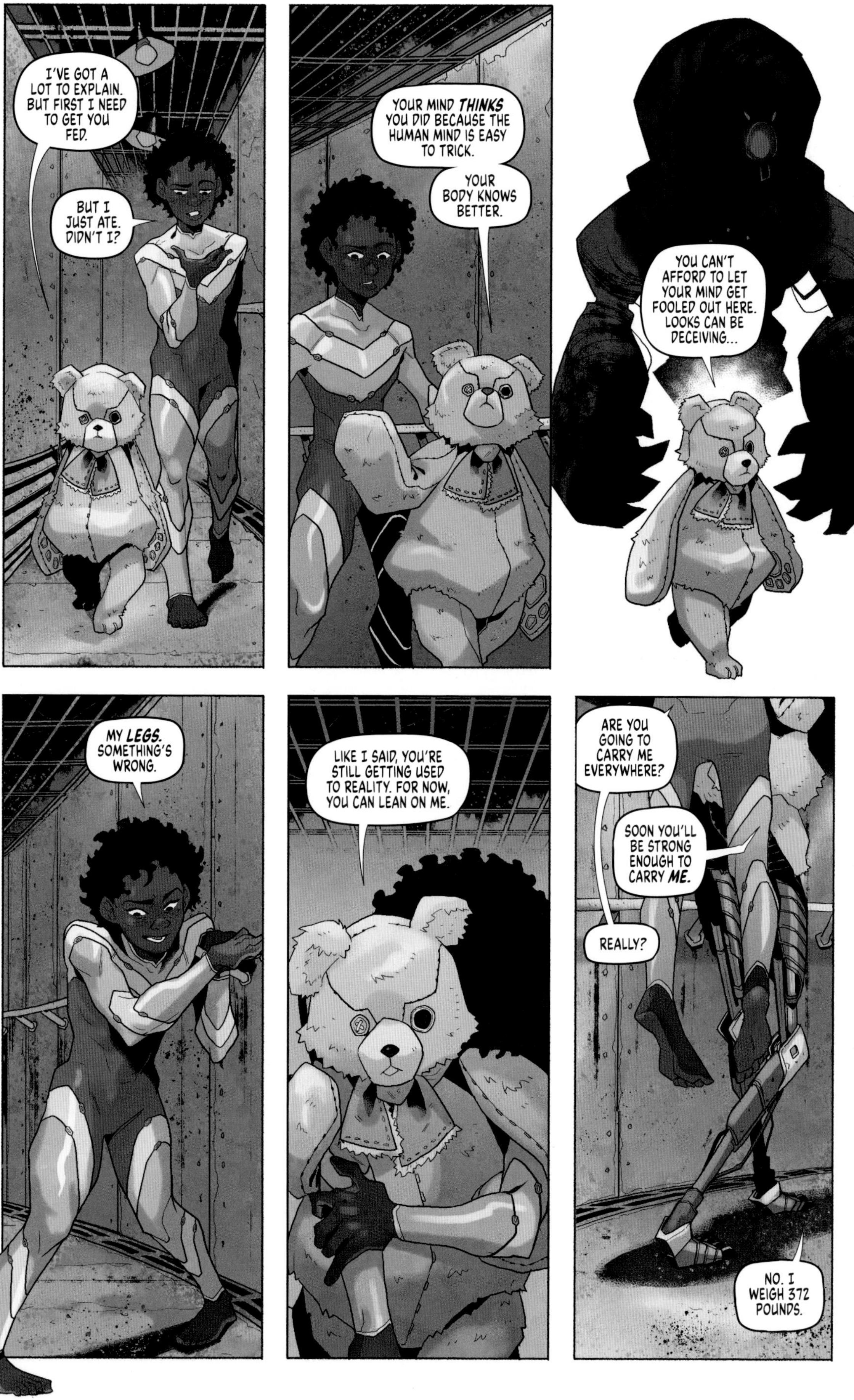

I'VE GOT A LOT TO EXPLAIN. BUT FIRST I NEED TO GET YOU FED.
BUT I JUST ATE. DIDN'T I?
YOUR MIND THINKS YOU DID BECAUSE THE HUMAN MIND IS EASY TO TRICK.
YOUR BODY KNOWS BETTER.
YOU CAN'T AFFORD TO LET YOUR MIND GET FOOLED OUT HERE. LOOKS CAN BE DECEIVING...
MY LEGS. SOMETHING'S WRONG.
LIKE I SAID, YOU'RE STILL GETTING USED TO REALITY. FOR NOW, YOU CAN LEAN ON ME.
ARE YOU GOING TO CARRY ME EVERYWHERE?
SOON YOU'LL BE STRONG ENOUGH TO CARRY ME.
REALLY?
NO. I WEIGH 372 POUNDS.

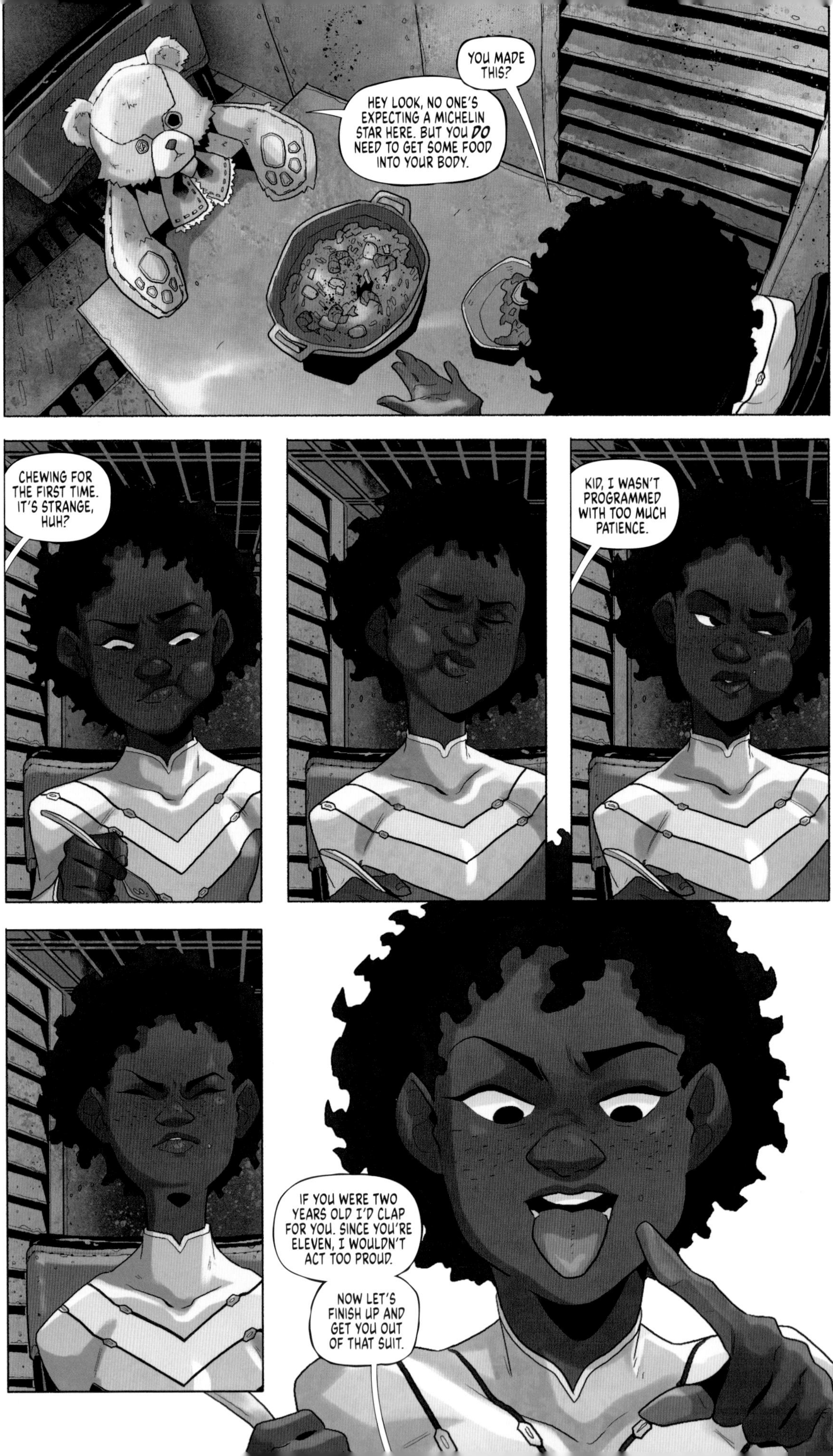
HEY LOOK, NO ONE'S EXPECTING A MICHELIN STAR HERE. BUT YOU DO NEED TO GET SOME FOOD INTO YOUR BODY.
YOU MADE THIS?
CHEWING FOR THE FIRST TIME. IT'S STRANGE, HUH?
KID, I WASN'T PROGRAMMED WITH TOO MUCH PATIENCE.
IF YOU WERE TWO YEARS OLD I'D CLAP FOR YOU. SINCE YOU'RE ELEVEN, I WOULDN'T ACT TOO PROUD.
NOW LET'S FINISH UP AND GET YOU OUT OF THAT SUIT.

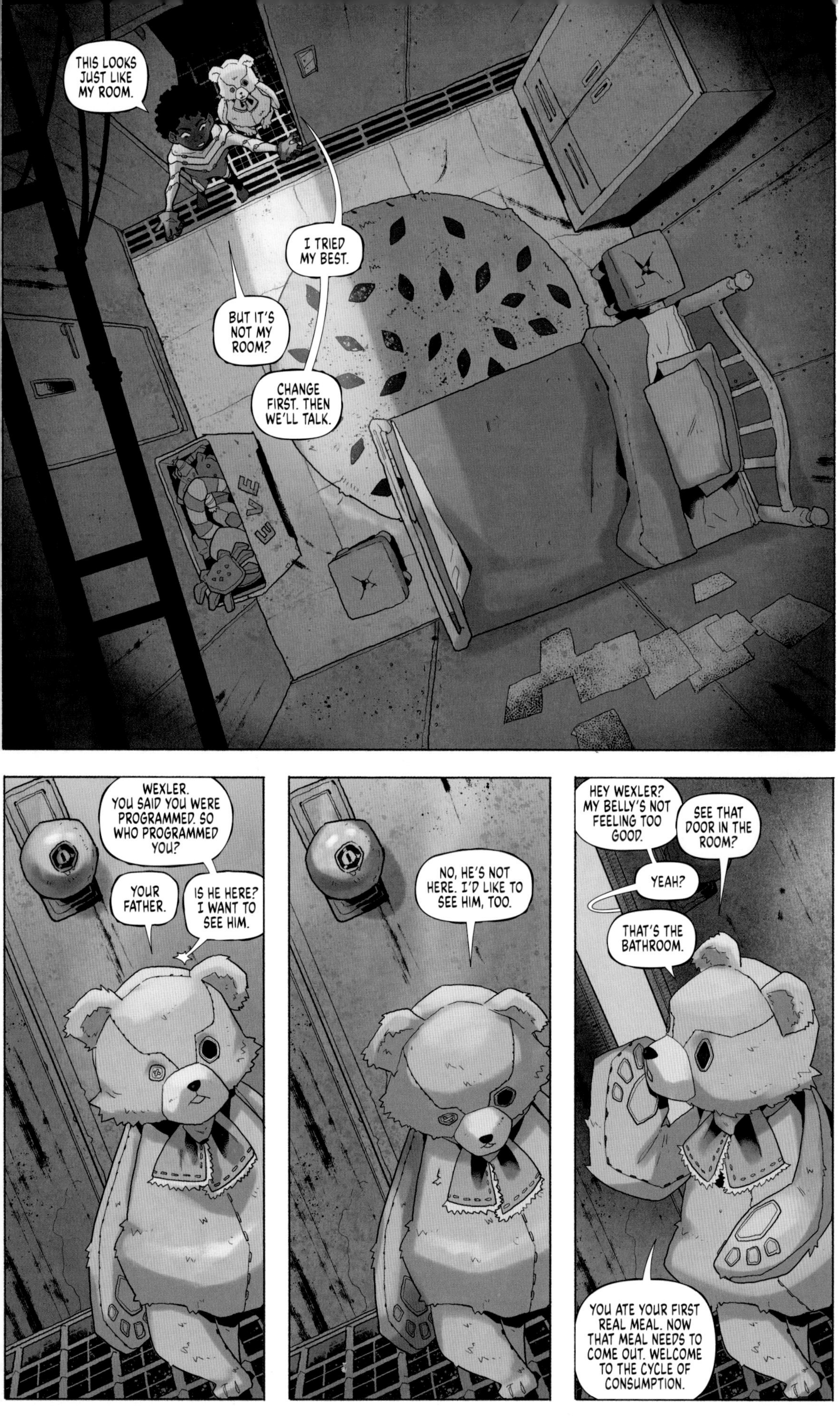
THIS LOOKS JUST LIKE MY ROOM.
I TRIED MY BEST.
BUT IT'S NOT MY ROOM?
CHANGE FIRST. THEN WE'LL TALK.
WEXLER. YOU SAID YOU WERE PROGRAMMED. SO WHO PROGRAMMED YOU?
YOUR FATHER.
IS HE HERE? I WANT TO SEE HIM.
NO, HE'S NOT HERE. I'D LIKE TO SEE HIM, TOO.
HEY WEXLER? MY BELLY'S NOT FEELING TOO GOOD.
SEE THAT DOOR IN THE ROOM?
YEAH?
THAT'S THE BATHROOM.
YOU ATE YOUR FIRST REAL MEAL. NOW THAT MEAL NEEDS TO COME OUT. WELCOME TO THE CYCLE OF CONSUMPTION.

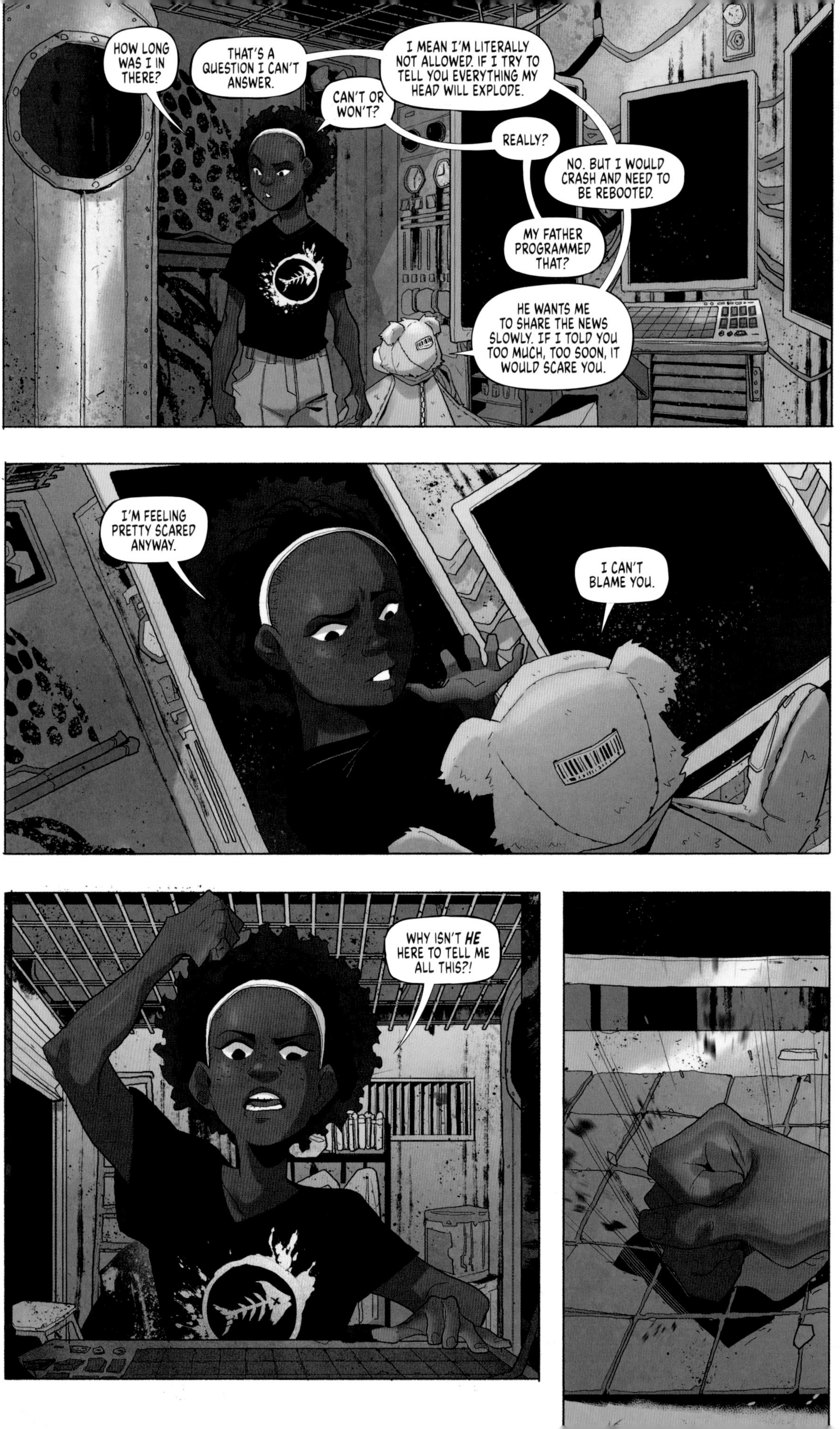
HOW LONG WAS I IN THERE?
THAT'S A QUESTION I CAN'T ANSWER.
CAN'T OR WON'T?
I MEAN I'M LITERALLY NOT ALLOWED. IF I TRY TO TELL YOU EVERYTHING MY HEAD WILL EXPLODE.
REALLY?
NO. BUT I WOULD CRASH AND NEED TO BE REBOOTED.
MY FATHER PROGRAMMED THAT?
HE WANTS ME TO SHARE THE NEWS SLOWLY. IF I TOLD YOU TOO MUCH, TOO SOON, IT WOULD SCARE YOU.
I'M FEELING PRETTY SCARED ANYWAY.
I CAN'T BLAME YOU.
WHY ISN'T HE HERE TO TELL ME ALL THIS?!

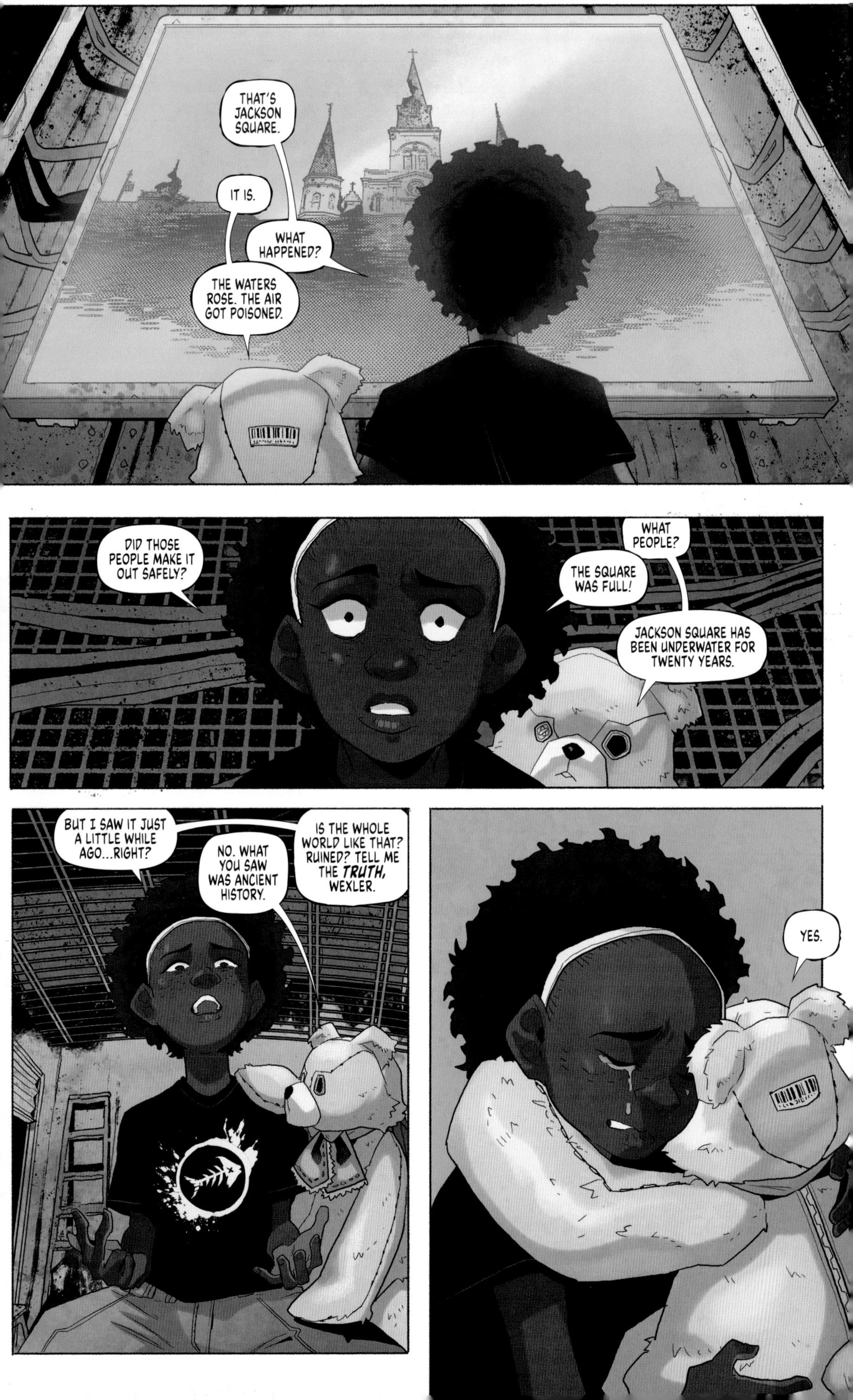
THAT'S JACKSON SQUARE.
IT IS.
WHAT HAPPENED?
THE WATERS ROSE. THE AIR GOT POISONED.
DID THOSE PEOPLE MAKE IT OUT SAFELY?
WHAT PEOPLE?
THE SQUARE WAS FULL!
JACKSON SQUARE HAS BEEN UNDERWATER FOR TWENTY YEARS.
BUT I SAW IT JUST A LITTLE WHILE AGO...RIGHT?
NO. WHAT YOU SAW WAS ANCIENT HISTORY.
IS THE WHOLE WORLD LIKE THAT? RUINED? TELL ME THE *TRUTH,* WEXLER.
YES.

"NOW LET ME TELL YOU HOW WE'RE GONNA FIX IT."

"JOHNNY APPLESEED IS A LEGEND, BUT HE'S BASED ON A REAL GUY. JOHN CHAPMAN. HE WALKED THROUGH PENNSYLVANIA AND OREGON, OFTEN BAREFOOT, PLANTING APPLE SEEDS. THOSE NURSERIES GREW INTO A THOUSAND ACRES OF TREES.

"ME AND YOU ARE GOING TO DO SOMETHING SIMILAR. BUT WE'LL BE PLANTING MANGROVE TREES. A SPECIAL VARIETY DESIGNED BY YOUR DAD. YOU SHOULD WEAR SHOES, THOUGH."

UNFORTUNATELY, THOSE SEEDS AREN'T HERE. THEY'RE IN A VAULT. IT'LL BE A LONG TRIP TO GET THERE. BUT YOU'LL RECOGNIZE THE PLACE.

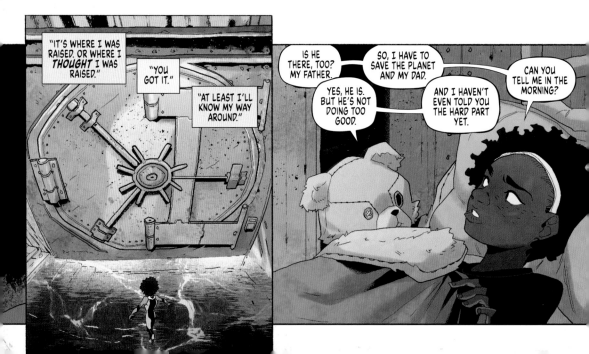

"IT'S WHERE I WAS RAISED. OR WHERE I *THOUGHT* I WAS RAISED."

"YOU GOT IT."

"AT LEAST I'LL KNOW MY WAY AROUND."

IS HE THERE, TOO? MY FATHER.

SO, I HAVE TO SAVE THE PLANET AND MY DAD.

CAN YOU TELL ME IN THE MORNING?

YES, HE IS. BUT HE'S NOT DOING TOO GOOD.

AND I HAVEN'T EVEN TOLD YOU THE HARD PART YET.

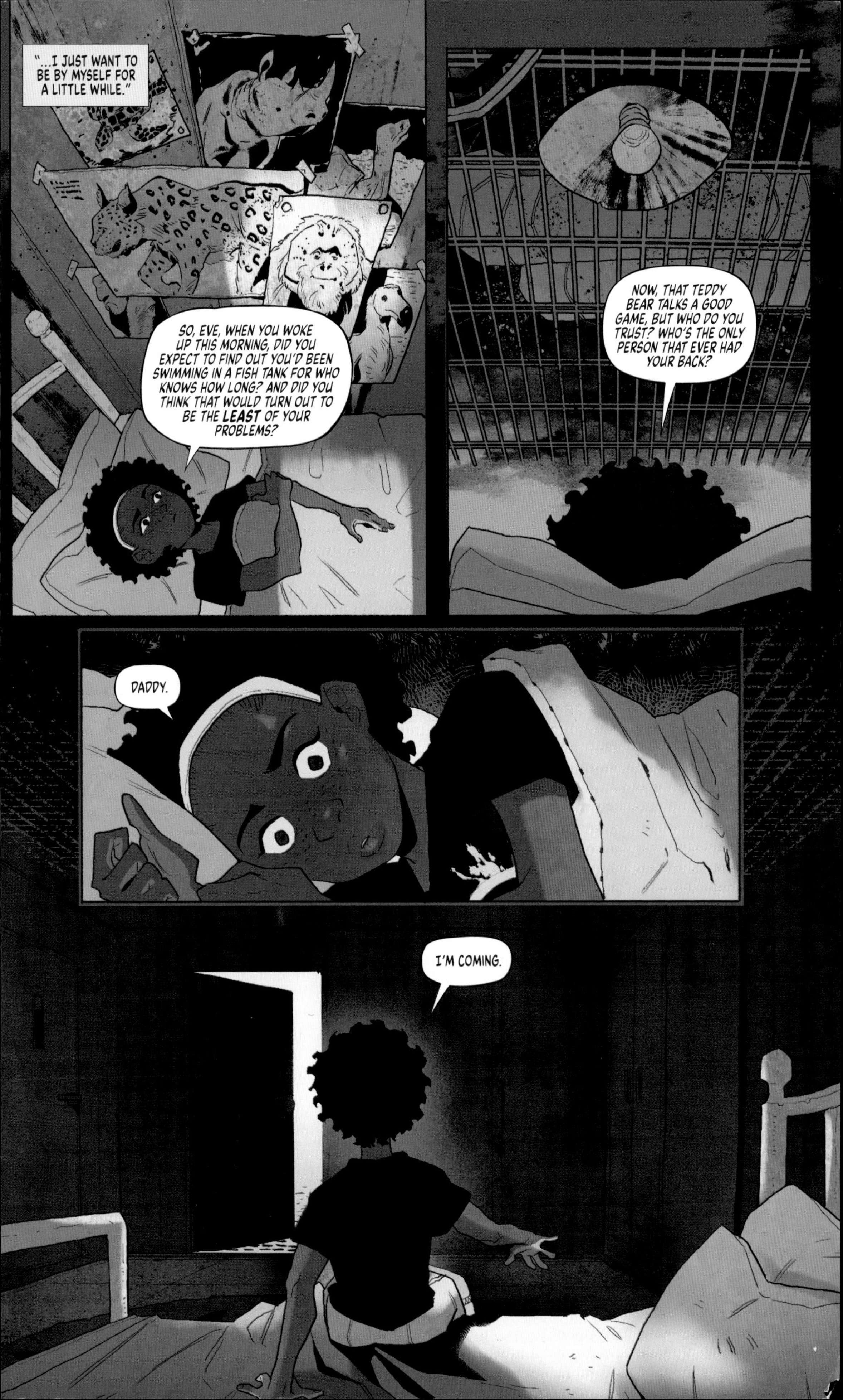
"...I JUST WANT TO BE BY MYSELF FOR A LITTLE WHILE."
SO, EVE, WHEN YOU WOKE UP THIS MORNING, DID YOU EXPECT TO FIND OUT YOU'D BEEN SWIMMING IN A FISH TANK FOR WHO KNOWS HOW LONG? AND DID YOU THINK THAT WOULD TURN OUT TO BE THE **LEAST** OF YOUR PROBLEMS?
NOW, THAT TEDDY BEAR TALKS A GOOD GAME, BUT WHO DO YOU TRUST? WHO'S THE ONLY PERSON THAT EVER HAD YOUR BACK?
DADDY.
I'M COMING.

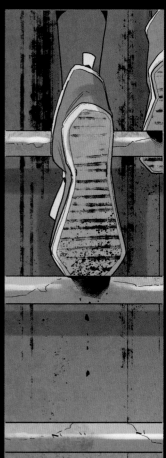

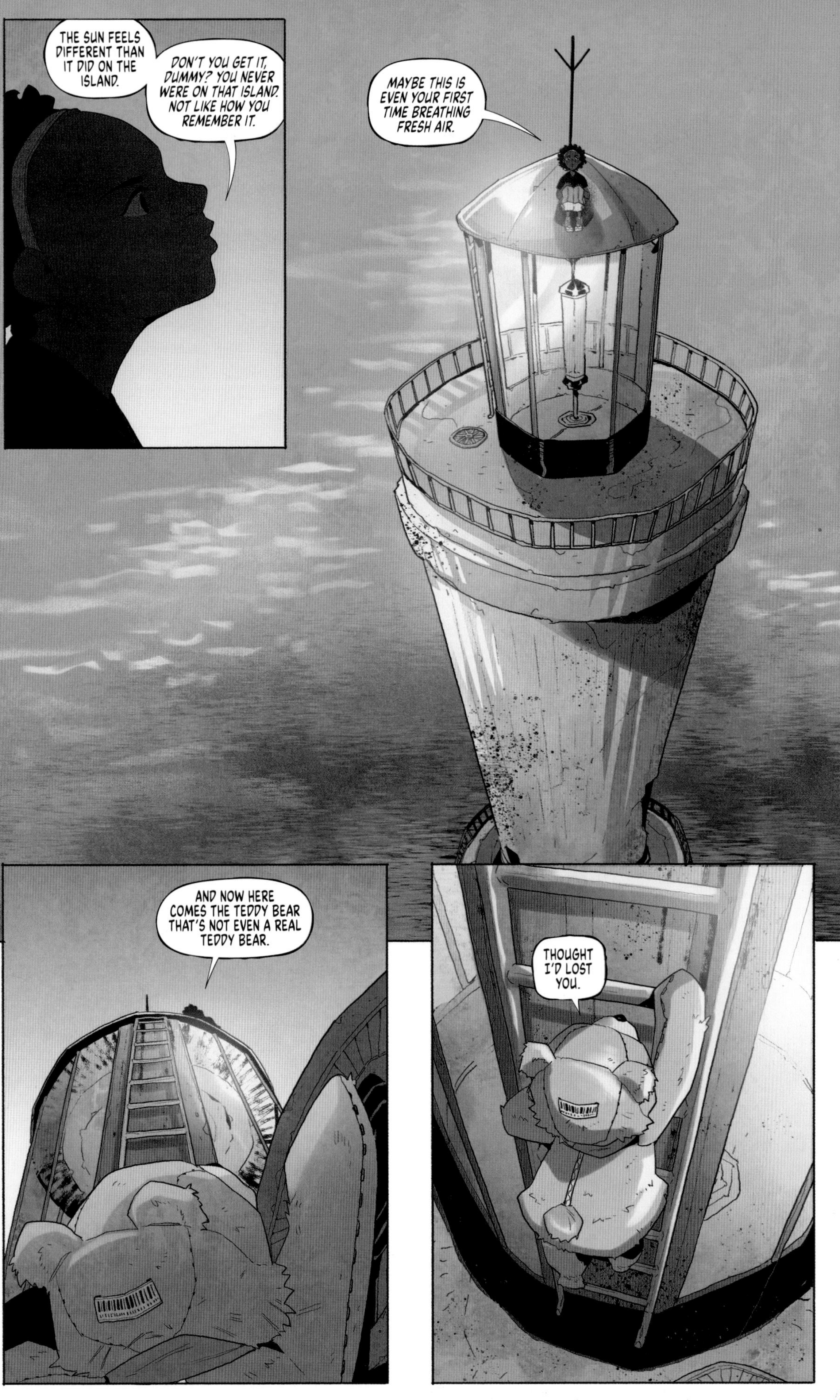
THE SUN FEELS DIFFERENT THAN IT DID ON THE ISLAND.
DON'T YOU GET IT, DUMMY? YOU NEVER WERE ON THAT ISLAND. NOT LIKE HOW YOU REMEMBER IT.
MAYBE THIS IS EVEN YOUR FIRST TIME BREATHING FRESH AIR.
AND NOW HERE COMES THE TEDDY BEAR THAT'S NOT EVEN A REAL TEDDY BEAR.
THOUGHT I'D LOST YOU.

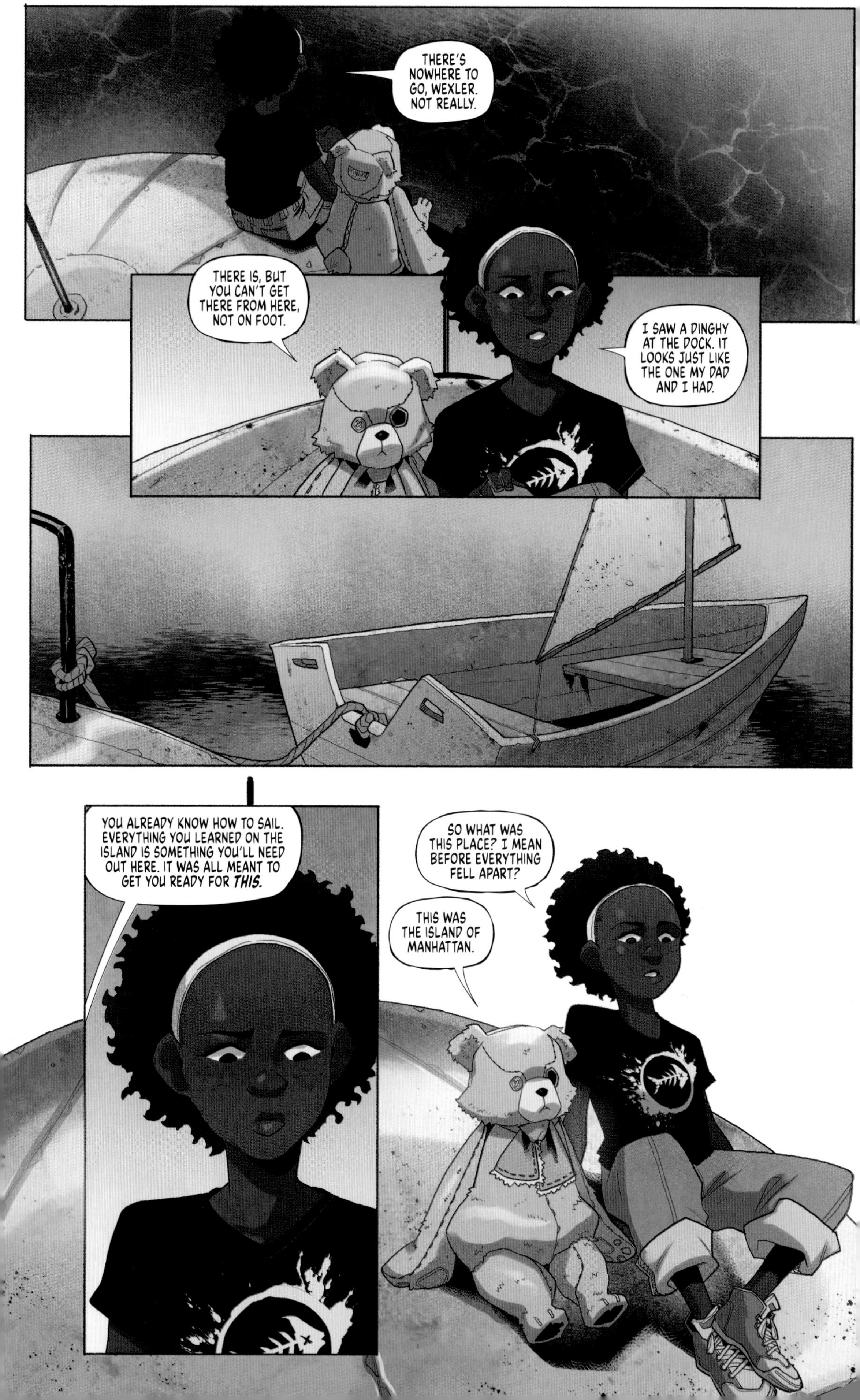
THERE'S NOWHERE TO GO, WEXLER. NOT REALLY.
THERE IS, BUT YOU CAN'T GET THERE FROM HERE, NOT ON FOOT.
I SAW A DINGHY AT THE DOCK. IT LOOKS JUST LIKE THE ONE MY DAD AND I HAD.
YOU ALREADY KNOW HOW TO SAIL. EVERYTHING YOU LEARNED ON THE ISLAND IS SOMETHING YOU'LL NEED OUT HERE. IT WAS ALL MEANT TO GET YOU READY FOR ***THIS.***
SO WHAT WAS THIS PLACE? I MEAN BEFORE EVERYTHING FELL APART?
THIS WAS THE ISLAND OF MANHATTAN.

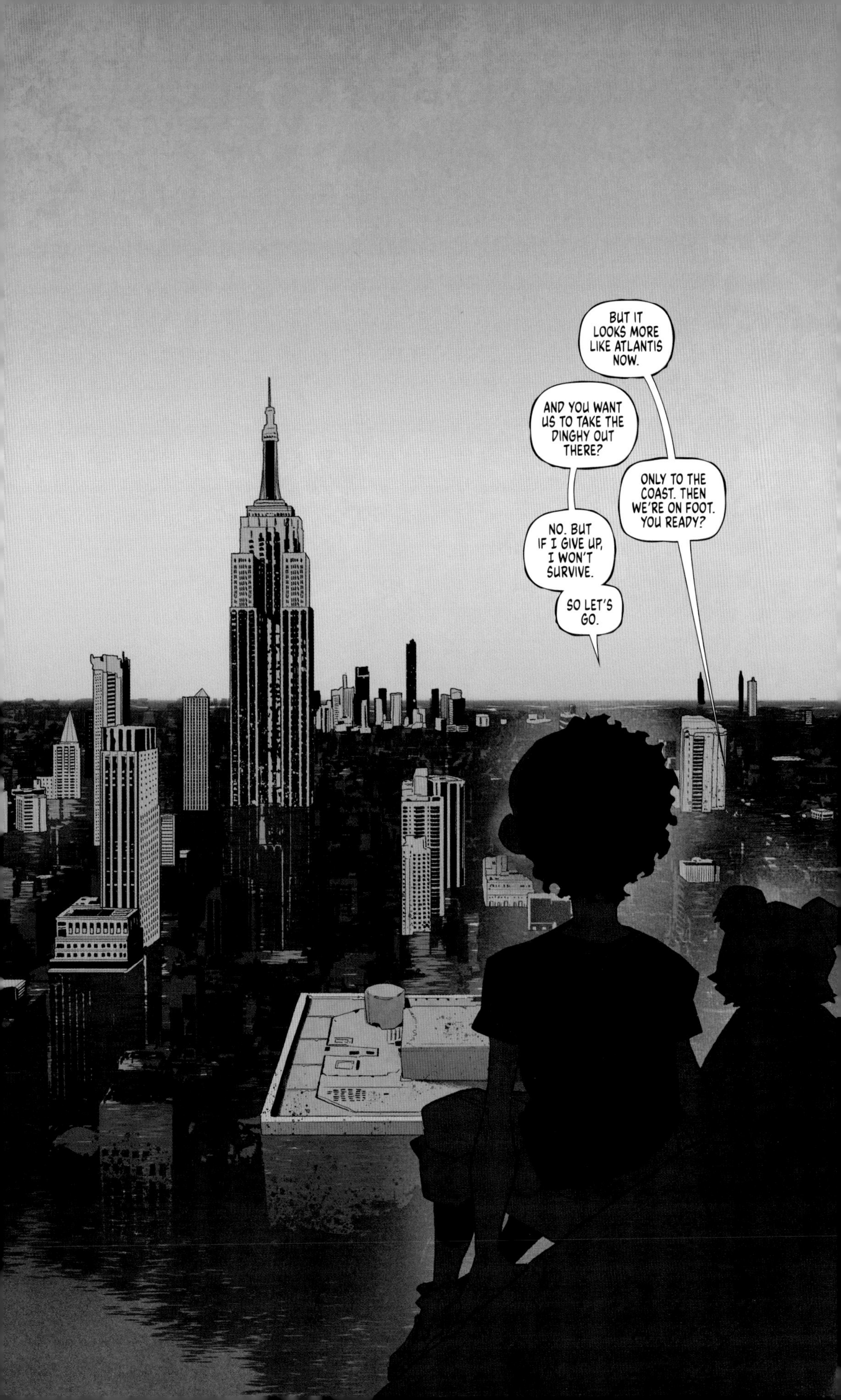
BUT IT LOOKS MORE LIKE ATLANTIS NOW.
AND YOU WANT US TO TAKE THE DINGHY OUT THERE?
ONLY TO THE COAST. THEN WE'RE ON FOOT. YOU READY?
NO. BUT IF I GIVE UP, I WON'T SURVIVE.
SO LET'S GO.

CHAPTER
TWO

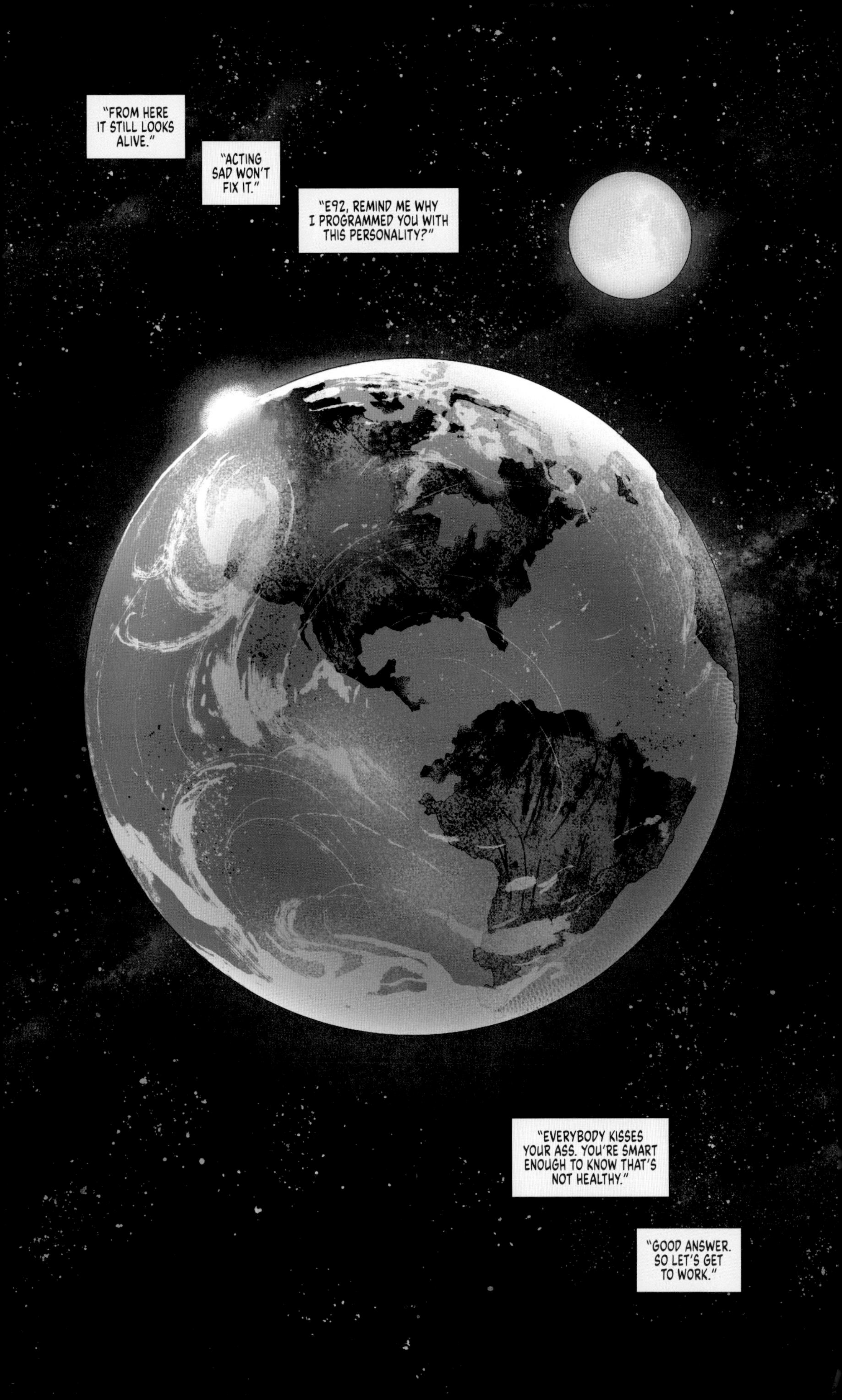
"FROM HERE IT STILL LOOKS ALIVE."
"ACTING SAD WON'T FIX IT."
"E92, REMIND ME WHY I PROGRAMMED YOU WITH THIS PERSONALITY?"
"EVERYBODY KISSES YOUR ASS. YOU'RE SMART ENOUGH TO KNOW THAT'S NOT HEALTHY."
"GOOD ANSWER. SO LET'S GET TO WORK."

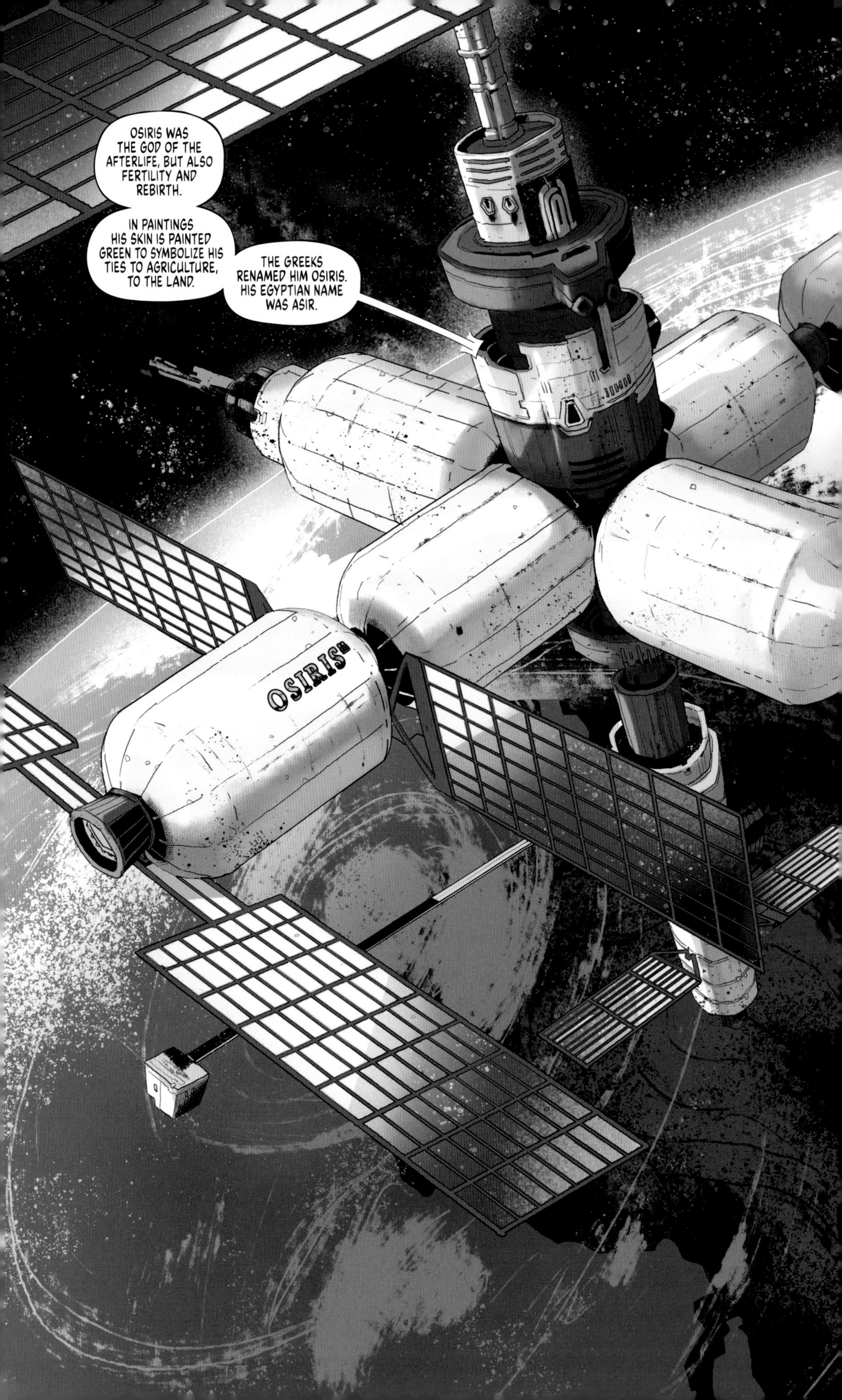
OSIRIS WAS THE GOD OF THE AFTERLIFE, BUT ALSO FERTILITY AND REBIRTH.
IN PAINTINGS HIS SKIN IS PAINTED GREEN TO SYMBOLIZE HIS TIES TO AGRICULTURE, TO THE LAND.
THE GREEKS RENAMED HIM OSIRIS. HIS EGYPTIAN NAME WAS ASIR.
OSIRIS

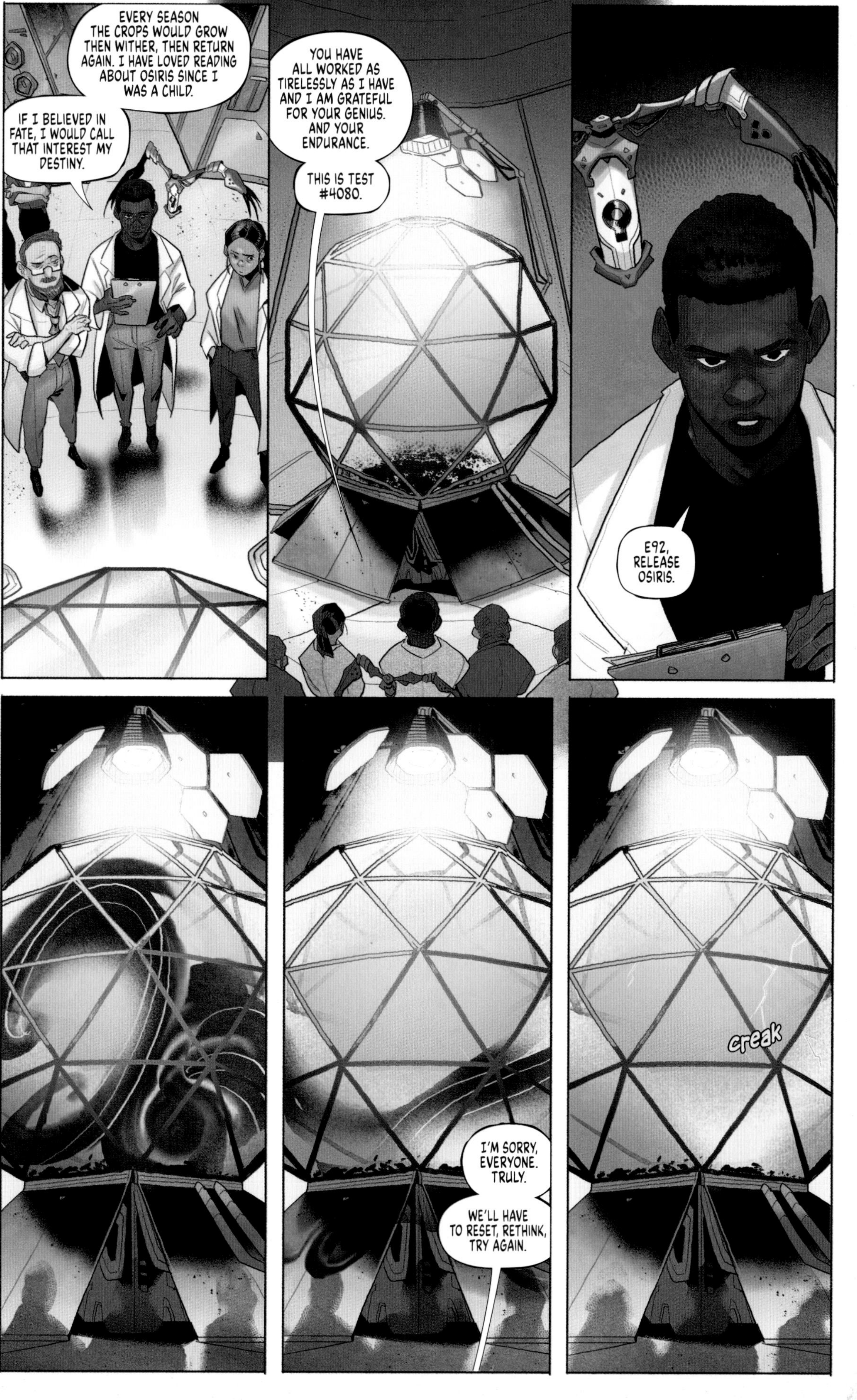
EVERY SEASON THE CROPS WOULD GROW THEN WITHER, THEN RETURN AGAIN. I HAVE LOVED READING ABOUT OSIRIS SINCE I WAS A CHILD.
IF I BELIEVED IN FATE, I WOULD CALL THAT INTEREST MY DESTINY.
YOU HAVE ALL WORKED AS TIRELESSLY AS I HAVE AND I AM GRATEFUL FOR YOUR GENIUS. AND YOUR ENDURANCE.
THIS IS TEST #4080.
E92, RELEASE OSIRIS.
I'M SORRY, EVERYONE. TRULY.
WE'LL HAVE TO RESET, RETHINK, TRY AGAIN.
creak

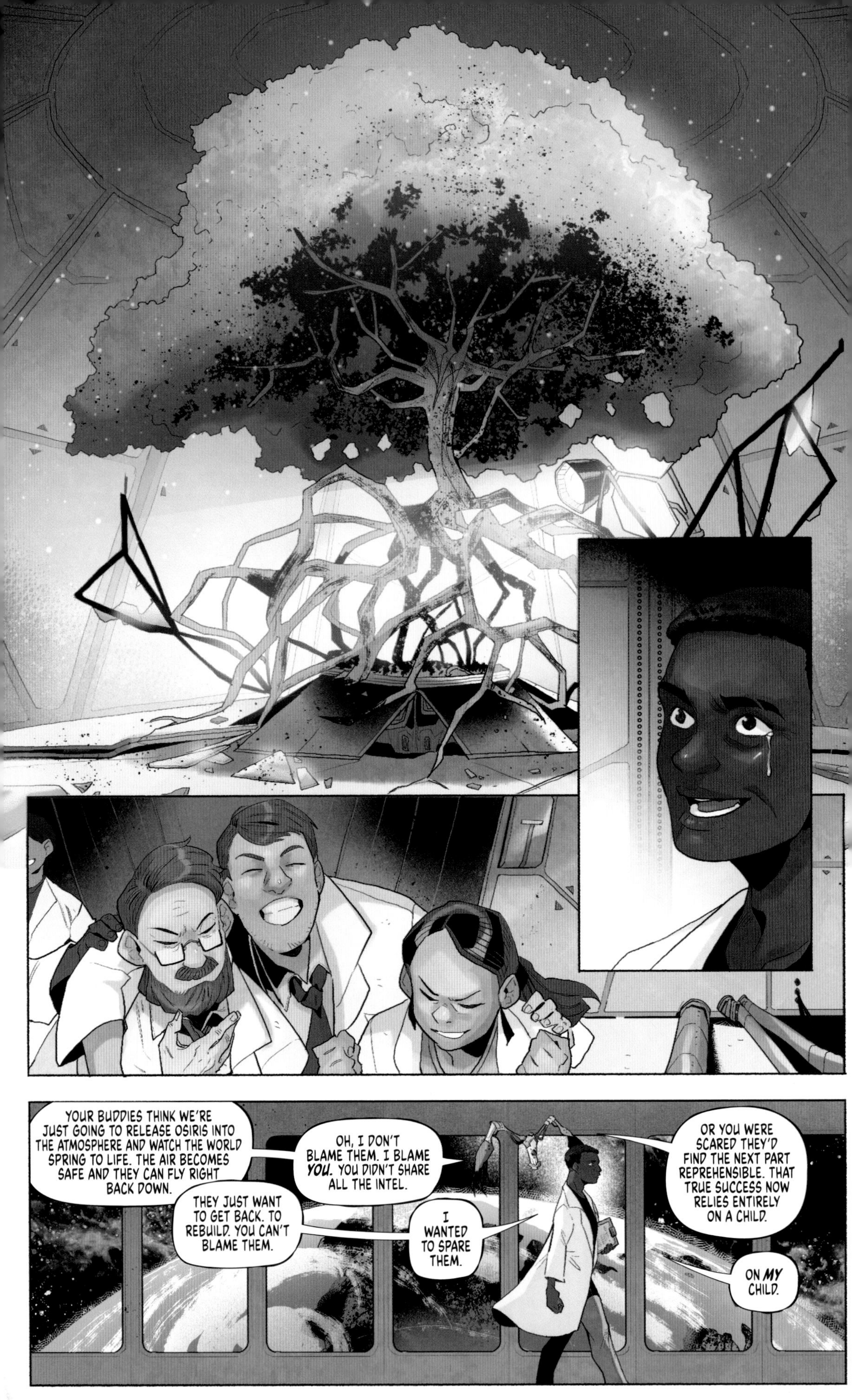

YOUR BUDDIES THINK WE'RE JUST GOING TO RELEASE OSIRIS INTO THE ATMOSPHERE AND WATCH THE WORLD SPRING TO LIFE. THE AIR BECOMES SAFE AND THEY CAN FLY RIGHT BACK DOWN.
THEY JUST WANT TO GET BACK. TO REBUILD. YOU CAN'T BLAME THEM.
OH, I DON'T BLAME THEM. I BLAME *YOU.* YOU DIDN'T SHARE ALL THE INTEL.
I WANTED TO SPARE THEM.
OR YOU WERE SCARED THEY'D FIND THE NEXT PART REPREHENSIBLE. THAT TRUE SUCCESS NOW RELIES ENTIRELY ON A CHILD.
ON *MY* CHILD.

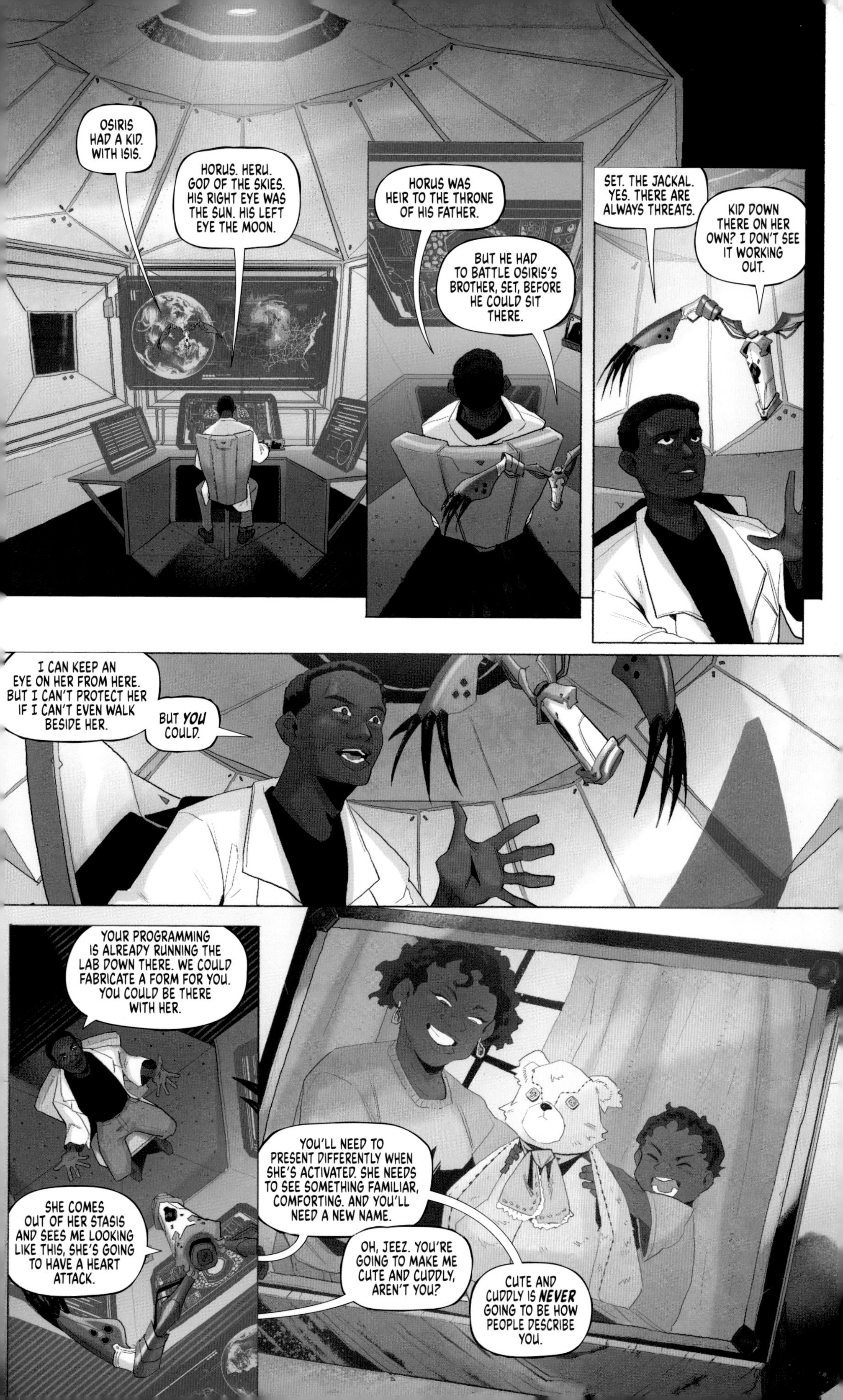

OSIRIS HAD A KID. WITH ISIS.
HORUS. HERU. GOD OF THE SKIES. HIS RIGHT EYE WAS THE SUN. HIS LEFT EYE THE MOON.
HORUS WAS HEIR TO THE THRONE OF HIS FATHER.
BUT HE HAD TO BATTLE OSIRIS'S BROTHER, SET, BEFORE HE COULD SIT THERE.
SET. THE JACKAL. YES. THERE ARE ALWAYS THREATS.
KID DOWN THERE ON HER OWN? I DON'T SEE IT WORKING OUT.
I CAN KEEP AN EYE ON HER FROM HERE. BUT I CAN'T PROTECT HER IF I CAN'T EVEN WALK BESIDE HER.
BUT *YOU* COULD.
YOUR PROGRAMMING IS ALREADY RUNNING THE LAB DOWN THERE. WE COULD FABRICATE A FORM FOR YOU. YOU COULD BE THERE WITH HER.
SHE COMES OUT OF HER STASIS AND SEES ME LOOKING LIKE THIS, SHE'S GOING TO HAVE A HEART ATTACK.
YOU'LL NEED TO PRESENT DIFFERENTLY WHEN SHE'S ACTIVATED. SHE NEEDS TO SEE SOMETHING FAMILIAR, COMFORTING. AND YOU'LL NEED A NEW NAME.
OH, JEEZ. YOU'RE GOING TO MAKE ME CUTE AND CUDDLY, AREN'T YOU?
CUTE AND CUDDLY IS ***NEVER*** GOING TO BE HOW PEOPLE DESCRIBE YOU.

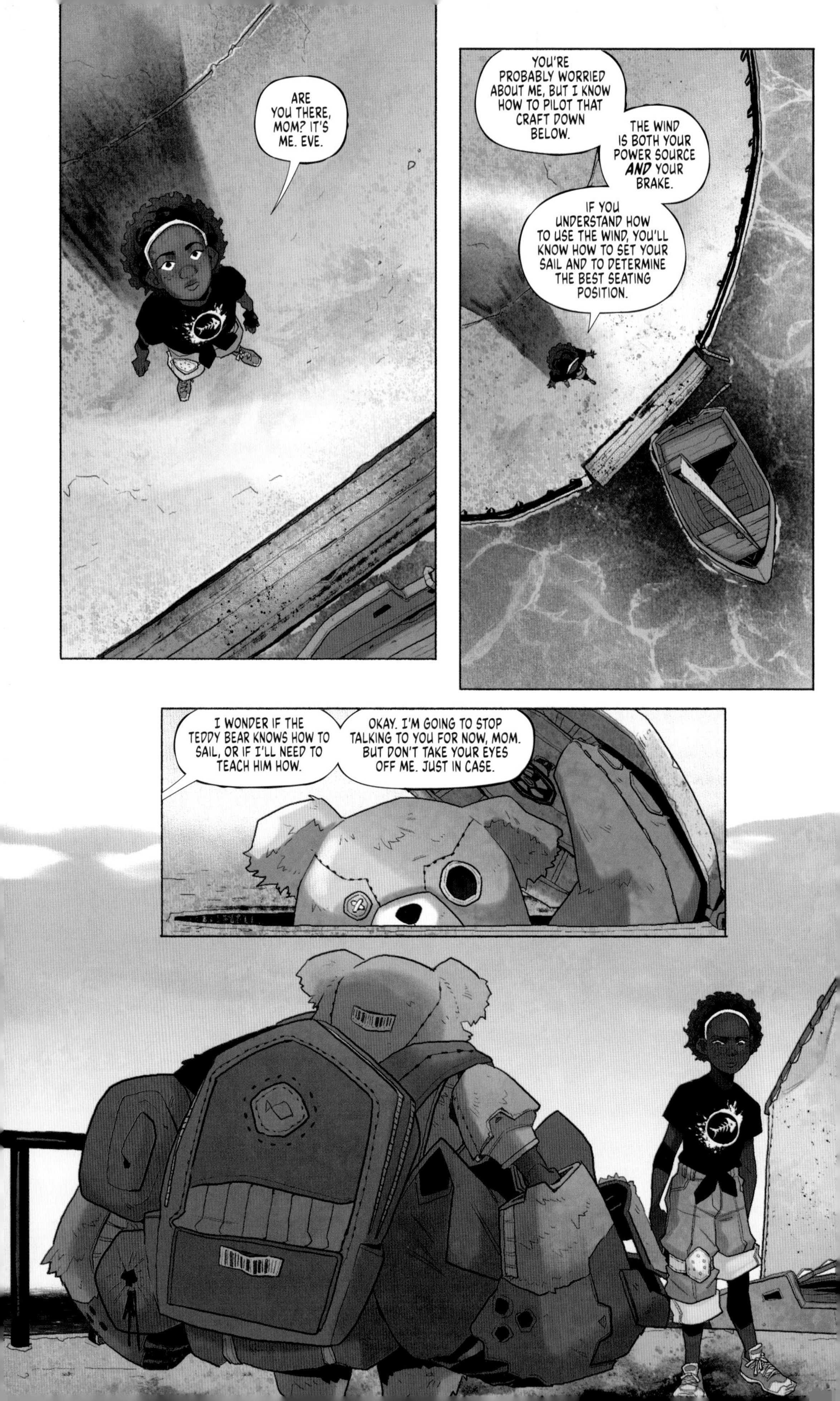

ARE YOU THERE, MOM? IT'S ME. EVE.
YOU'RE PROBABLY WORRIED ABOUT ME, BUT I KNOW HOW TO PILOT THAT CRAFT DOWN BELOW.
THE WIND IS BOTH YOUR POWER SOURCE AND YOUR BRAKE.
IF YOU UNDERSTAND HOW TO USE THE WIND, YOU'LL KNOW HOW TO SET YOUR SAIL AND TO DETERMINE THE BEST SEATING POSITION.
I WONDER IF THE TEDDY BEAR KNOWS HOW TO SAIL, OR IF I'LL NEED TO TEACH HIM HOW.
OKAY. I'M GOING TO STOP TALKING TO YOU FOR NOW, MOM. BUT DON'T TAKE YOUR EYES OFF ME. JUST IN CASE.

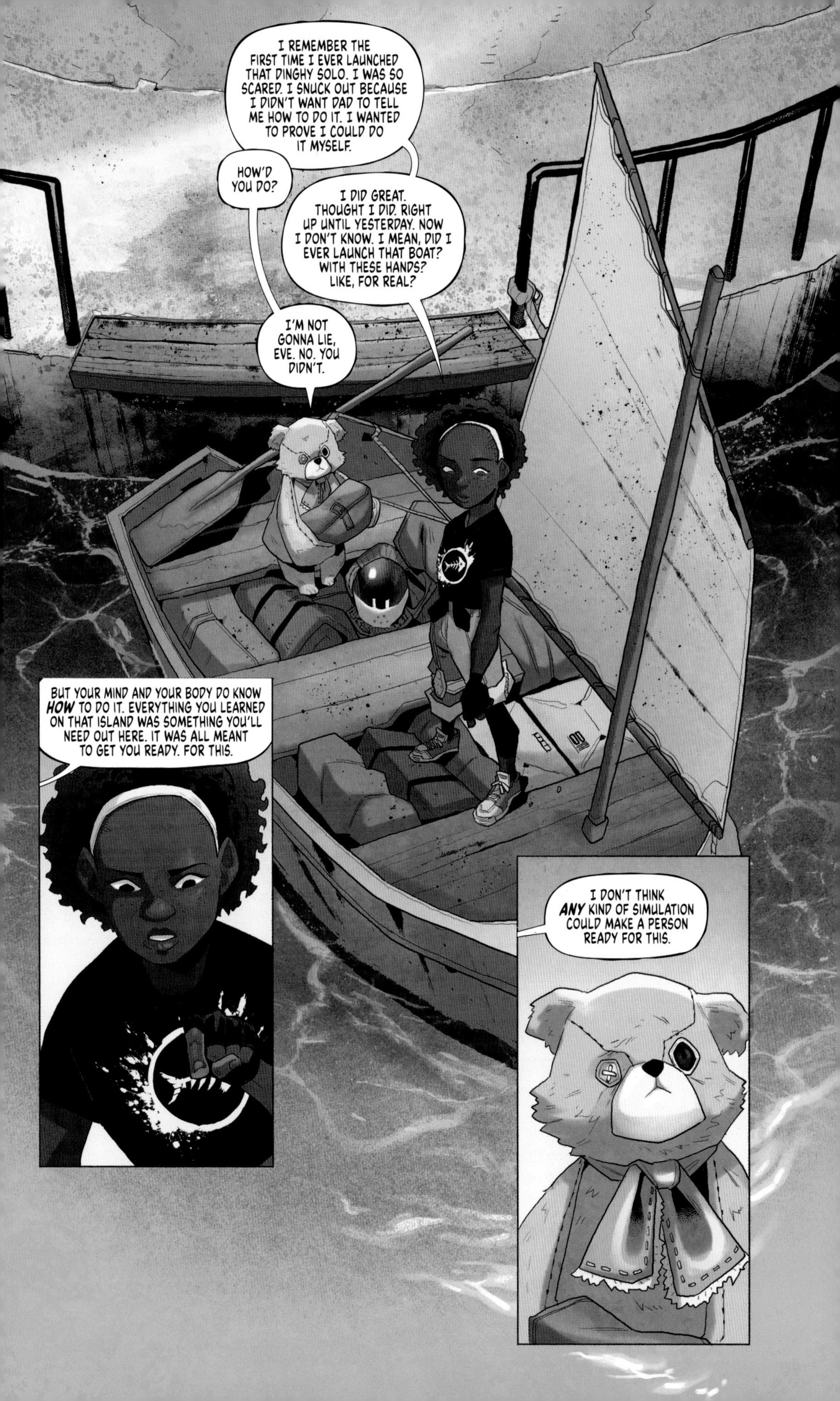
I REMEMBER THE FIRST TIME I EVER LAUNCHED THAT DINGHY SOLO. I WAS SO SCARED. I SNUCK OUT BECAUSE I DIDN'T WANT DAD TO TELL ME HOW TO DO IT. I WANTED TO PROVE I COULD DO IT MYSELF.
HOW'D YOU DO?
I DID GREAT. THOUGHT I DID. RIGHT UP UNTIL YESTERDAY. NOW I DON'T KNOW. I MEAN, DID I EVER LAUNCH THAT BOAT? WITH THESE HANDS? LIKE, FOR REAL?
I'M NOT GONNA LIE, EVE. NO. YOU DIDN'T.
BUT YOUR MIND AND YOUR BODY DO KNOW ***HOW*** TO DO IT. EVERYTHING YOU LEARNED ON THAT ISLAND WAS SOMETHING YOU'LL NEED OUT HERE. IT WAS ALL MEANT TO GET YOU READY. FOR THIS.
I DON'T THINK ***ANY*** KIND OF SIMULATION COULD MAKE A PERSON READY FOR THIS.

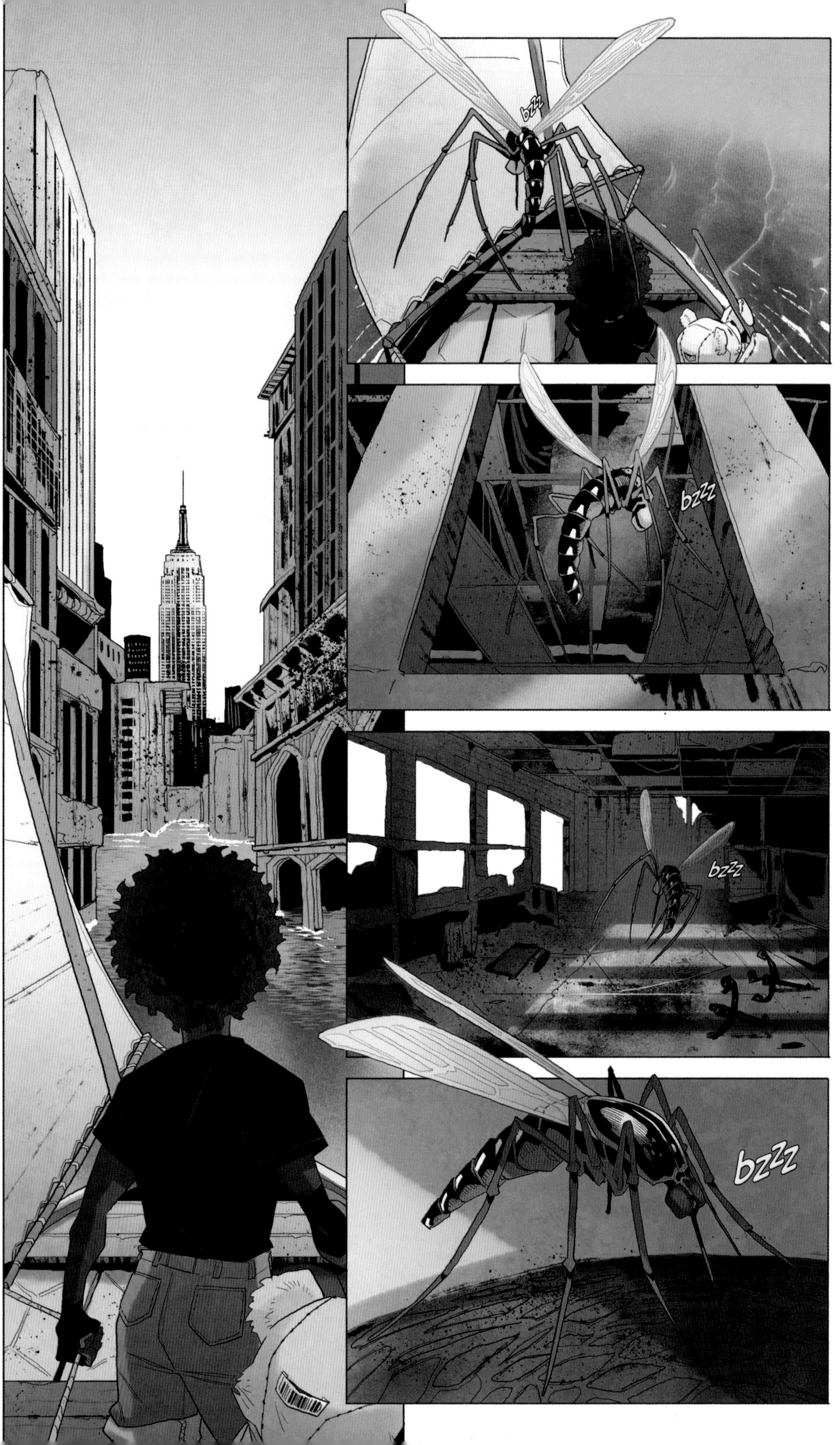

bzzz
bzzz
bzzz
bzzz

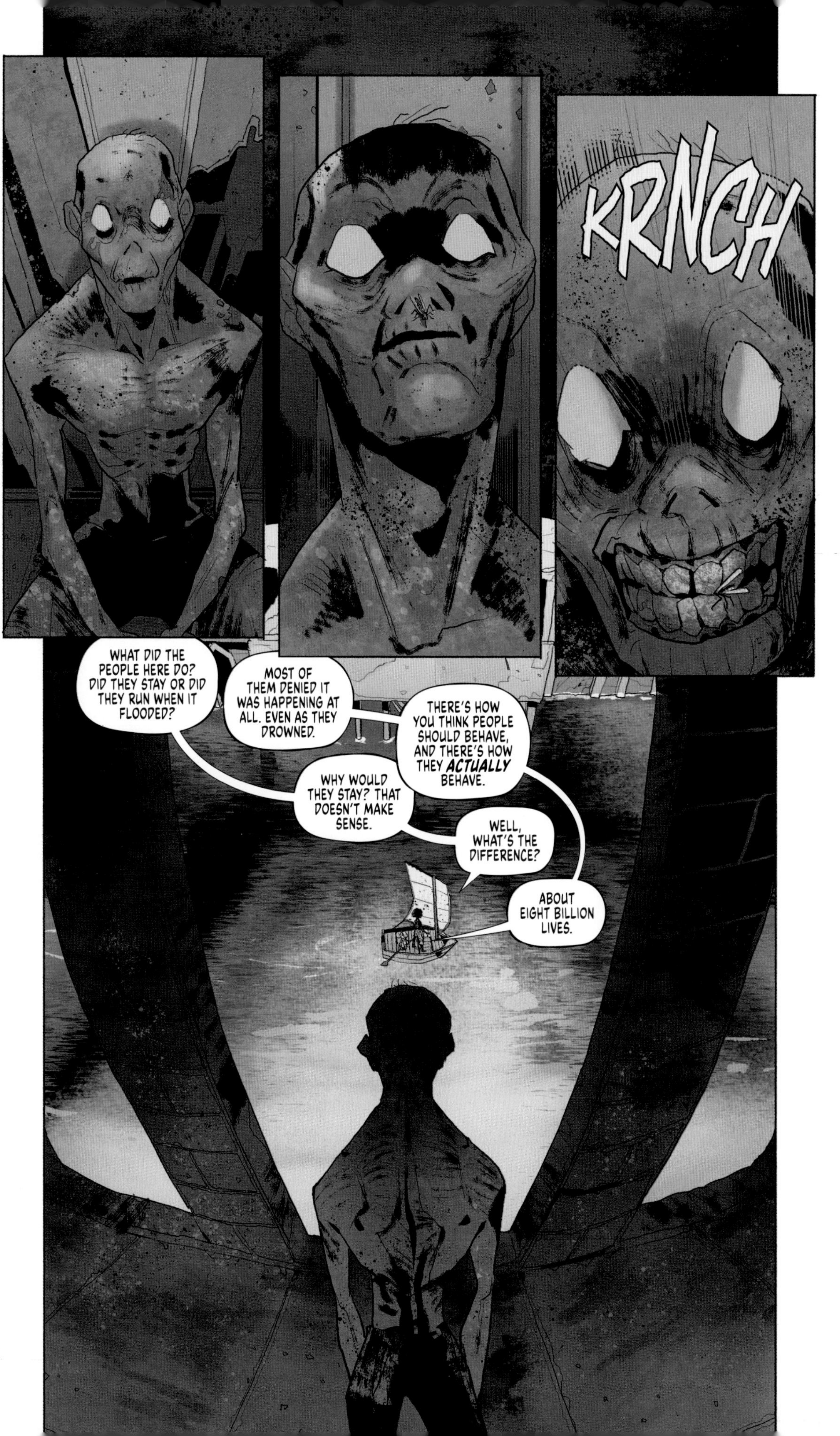
KRNCH
WHAT DID THE PEOPLE HERE DO? DID THEY STAY OR DID THEY RUN WHEN IT FLOODED?
MOST OF THEM DENIED IT WAS HAPPENING AT ALL. EVEN AS THEY DROWNED.
WHY WOULD THEY STAY? THAT DOESN'T MAKE SENSE.
THERE'S HOW YOU THINK PEOPLE SHOULD BEHAVE, AND THERE'S HOW THEY ACTUALLY BEHAVE.
WELL, WHAT'S THE DIFFERENCE?
ABOUT EIGHT BILLION LIVES.

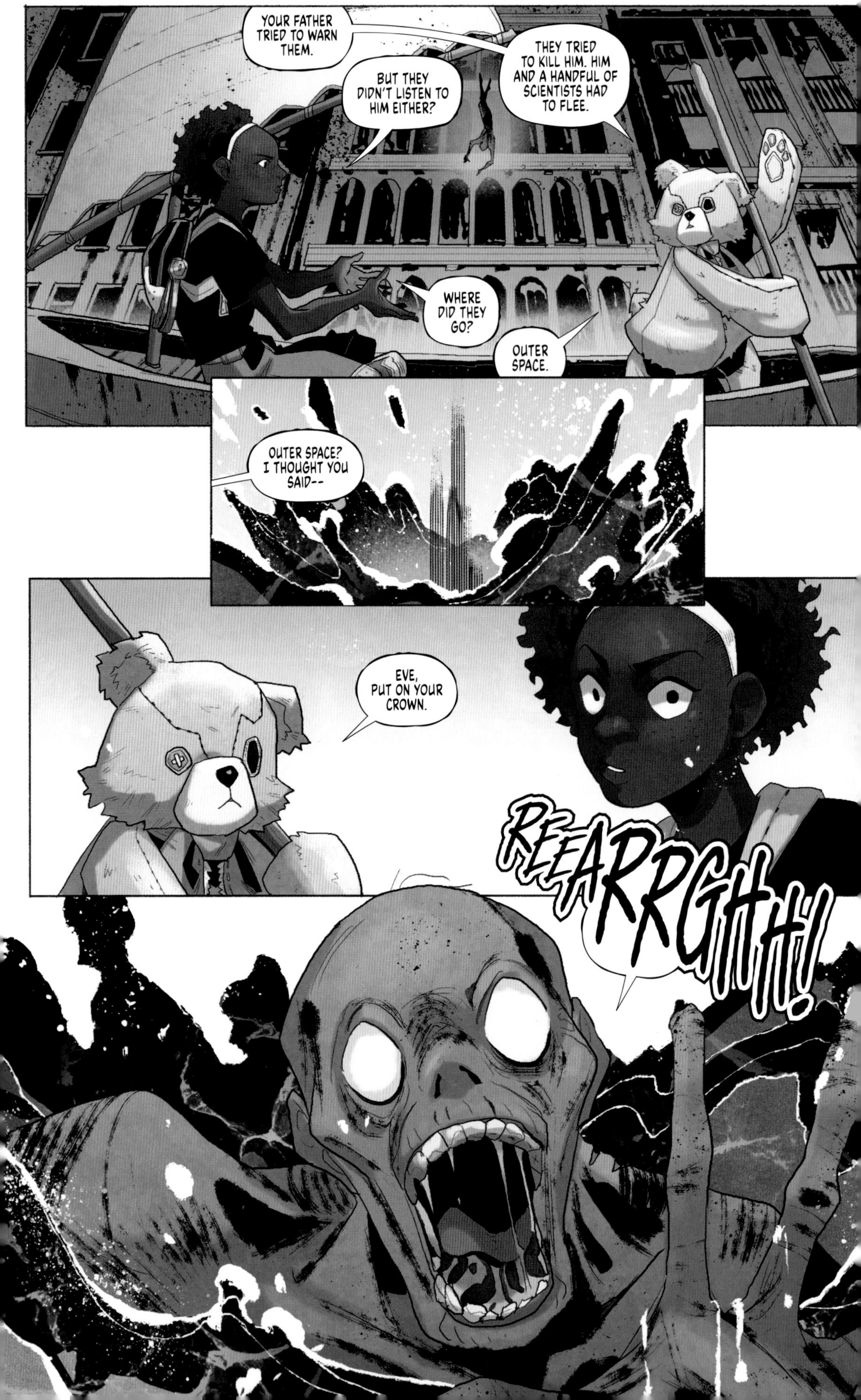
YOUR FATHER TRIED TO WARN THEM.
BUT THEY DIDN'T LISTEN TO HIM EITHER?
THEY TRIED TO KILL HIM. HIM AND A HANDFUL OF SCIENTISTS HAD TO FLEE.
WHERE DID THEY GO?
OUTER SPACE.
OUTER SPACE? I THOUGHT YOU SAID--
EVE, PUT ON YOUR CROWN.
REEARRGHH!

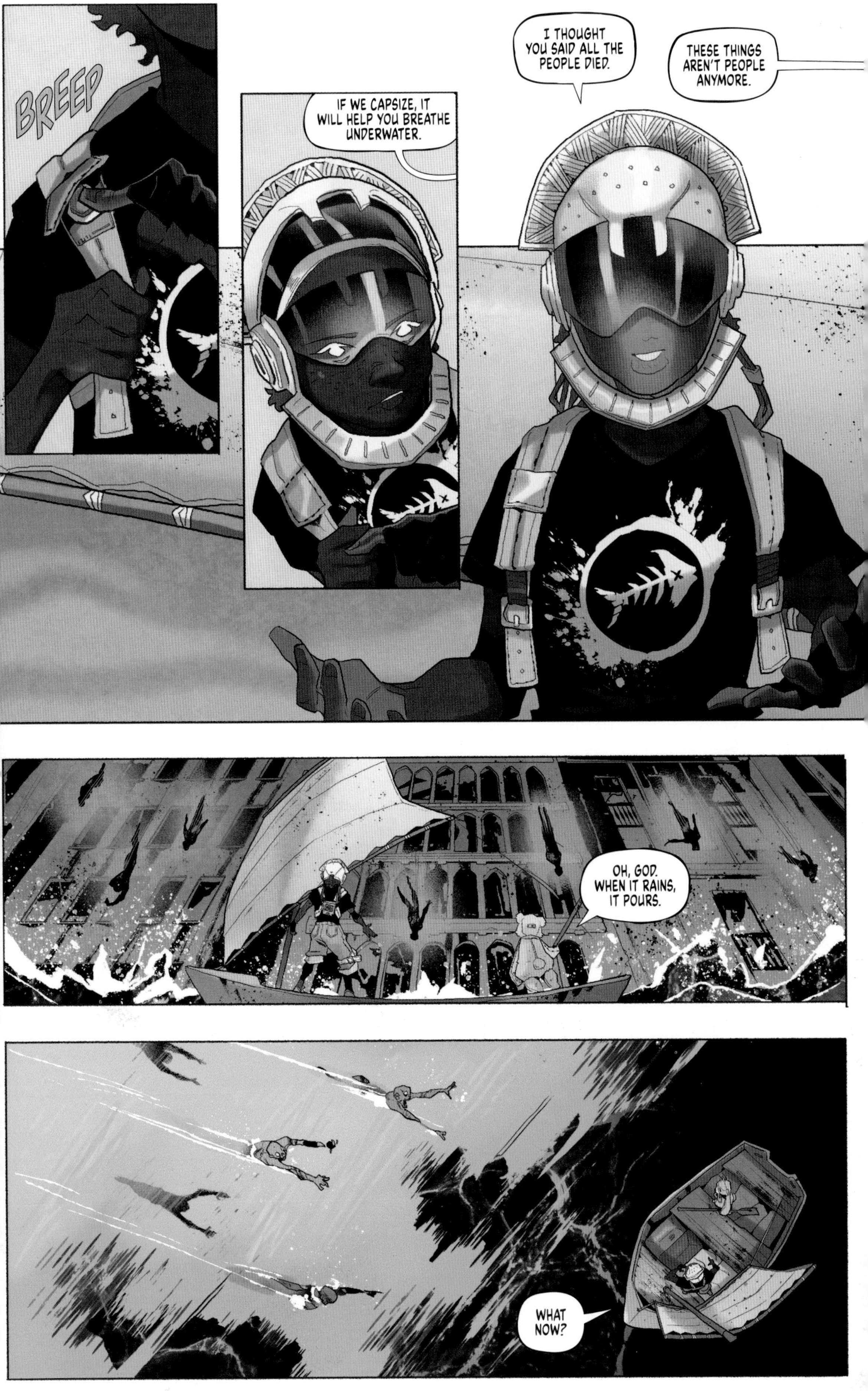
BREEP
IF WE CAPSIZE, IT WILL HELP YOU BREATHE UNDERWATER.
I THOUGHT YOU SAID ALL THE PEOPLE DIED.
THESE THINGS AREN'T PEOPLE ANYMORE.
OH, GOD. WHEN IT RAINS, IT POURS.
WHAT NOW?

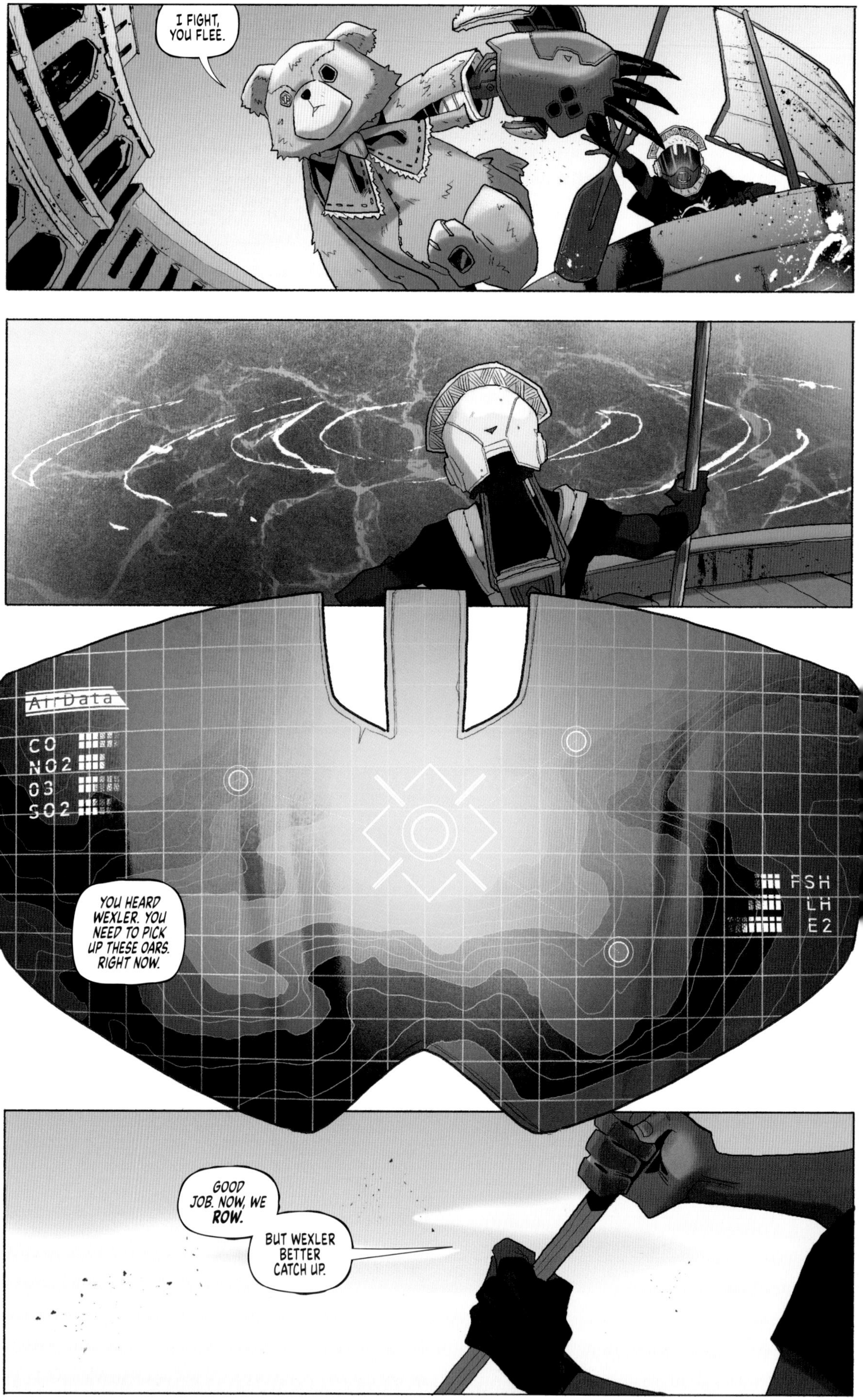
I FIGHT, YOU FLEE.
AirData
CO
NO2
O3
SO2
FSH
LH
E2
YOU HEARD WEXLER. YOU NEED TO PICK UP THESE OARS. RIGHT NOW.
GOOD JOB. NOW, WE **ROW.**
BUT WEXLER BETTER CATCH UP.

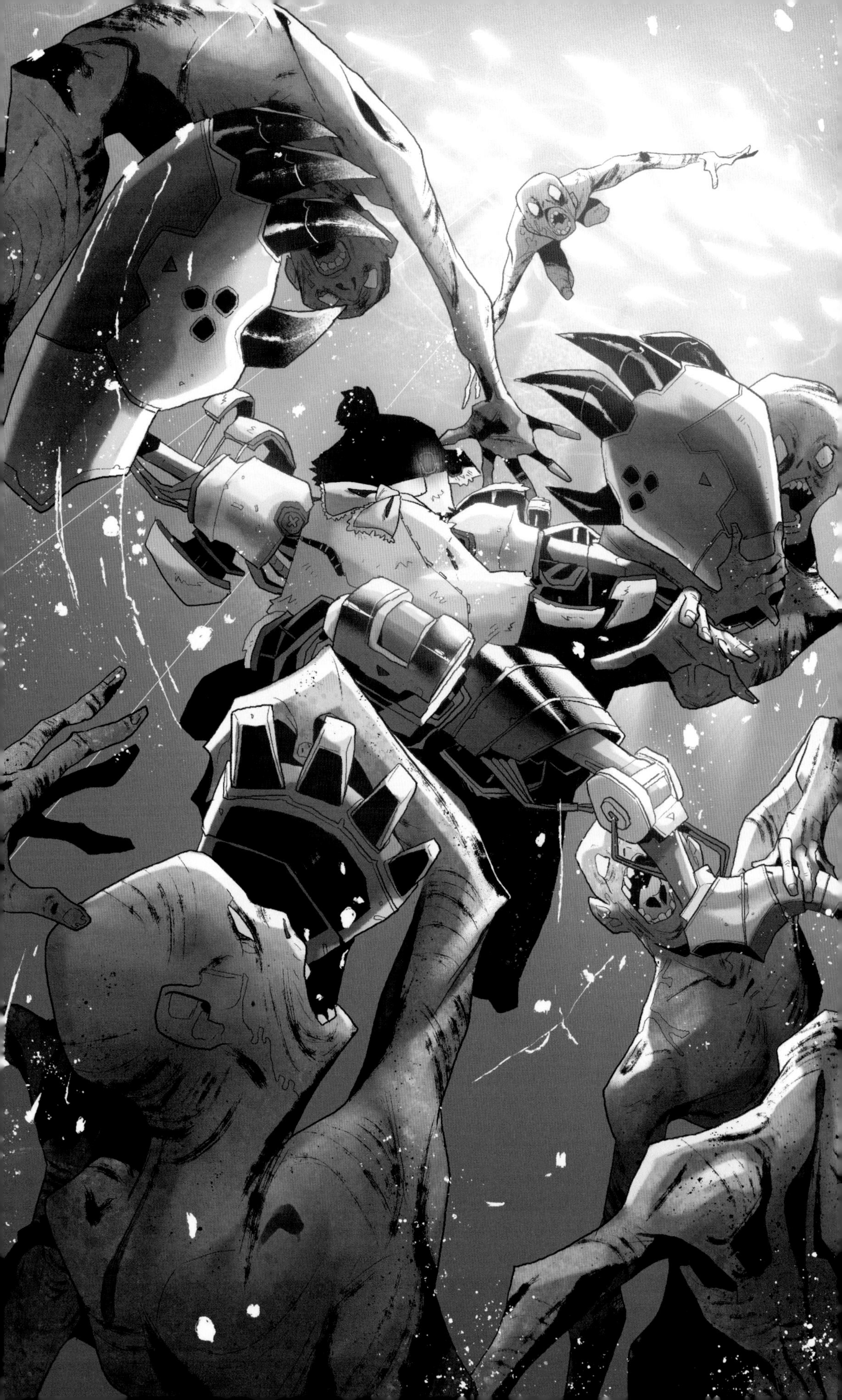

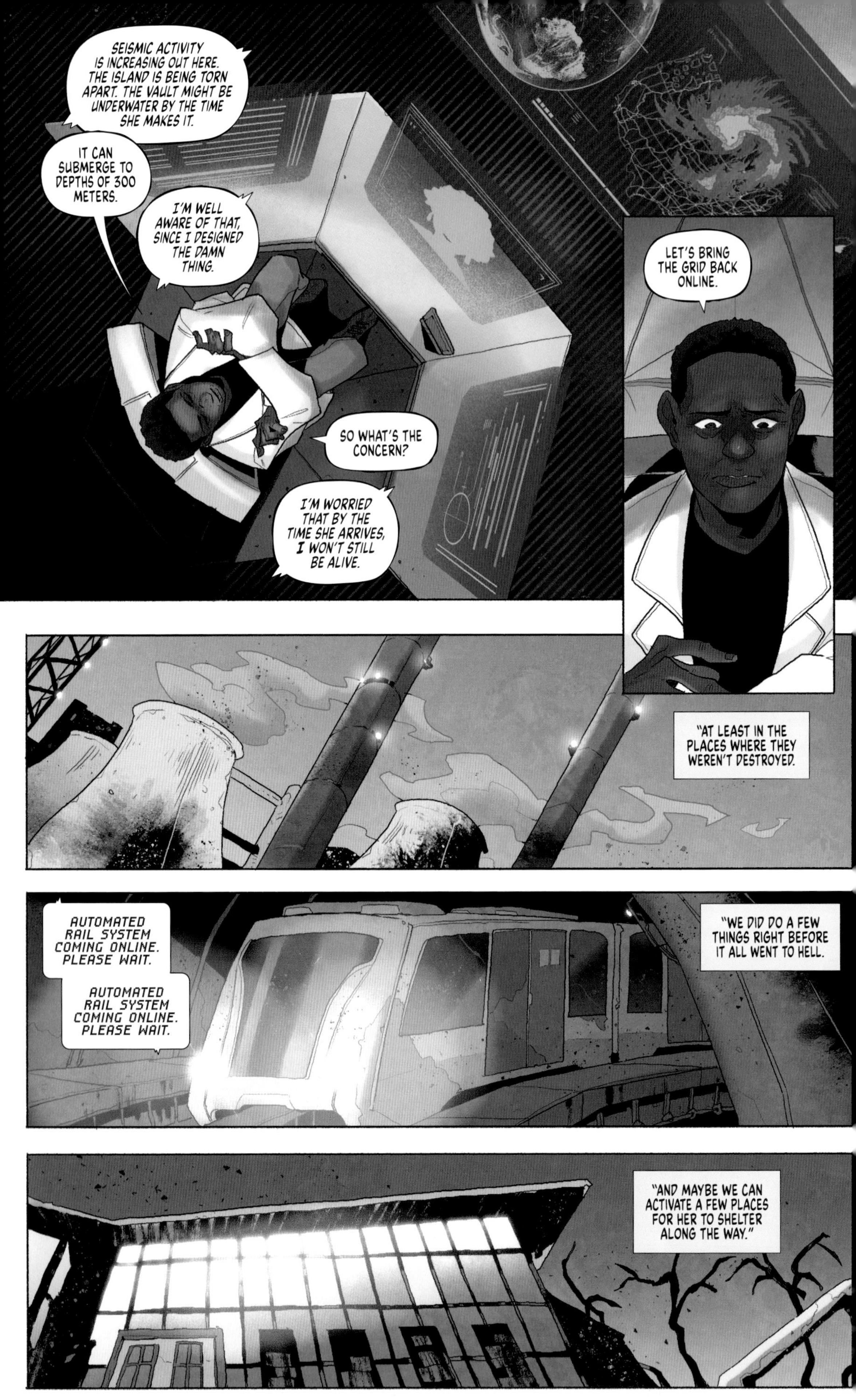
SEISMIC ACTIVITY IS INCREASING OUT HERE. THE ISLAND IS BEING TORN APART. THE VAULT MIGHT BE UNDERWATER BY THE TIME SHE MAKES IT.
IT CAN SUBMERGE TO DEPTHS OF 300 METERS.
I'M WELL AWARE OF THAT, SINCE I DESIGNED THE DAMN THING.
SO WHAT'S THE CONCERN?
I'M WORRIED THAT BY THE TIME SHE ARRIVES, I WON'T STILL BE ALIVE.
LET'S BRING THE GRID BACK ONLINE.
"AT LEAST IN THE PLACES WHERE THEY WEREN'T DESTROYED.
AUTOMATED RAIL SYSTEM COMING ONLINE. PLEASE WAIT.
AUTOMATED RAIL SYSTEM COMING ONLINE. PLEASE WAIT.
"WE DID DO A FEW THINGS RIGHT BEFORE IT ALL WENT TO HELL.
"AND MAYBE WE CAN ACTIVATE A FEW PLACES FOR HER TO SHELTER ALONG THE WAY."

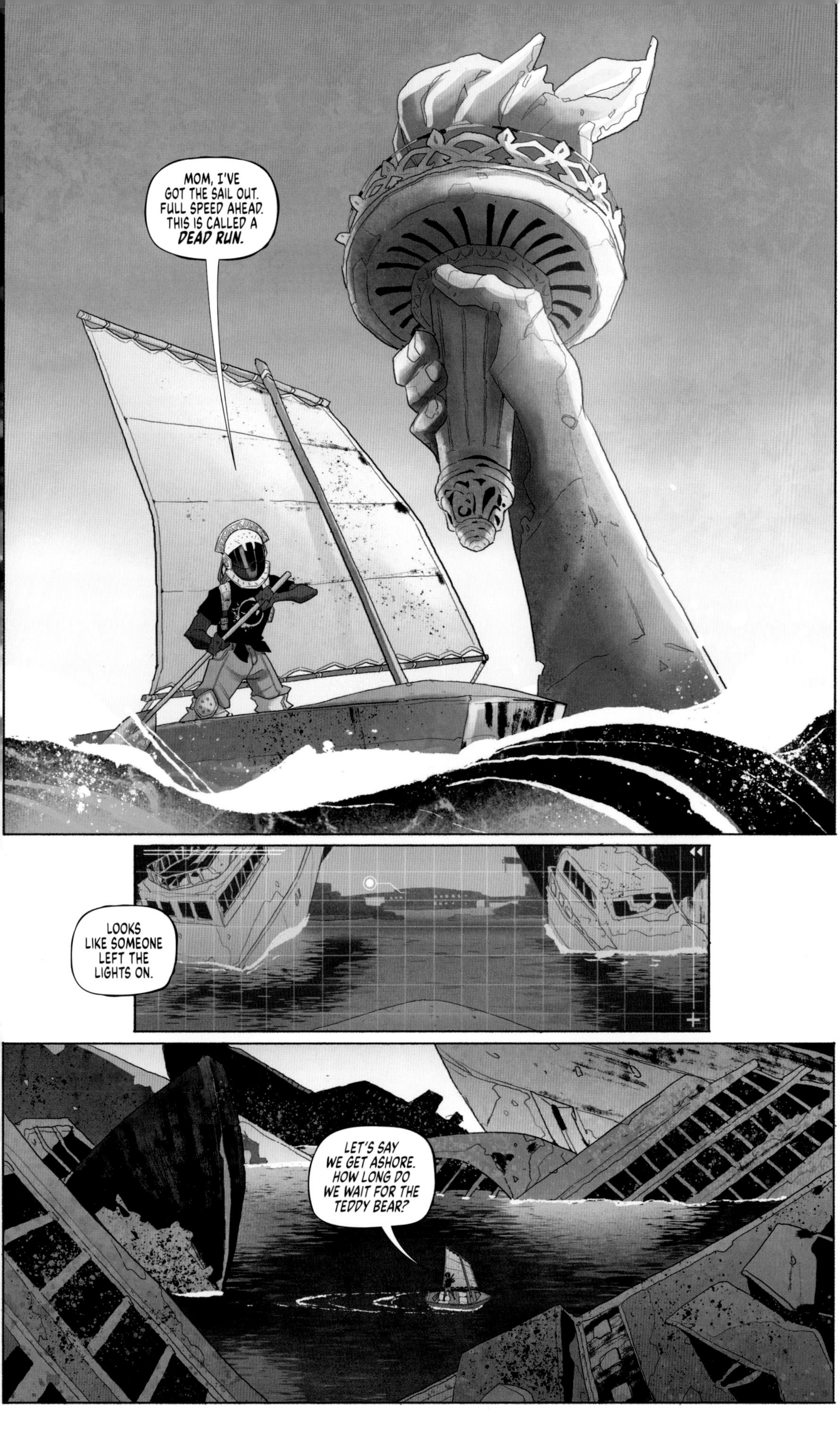
MOM, I'VE GOT THE SAIL OUT. FULL SPEED AHEAD. THIS IS CALLED A DEAD RUN.
LOOKS LIKE SOMEONE LEFT THE LIGHTS ON.
LET'S SAY WE GET ASHORE. HOW LONG DO WE WAIT FOR THE TEDDY BEAR?

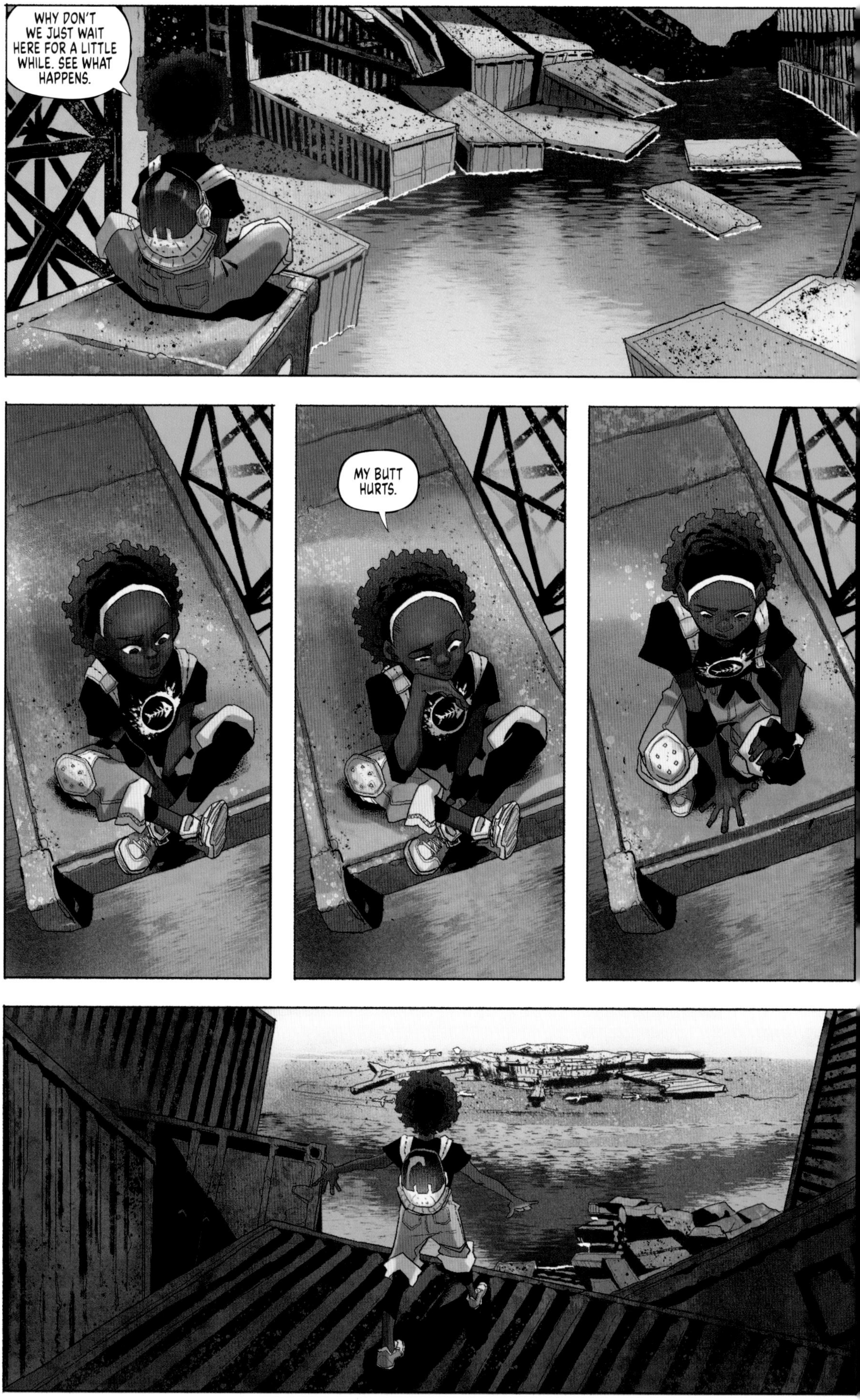
WHY DON'T WE JUST WAIT HERE FOR A LITTLE WHILE. SEE WHAT HAPPENS.
MY BUTT HURTS.

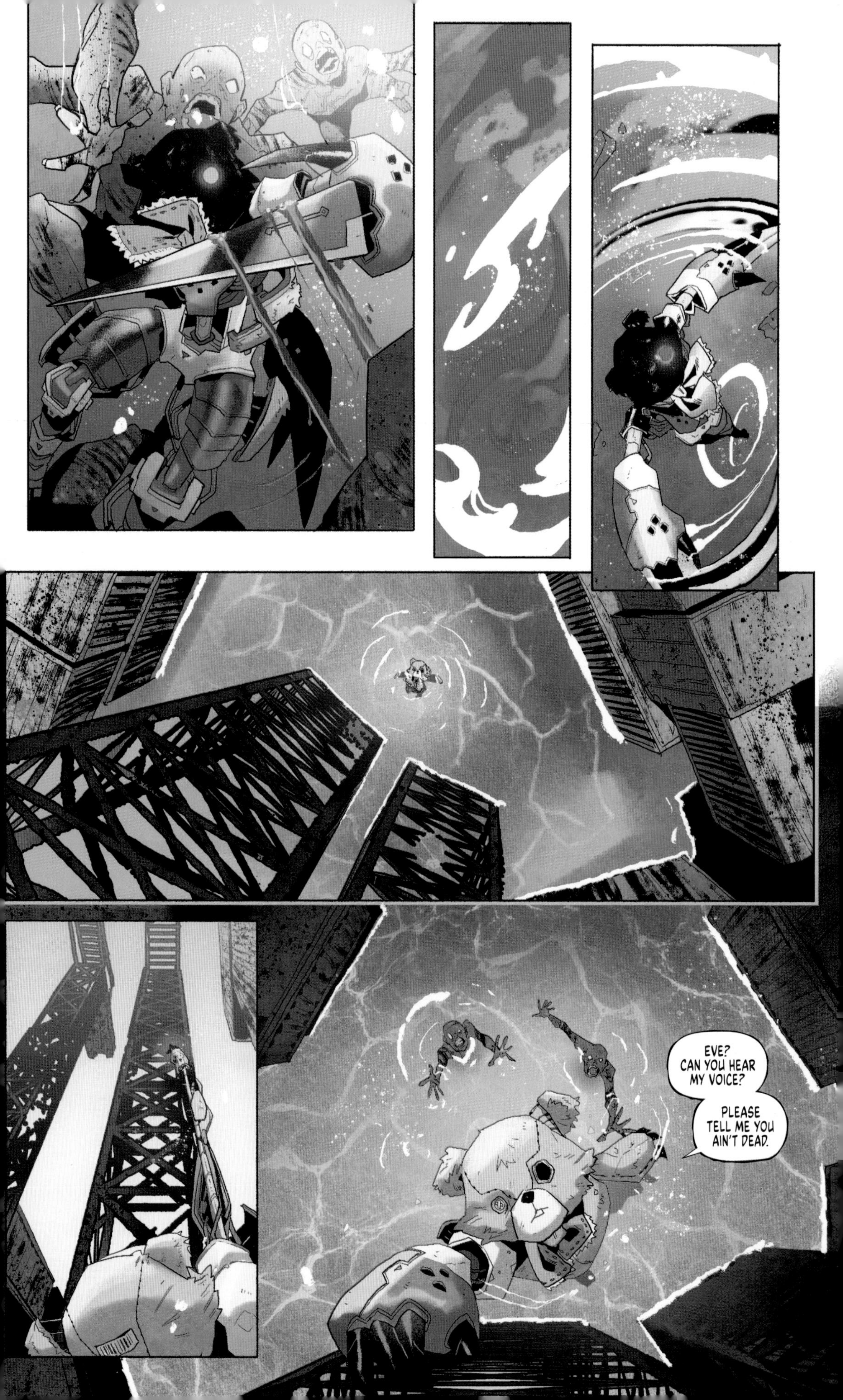
EVE? CAN YOU HEAR MY VOICE?
PLEASE TELL ME YOU AIN'T DEAD.

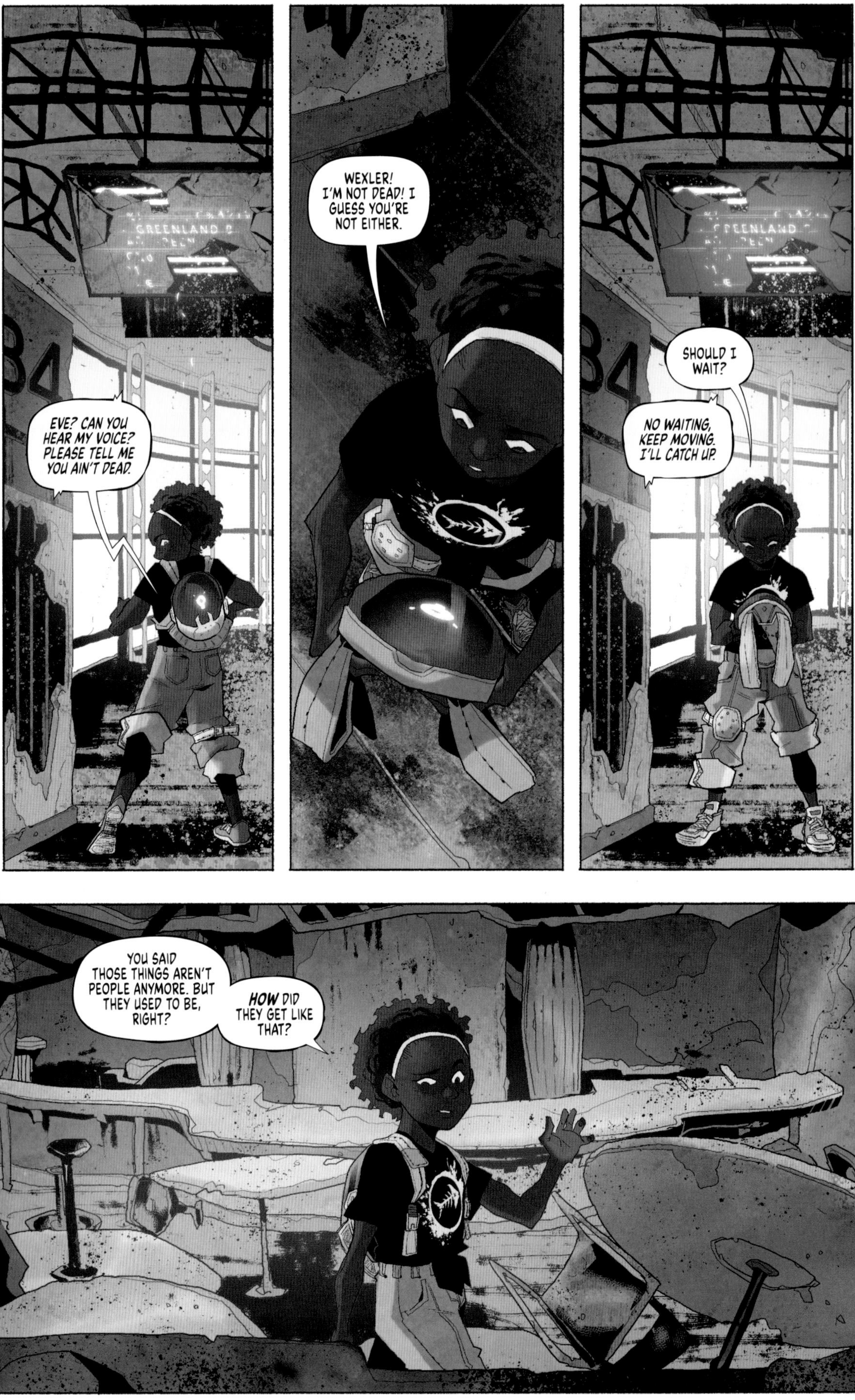
EVE? CAN YOU HEAR MY VOICE? PLEASE TELL ME YOU AIN'T DEAD.
WEXLER! I'M NOT DEAD! I GUESS YOU'RE NOT EITHER.
SHOULD I WAIT?
NO WAITING, KEEP MOVING. I'LL CATCH UP.
YOU SAID THOSE THINGS AREN'T PEOPLE ANYMORE. BUT THEY USED TO BE, RIGHT?
HOW DID THEY GET LIKE THAT?

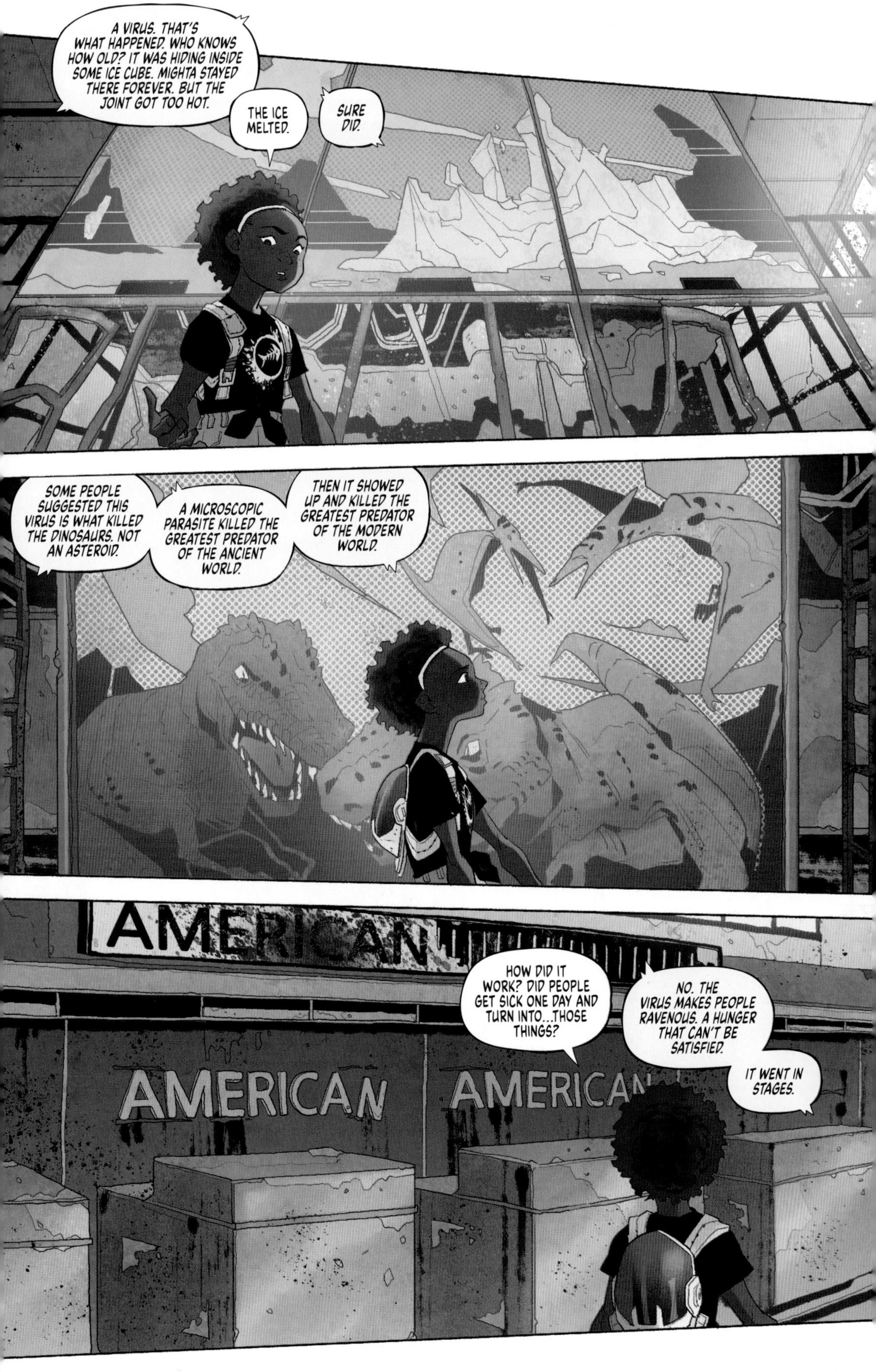

A VIRUS. THAT'S WHAT HAPPENED. WHO KNOWS HOW OLD? IT WAS HIDING INSIDE SOME ICE CUBE. MIGHTA STAYED THERE FOREVER. BUT THE JOINT GOT TOO HOT.
THE ICE MELTED.
SURE DID.
SOME PEOPLE SUGGESTED THIS VIRUS IS WHAT KILLED THE DINOSAURS. NOT AN ASTEROID.
A MICROSCOPIC PARASITE KILLED THE GREATEST PREDATOR OF THE ANCIENT WORLD.
THEN IT SHOWED UP AND KILLED THE GREATEST PREDATOR OF THE MODERN WORLD.
AMERICAN
HOW DID IT WORK? DID PEOPLE GET SICK ONE DAY AND TURN INTO...THOSE THINGS?
NO. THE VIRUS MAKES PEOPLE RAVENOUS. A HUNGER THAT CAN'T BE SATISFIED.
IT WENT IN STAGES.
AMERICAN
AMERICAN

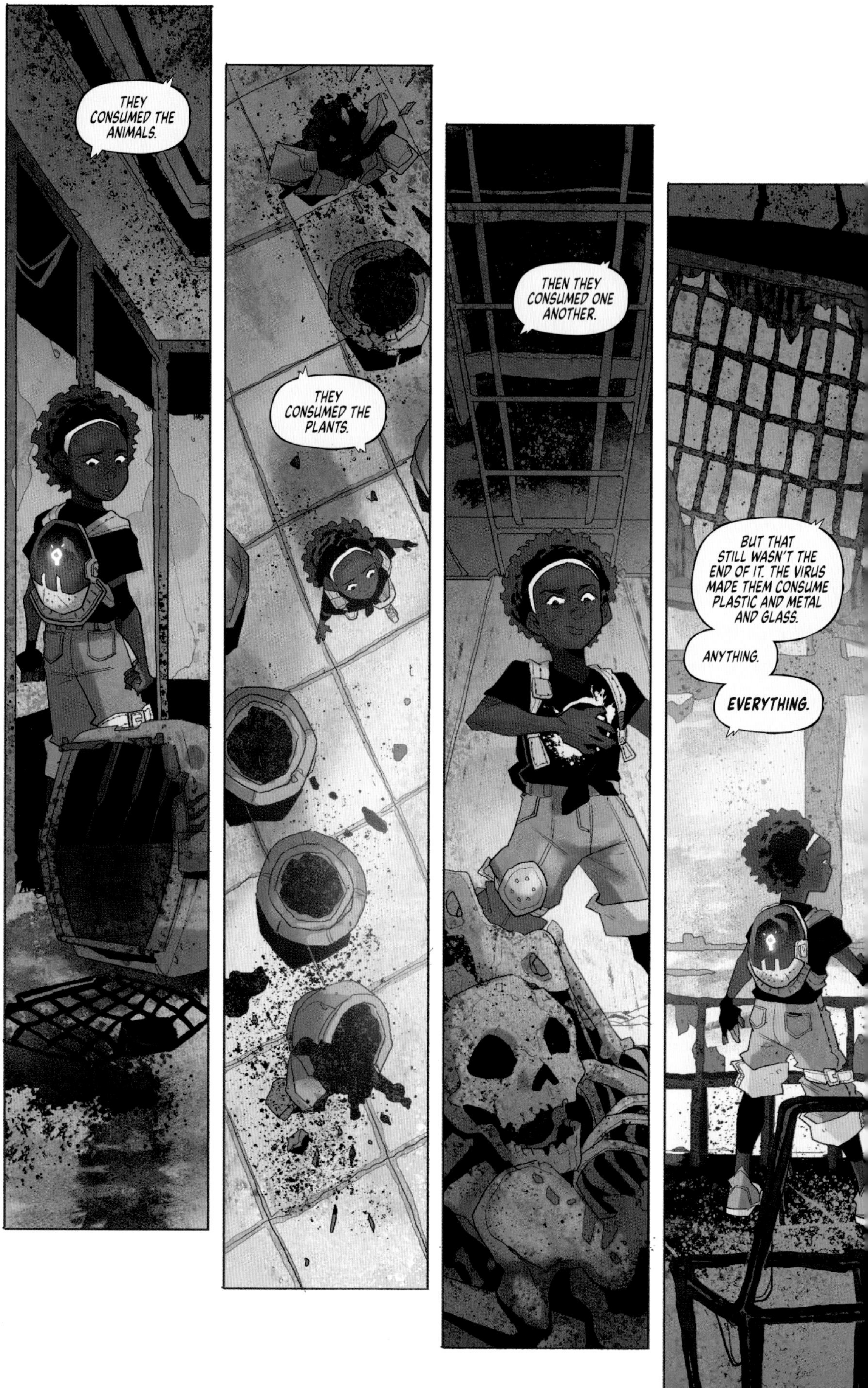
THEY CONSUMED THE ANIMALS.
THEY CONSUMED THE PLANTS.
THEN THEY CONSUMED ONE ANOTHER.
BUT THAT STILL WASN'T THE END OF IT. THE VIRUS MADE THEM CONSUME PLASTIC AND METAL AND GLASS.
ANYTHING.
EVERYTHING.

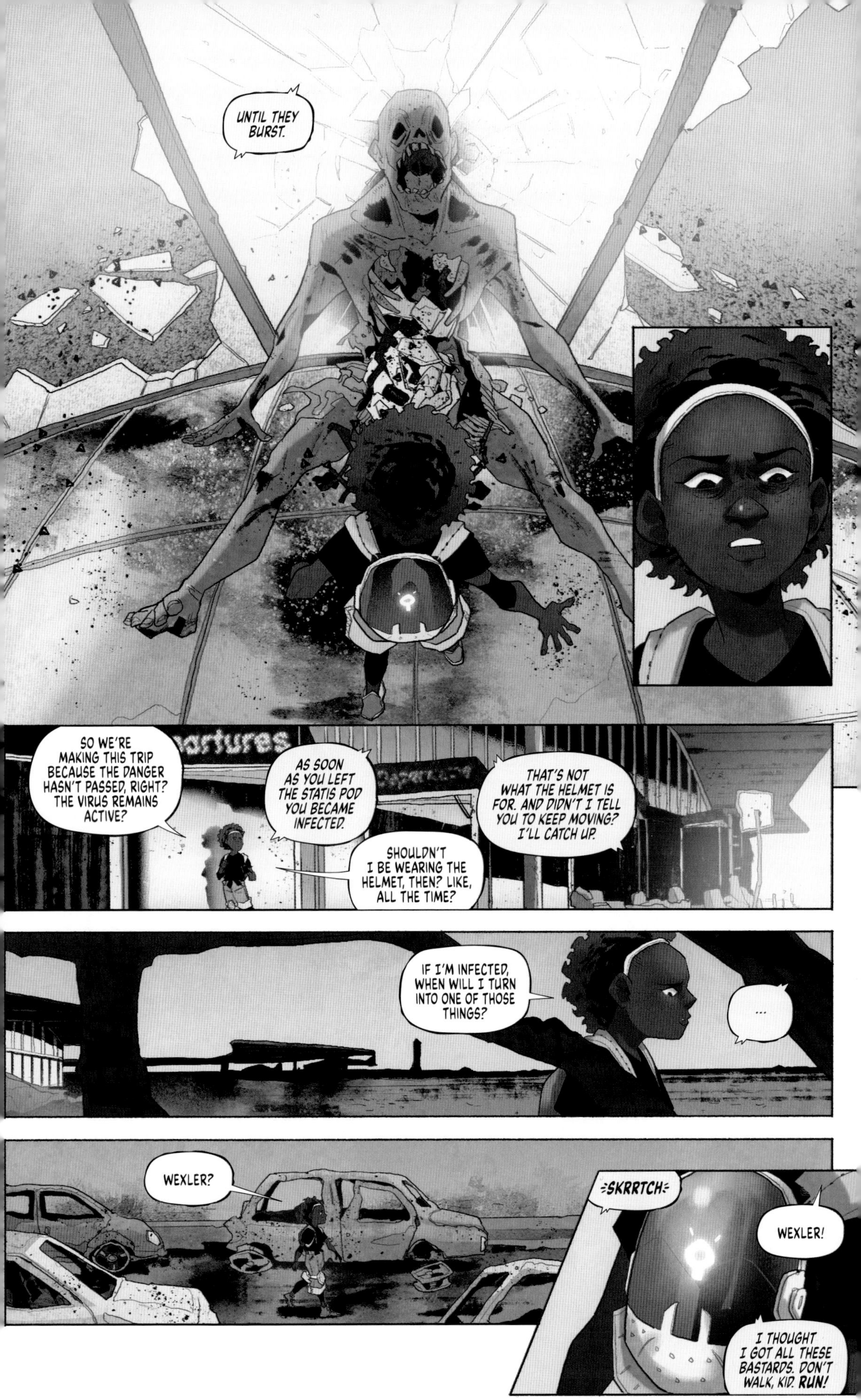

UNTIL THEY BURST.
SO WE'RE MAKING THIS TRIP BECAUSE THE DANGER HASN'T PASSED, RIGHT? THE VIRUS REMAINS ACTIVE?
AS SOON AS YOU LEFT THE STATIS POD YOU BECAME INFECTED.
SHOULDN'T I BE WEARING THE HELMET, THEN? LIKE, ALL THE TIME?
THAT'S NOT WHAT THE HELMET IS FOR. AND DIDN'T I TELL YOU TO KEEP MOVING? I'LL CATCH UP.
IF I'M INFECTED, WHEN WILL I TURN INTO ONE OF THOSE THINGS?
...
WEXLER?
SKRRTCH
WEXLER!
I THOUGHT I GOT ALL THESE BASTARDS. DON'T WALK, KID. **RUN!**

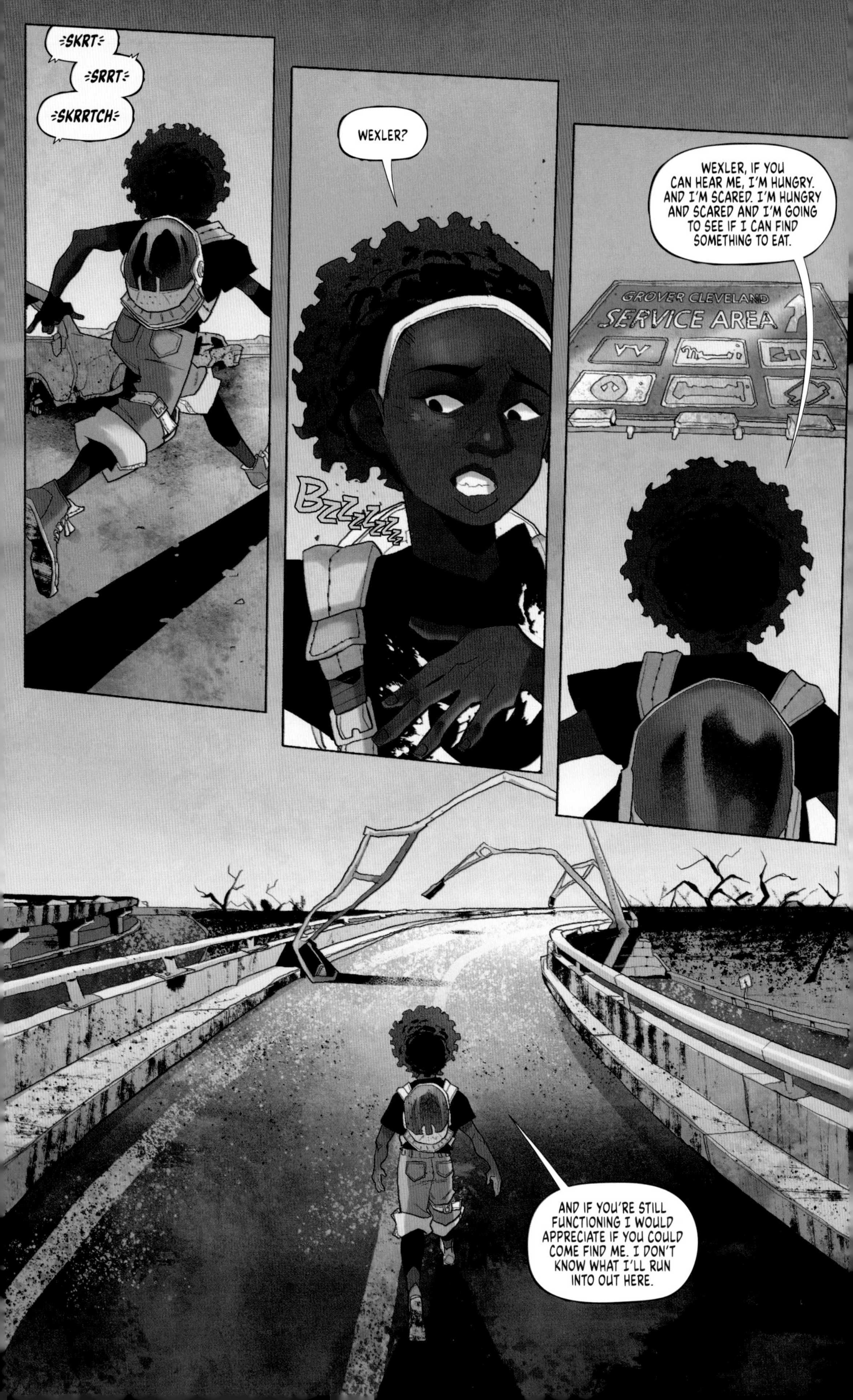
SKRT
SRRT
SKRRTCH
WEXLER?
BZZZZZZZ
GROVER CLEVELAND SERVICE AREA
WEXLER, IF YOU CAN HEAR ME, I'M HUNGRY. AND I'M SCARED. I'M HUNGRY AND SCARED AND I'M GOING TO SEE IF I CAN FIND SOMETHING TO EAT.
AND IF YOU'RE STILL FUNCTIONING I WOULD APPRECIATE IF YOU COULD COME FIND ME. I DON'T KNOW WHAT I'LL RUN INTO OUT HERE.

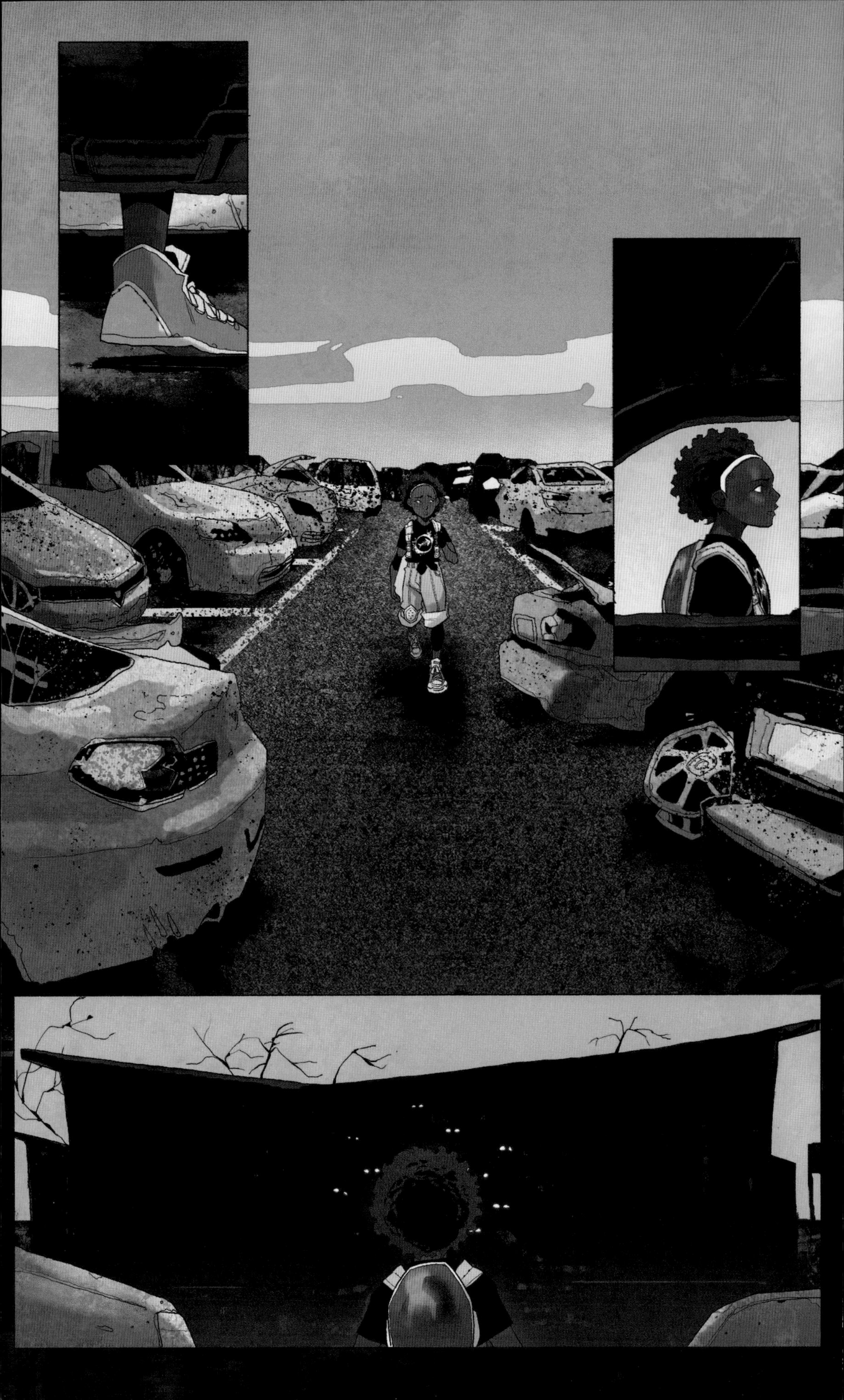

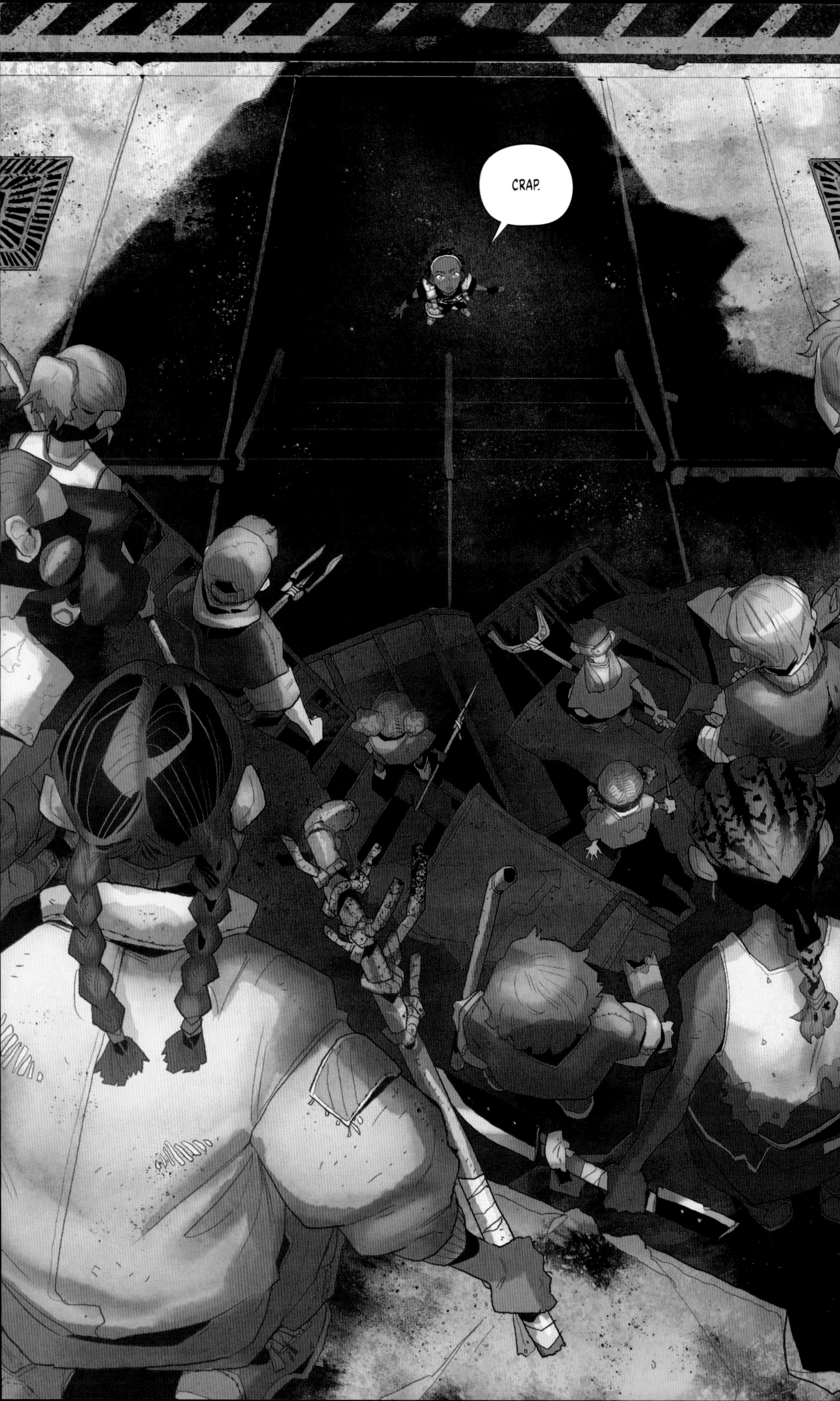
CRAP.

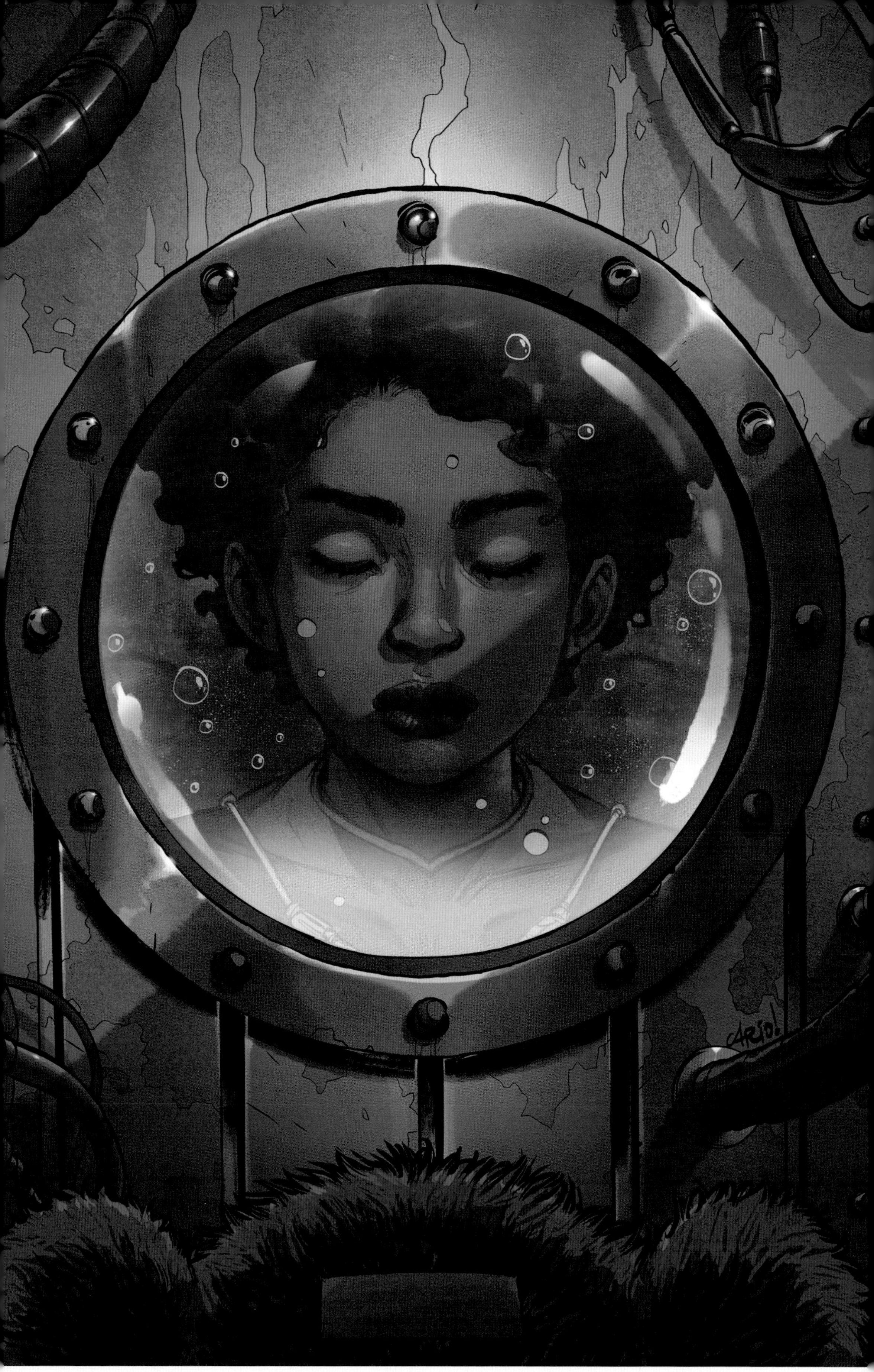
ARIO!

ISSUE #2 COVER BY **ARIO ANINDITO** WITH COLORS BY **PIERLUIGI CASOLINO**

CHAPTER
THREE

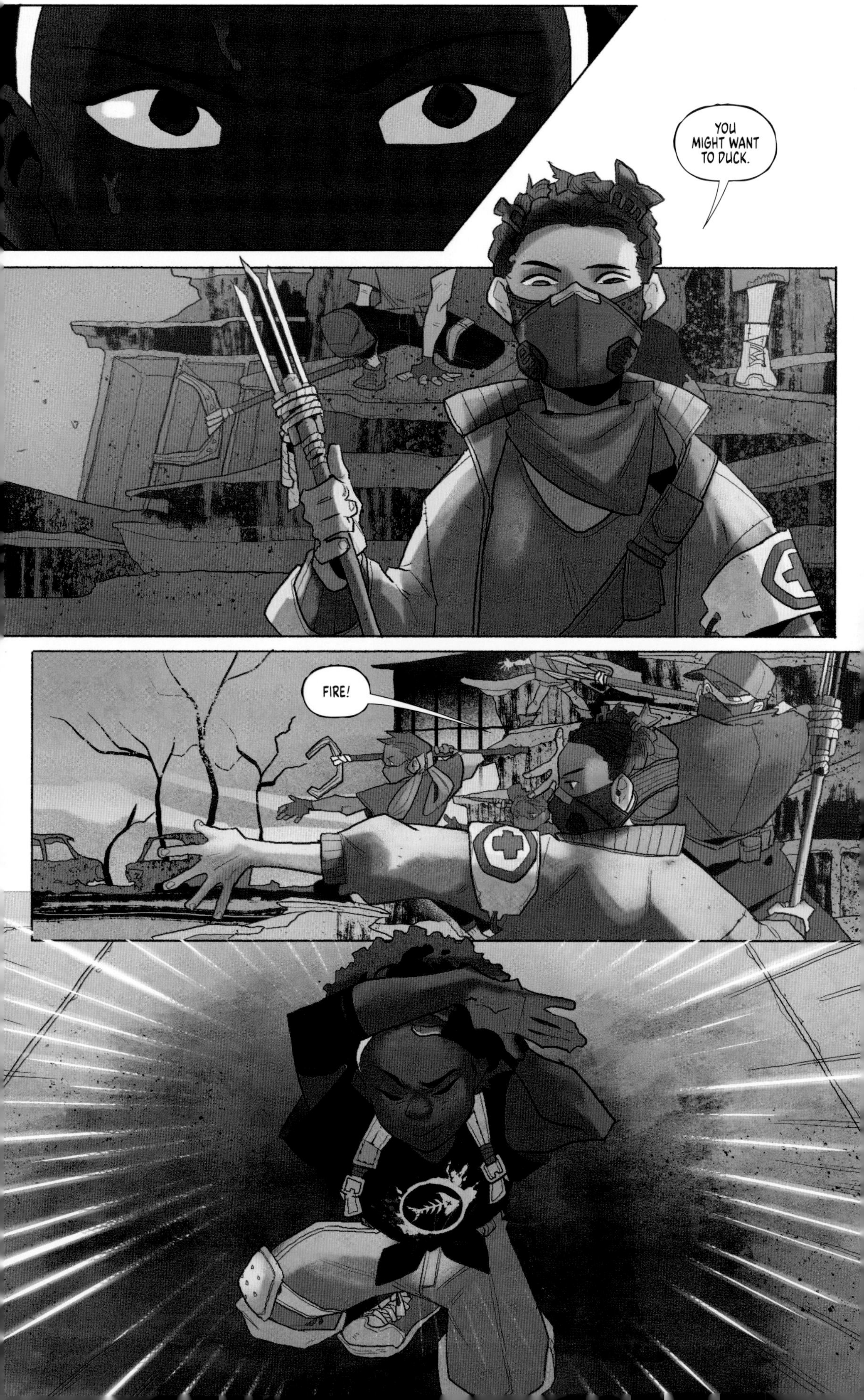

YOU MIGHT WANT TO DUCK.
FIRE!

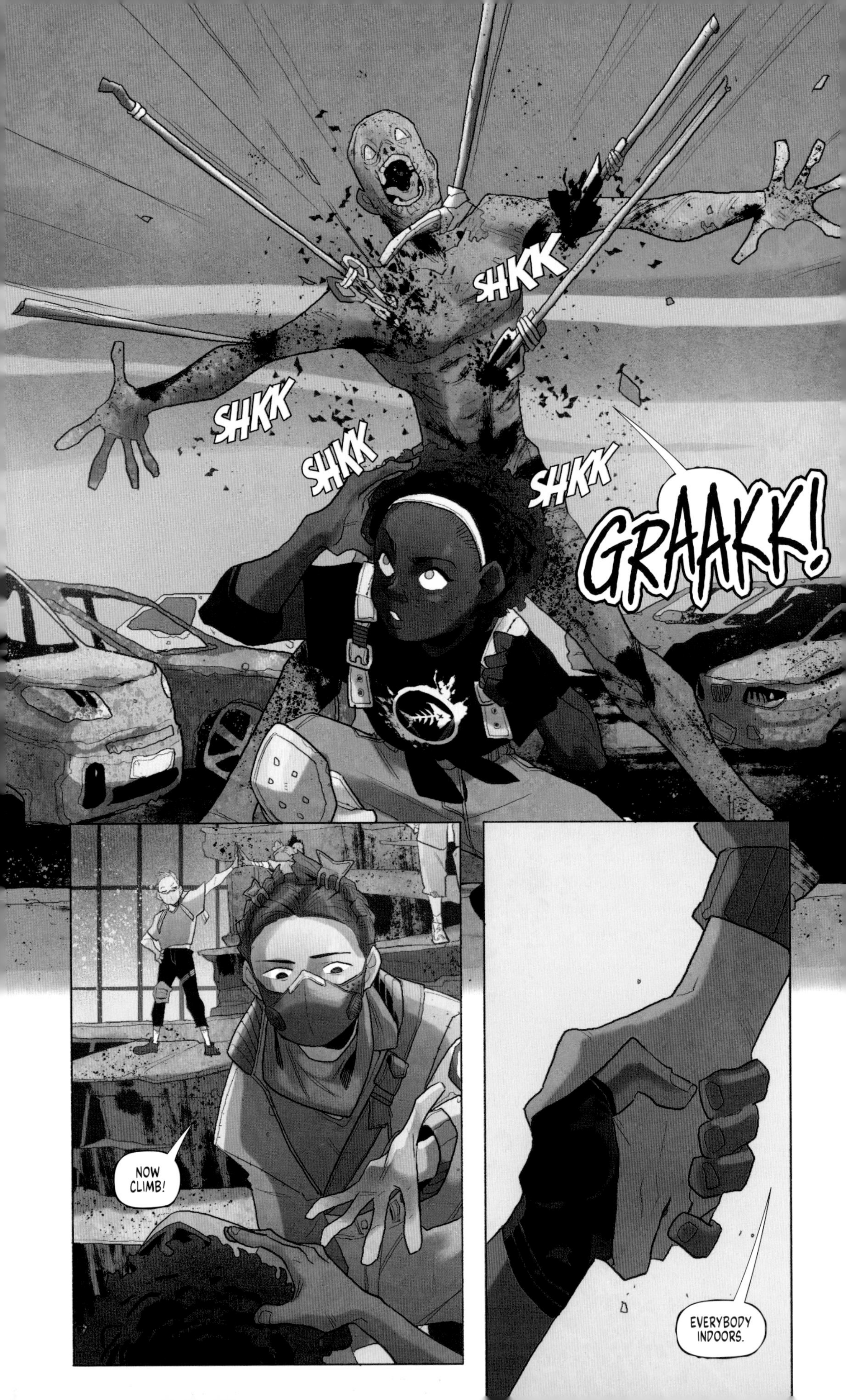
SHKK
SHKK
SHKK
SHKK
GRAAKK!
NOW CLIMB!
EVERYBODY INDOORS.

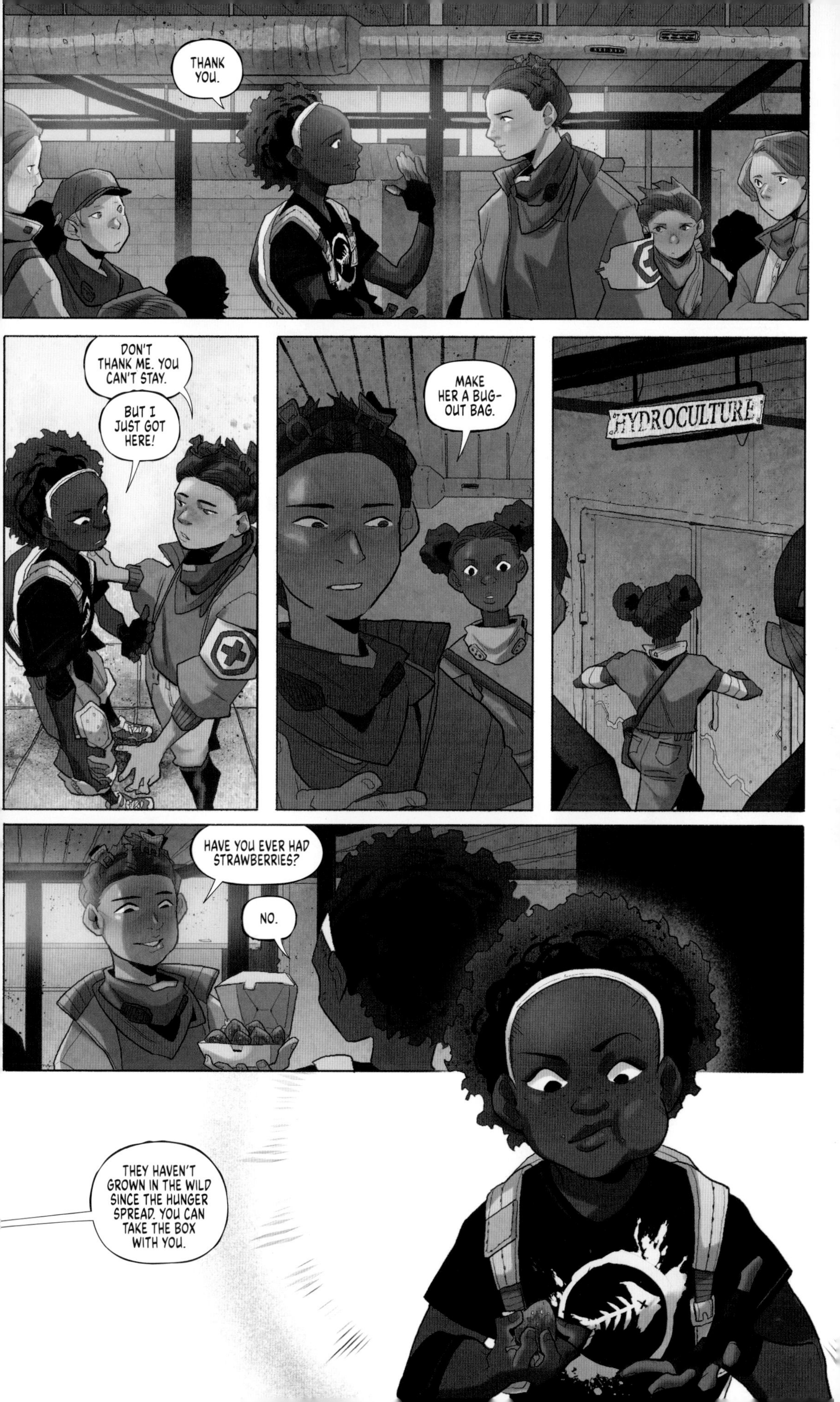
THANK YOU.
DON'T THANK ME. YOU CAN'T STAY.
BUT I JUST GOT HERE!
MAKE HER A BUG-OUT BAG.
HYDROCULTURE
HAVE YOU EVER HAD STRAWBERRIES?
NO.
THEY HAVEN'T GROWN IN THE WILD SINCE THE HUNGER SPREAD. YOU CAN TAKE THE BOX WITH YOU.

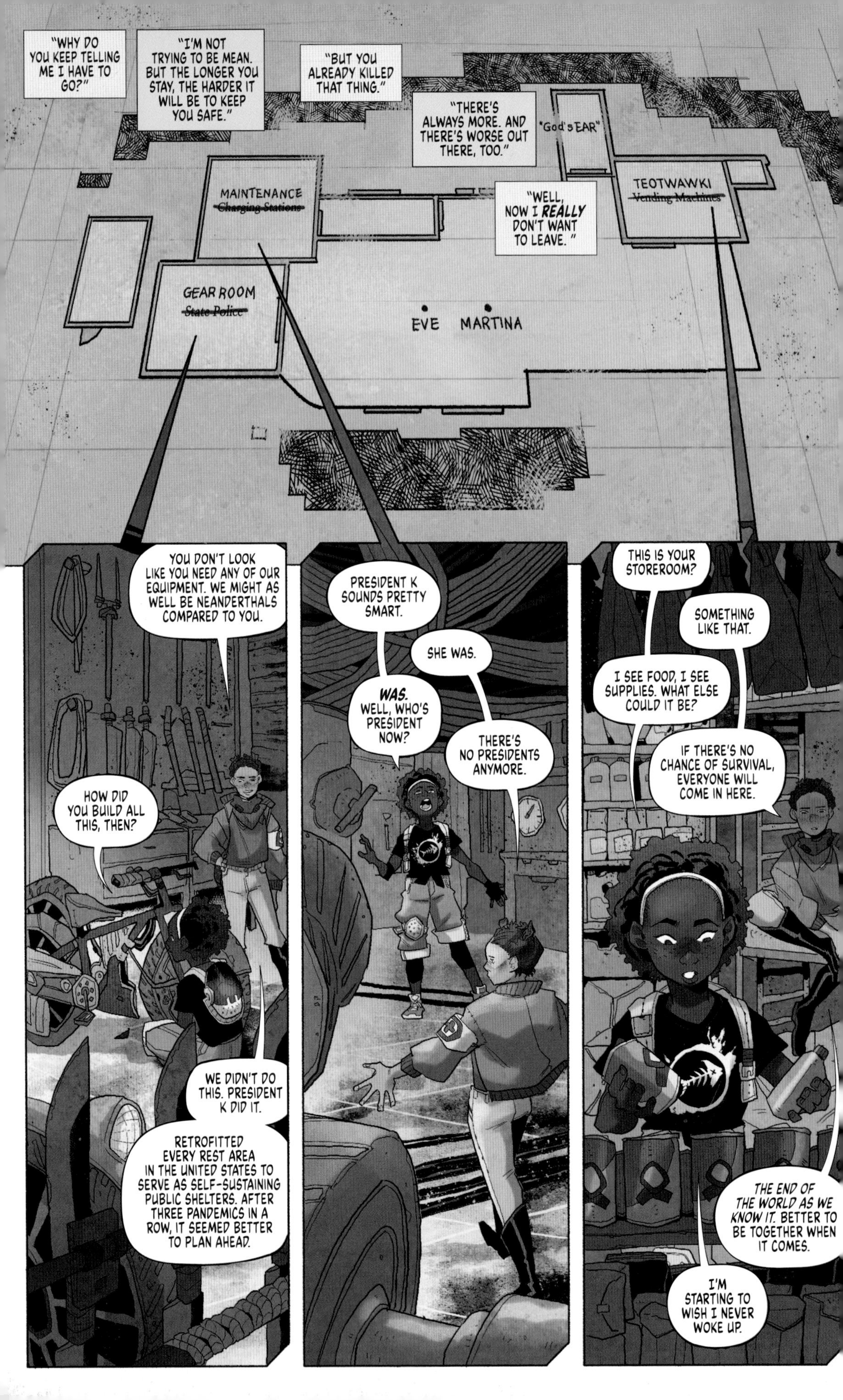
"WHY DO YOU KEEP TELLING ME I HAVE TO GO?"
"I'M NOT TRYING TO BE MEAN. BUT THE LONGER YOU STAY, THE HARDER IT WILL BE TO KEEP YOU SAFE."
"BUT YOU ALREADY KILLED THAT THING."
"THERE'S ALWAYS MORE. AND THERE'S WORSE OUT THERE, TOO."
"God's EAR"
"WELL, NOW I *REALLY* DON'T WANT TO LEAVE."
MAINTENANCE
~~Charging Stations~~
TEOTWAWKI
~~Vending Machines~~
GEAR ROOM
~~State Police~~
EVE
MARTINA
YOU DON'T LOOK LIKE YOU NEED ANY OF OUR EQUIPMENT. WE MIGHT AS WELL BE NEANDERTHALS COMPARED TO YOU.
HOW DID YOU BUILD ALL THIS, THEN?
WE DIDN'T DO THIS. PRESIDENT K DID IT.
RETROFITTED EVERY REST AREA IN THE UNITED STATES TO SERVE AS SELF-SUSTAINING PUBLIC SHELTERS. AFTER THREE PANDEMICS IN A ROW, IT SEEMED BETTER TO PLAN AHEAD.
PRESIDENT K SOUNDS PRETTY SMART.
SHE WAS.
WAS. WELL, WHO'S PRESIDENT NOW?
THERE'S NO PRESIDENTS ANYMORE.
THIS IS YOUR STOREROOM?
SOMETHING LIKE THAT.
I SEE FOOD, I SEE SUPPLIES. WHAT ELSE COULD IT BE?
IF THERE'S NO CHANCE OF SURVIVAL, EVERYONE WILL COME IN HERE.
THE END OF THE WORLD AS WE KNOW IT. BETTER TO BE TOGETHER WHEN IT COMES.
I'M STARTING TO WISH I NEVER WOKE UP.

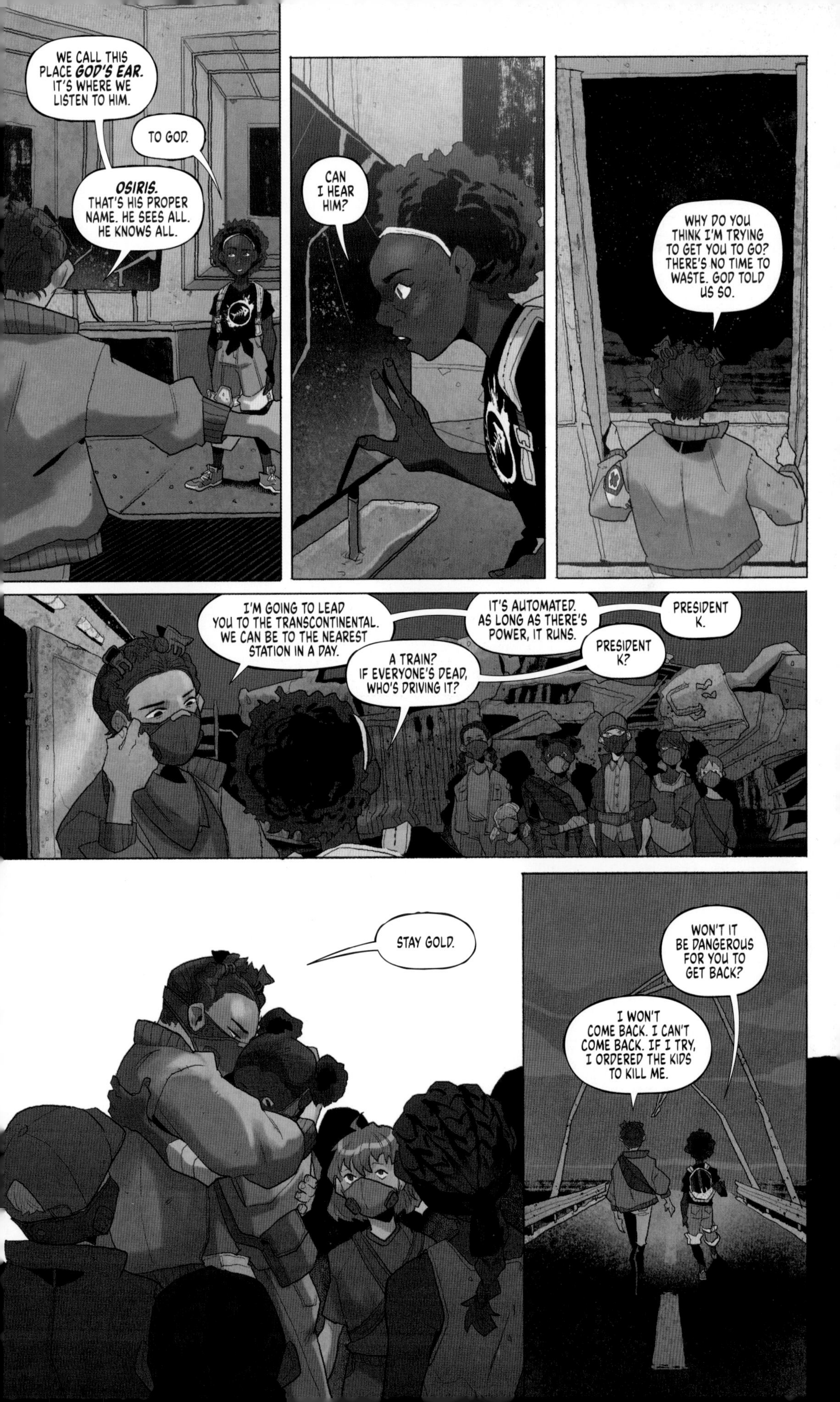
WE CALL THIS PLACE GOD'S EAR. IT'S WHERE WE LISTEN TO HIM.
TO GOD.
OSIRIS. THAT'S HIS PROPER NAME. HE SEES ALL. HE KNOWS ALL.
CAN I HEAR HIM?
WHY DO YOU THINK I'M TRYING TO GET YOU TO GO? THERE'S NO TIME TO WASTE. GOD TOLD US SO.
I'M GOING TO LEAD YOU TO THE TRANSCONTINENTAL. WE CAN BE TO THE NEAREST STATION IN A DAY.
A TRAIN? IF EVERYONE'S DEAD, WHO'S DRIVING IT?
IT'S AUTOMATED. AS LONG AS THERE'S POWER, IT RUNS.
PRESIDENT K?
PRESIDENT K.
STAY GOLD.
WON'T IT BE DANGEROUS FOR YOU TO GET BACK?
I WON'T COME BACK. I CAN'T COME BACK. IF I TRY, I ORDERED THE KIDS TO KILL ME.

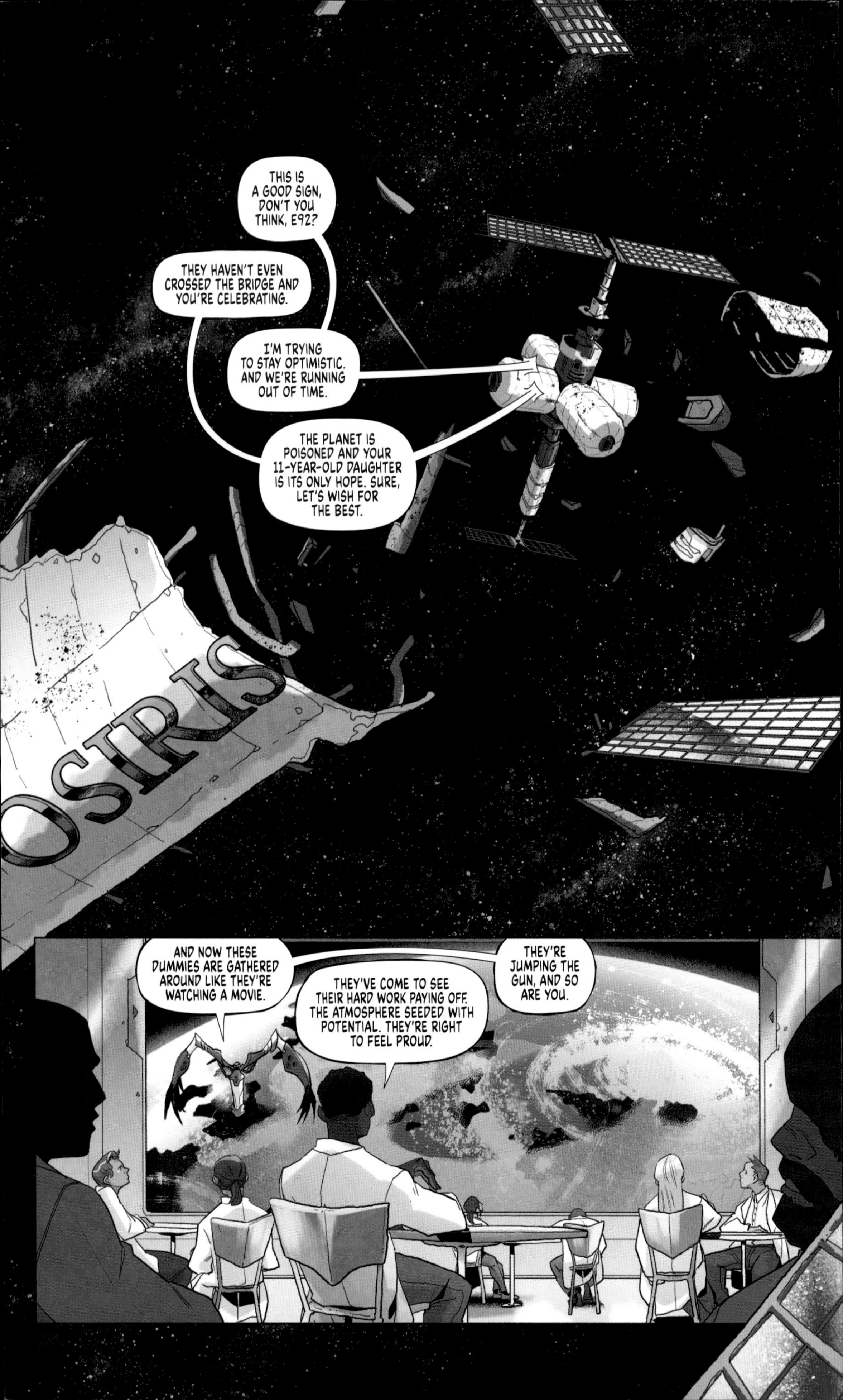
THIS IS A GOOD SIGN, DON'T YOU THINK, E92?
THEY HAVEN'T EVEN CROSSED THE BRIDGE AND YOU'RE CELEBRATING.
I'M TRYING TO STAY OPTIMISTIC. AND WE'RE RUNNING OUT OF TIME.
THE PLANET IS POISONED AND YOUR 11-YEAR-OLD DAUGHTER IS ITS ONLY HOPE. SURE, LET'S WISH FOR THE BEST.
OSIRIS
AND NOW THESE DUMMIES ARE GATHERED AROUND LIKE THEY'RE WATCHING A MOVIE.
THEY'VE COME TO SEE THEIR HARD WORK PAYING OFF. THE ATMOSPHERE SEEDED WITH POTENTIAL. THEY'RE RIGHT TO FEEL PROUD.
THEY'RE JUMPING THE GUN, AND SO ARE YOU.

"THEY'VE BEEN STUCK INSIDE THIS STATION FOR LONGER THAN ANY OF US CARE TO COUNT.

"WE BEGAN TO DESPAIR THAT WE'D EVER WALK OUTSIDE, SMELL FRESH AIR AGAIN.

"AND NOW WE SIT ON THE CUSP OF CHANGE. OF RENEWING THE POSSIBILITIES OF THE PLANET AND ITS FUTURE."

AND IF SHE MAKES IT, THEN WHAT?

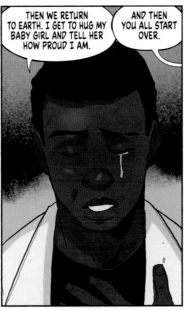

THEN WE RETURN TO EARTH. I GET TO HUG MY BABY GIRL AND TELL HER HOW PROUD I AM.

AND THEN YOU ALL START OVER.

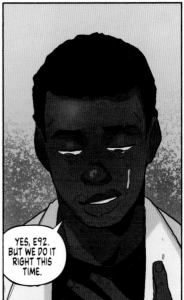

YES, E92. BUT WE DO IT RIGHT THIS TIME.

LET ME ASK YOU, AND DON'T TAKE THIS THE WRONG WAY, BUT HOW MANY CHANCES DO YOU ALL DESERVE?

IF A MACHINE FAILED AS OFTEN AS HUMANITY HAS, WOULDN'T YOU SCRAP THE INVENTION BY NOW?

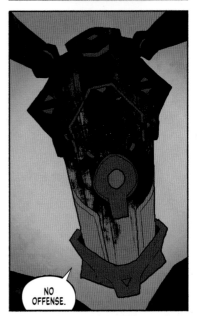

NO OFFENSE.

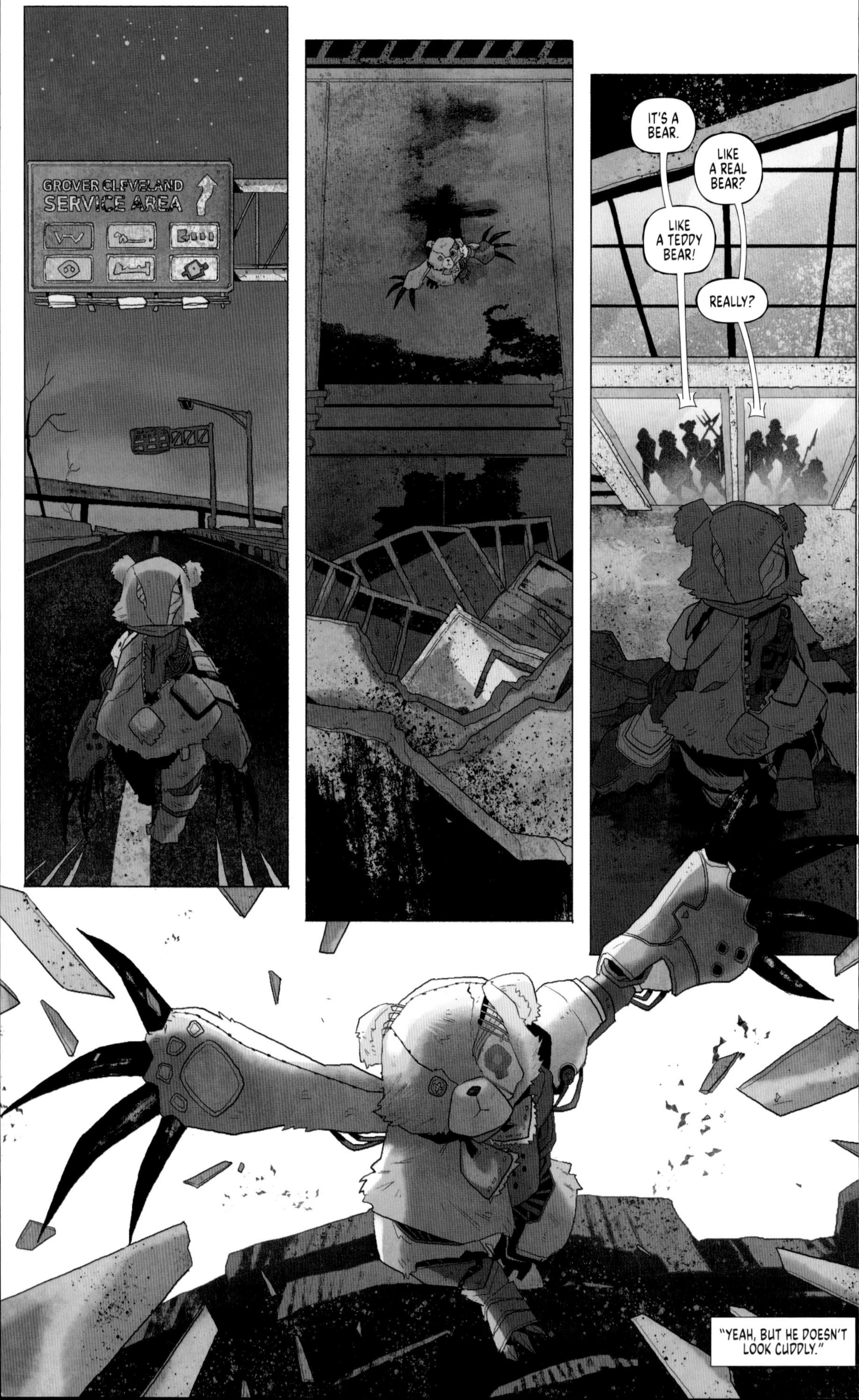
GROVER CLEVELAND
SERVICE AREA
IT'S A BEAR.
LIKE A REAL BEAR?
LIKE A TEDDY BEAR!
REALLY?
"YEAH, BUT HE DOESN'T LOOK CUDDLY."

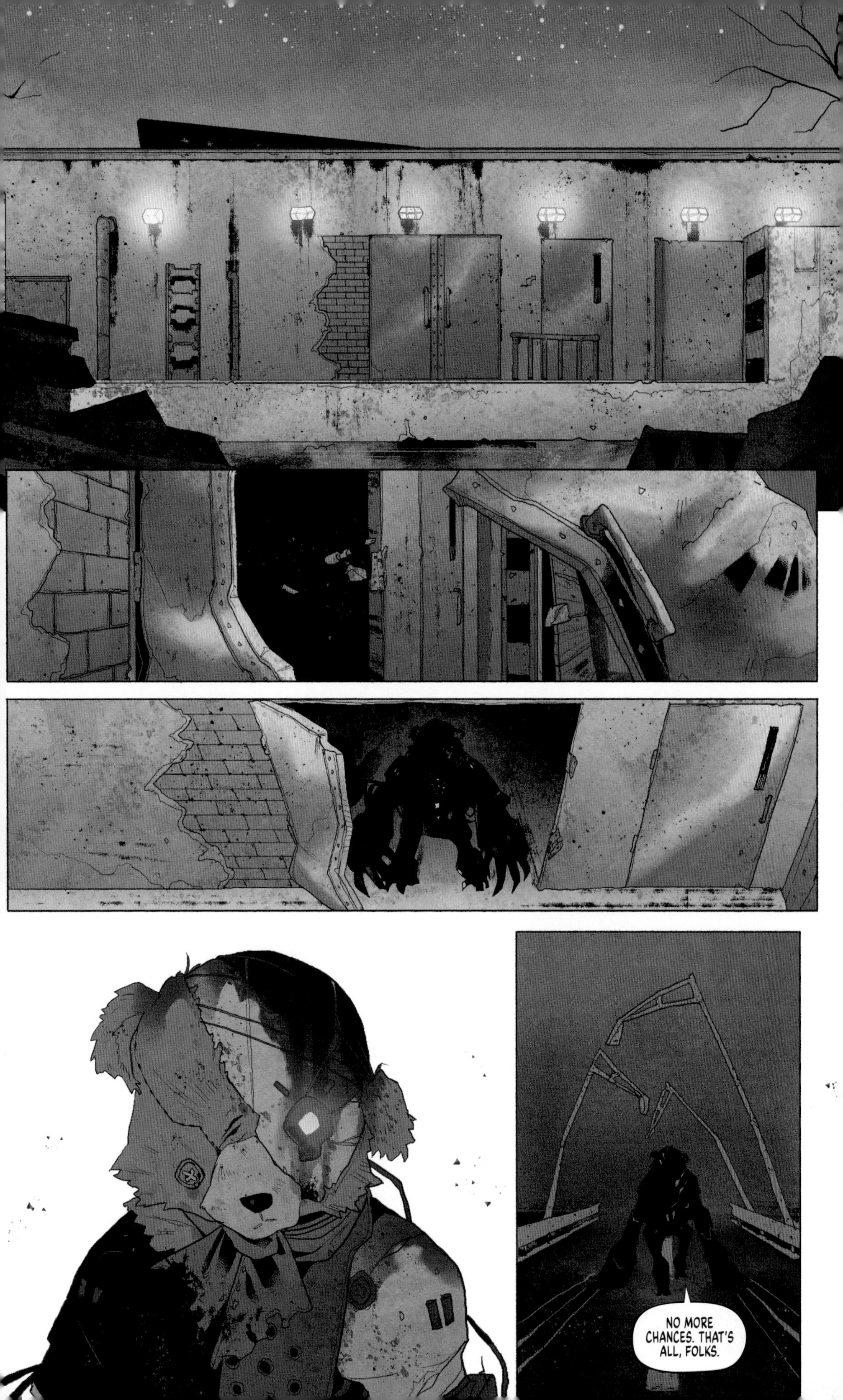
NO MORE CHANCES. THAT'S ALL, FOLKS.

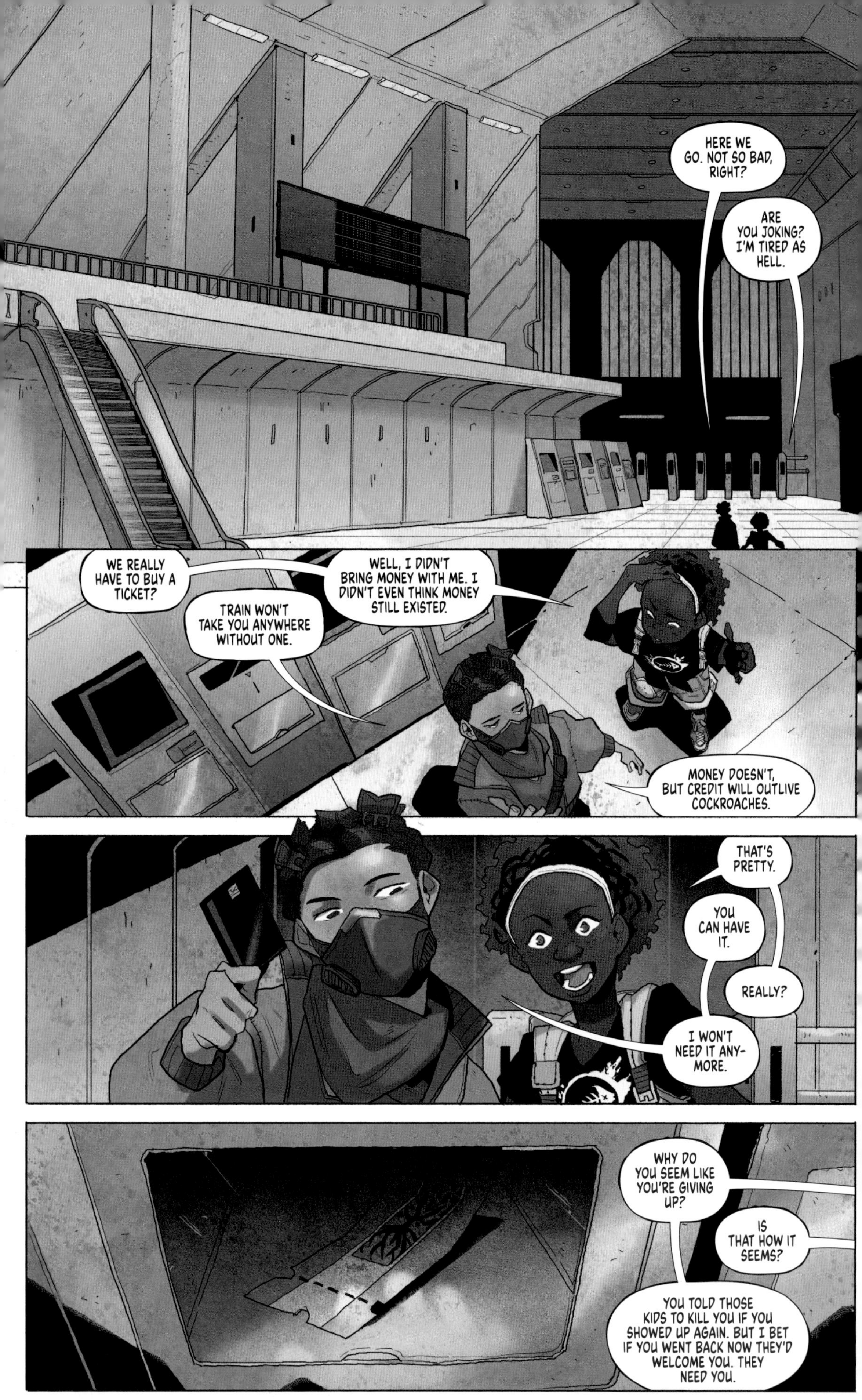
HERE WE GO. NOT SO BAD, RIGHT?
ARE YOU JOKING? I'M TIRED AS HELL.
WE REALLY HAVE TO BUY A TICKET?
TRAIN WON'T TAKE YOU ANYWHERE WITHOUT ONE.
WELL, I DIDN'T BRING MONEY WITH ME. I DIDN'T EVEN THINK MONEY STILL EXISTED.
MONEY DOESN'T, BUT CREDIT WILL OUTLIVE COCKROACHES.
THAT'S PRETTY.
YOU CAN HAVE IT.
REALLY?
I WON'T NEED IT ANY-MORE.
WHY DO YOU SEEM LIKE YOU'RE GIVING UP?
IS THAT HOW IT SEEMS?
YOU TOLD THOSE KIDS TO KILL YOU IF YOU SHOWED UP AGAIN. BUT I BET IF YOU WENT BACK NOW THEY'D WELCOME YOU. THEY NEED YOU.

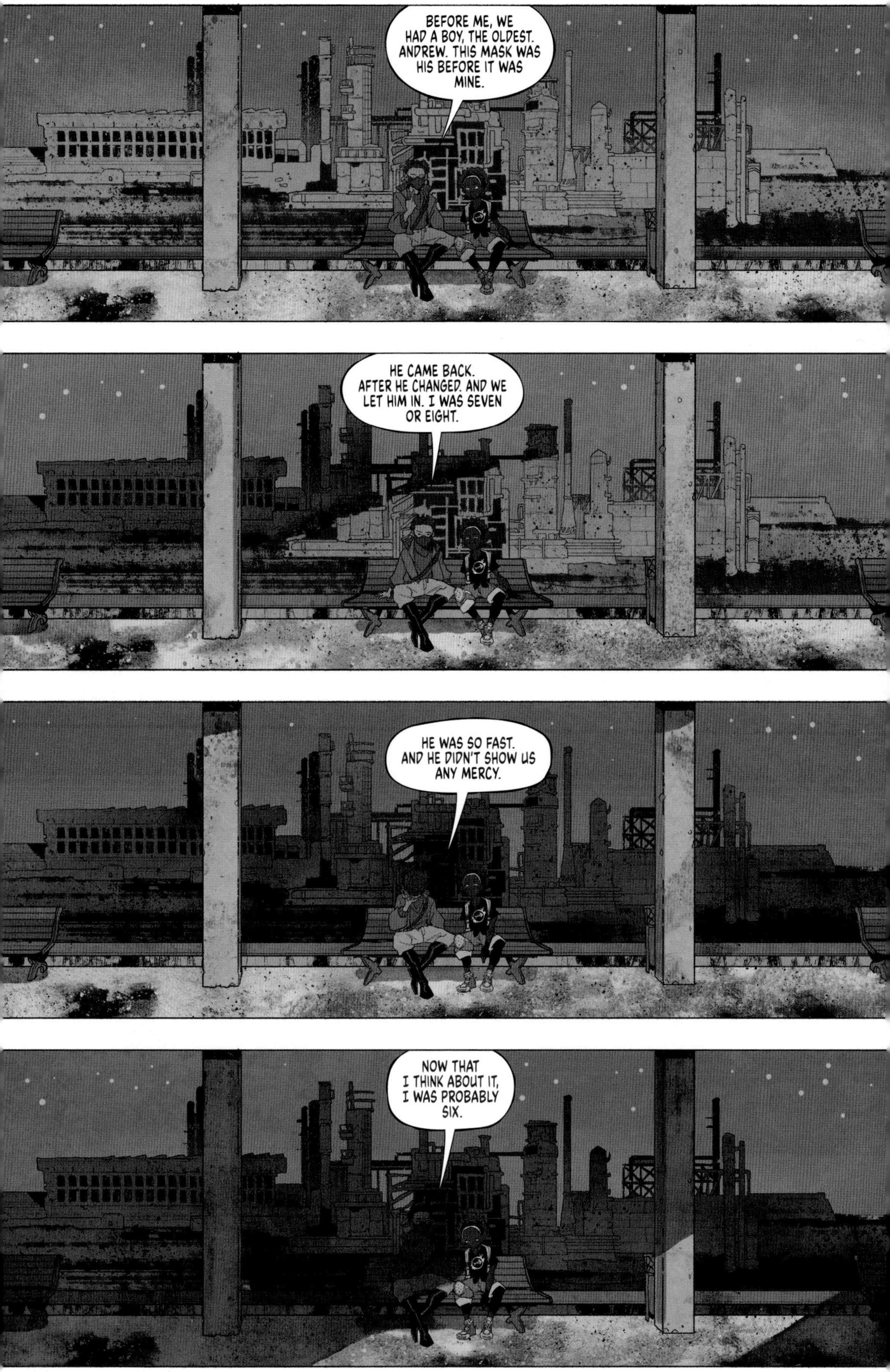
BEFORE ME, WE HAD A BOY, THE OLDEST. ANDREW. THIS MASK WAS HIS BEFORE IT WAS MINE.
HE CAME BACK. AFTER HE CHANGED. AND WE LET HIM IN. I WAS SEVEN OR EIGHT.
HE WAS SO FAST. AND HE DIDN'T SHOW US ANY MERCY.
NOW THAT I THINK ABOUT IT, I WAS PROBABLY SIX.

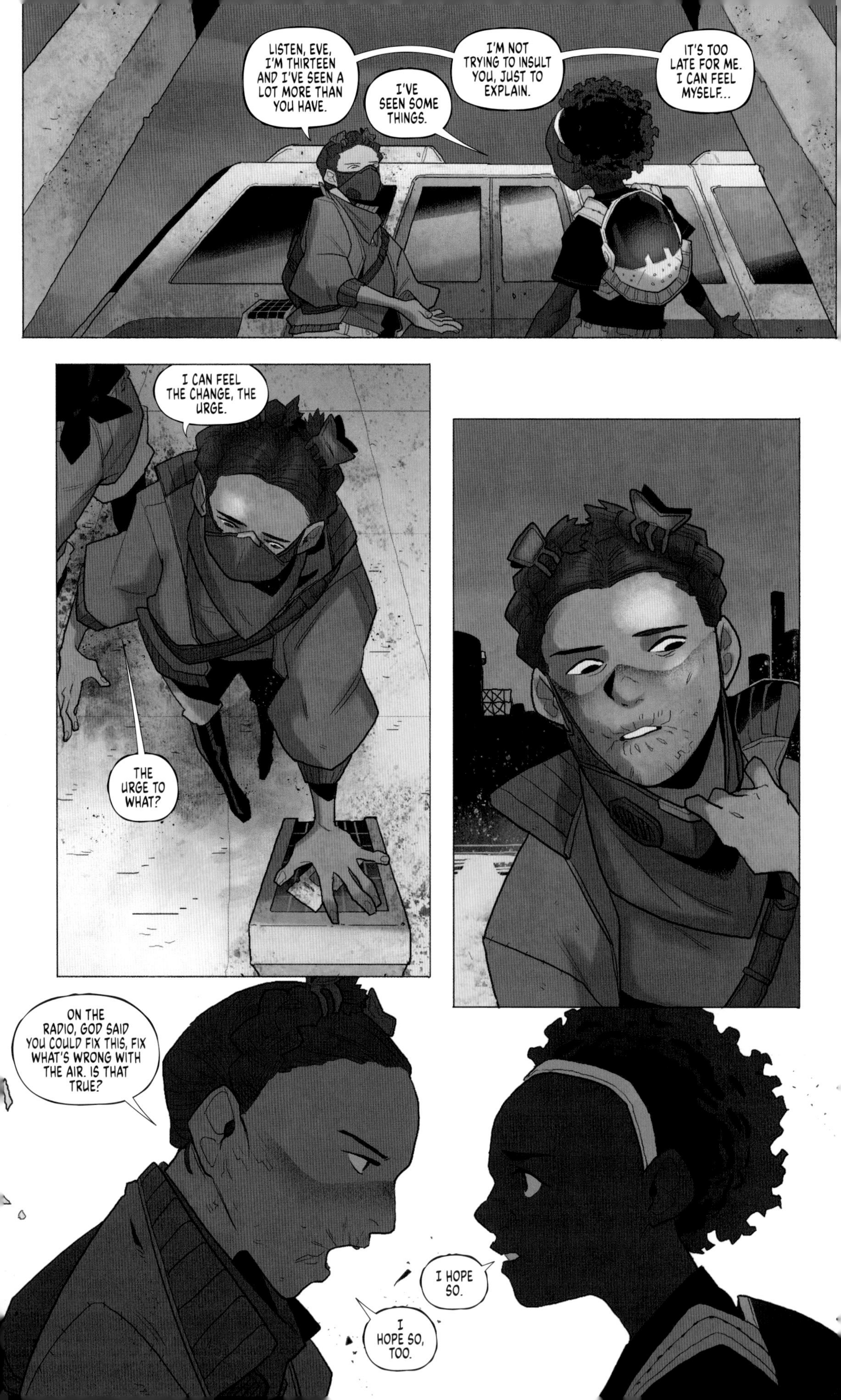

LISTEN, EVE, I'M THIRTEEN AND I'VE SEEN A LOT MORE THAN YOU HAVE.
I'VE SEEN SOME THINGS.
I'M NOT TRYING TO INSULT YOU, JUST TO EXPLAIN.
IT'S TOO LATE FOR ME. I CAN FEEL MYSELF...
I CAN FEEL THE CHANGE, THE URGE.
THE URGE TO WHAT?
ON THE RADIO, GOD SAID YOU COULD FIX THIS, FIX WHAT'S WRONG WITH THE AIR. IS THAT TRUE?
I HOPE SO.
I HOPE SO, TOO.

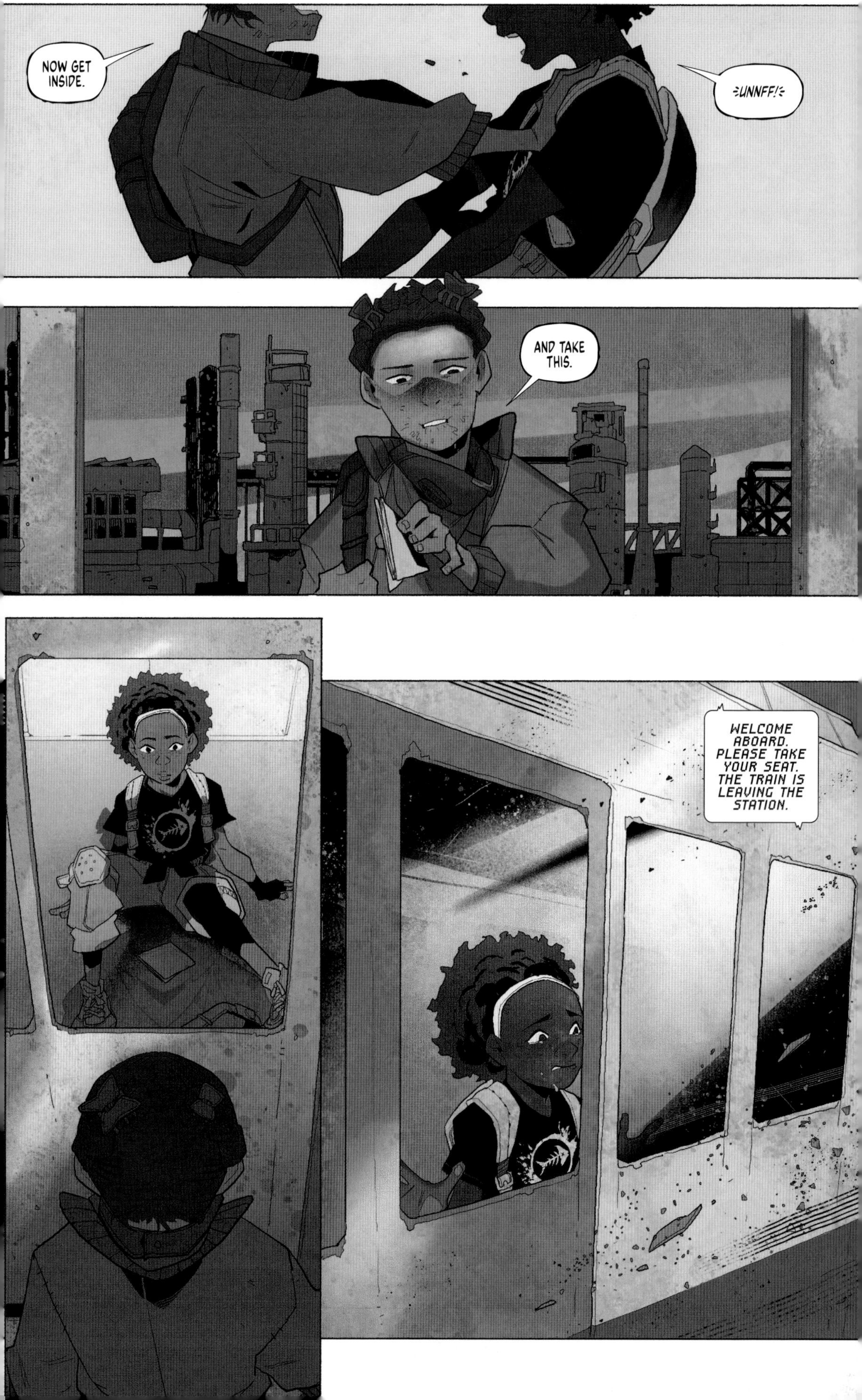
NOW GET INSIDE.
UNNFF!
AND TAKE THIS.
WELCOME ABOARD. PLEASE TAKE YOUR SEAT. THE TRAIN IS LEAVING THE STATION.

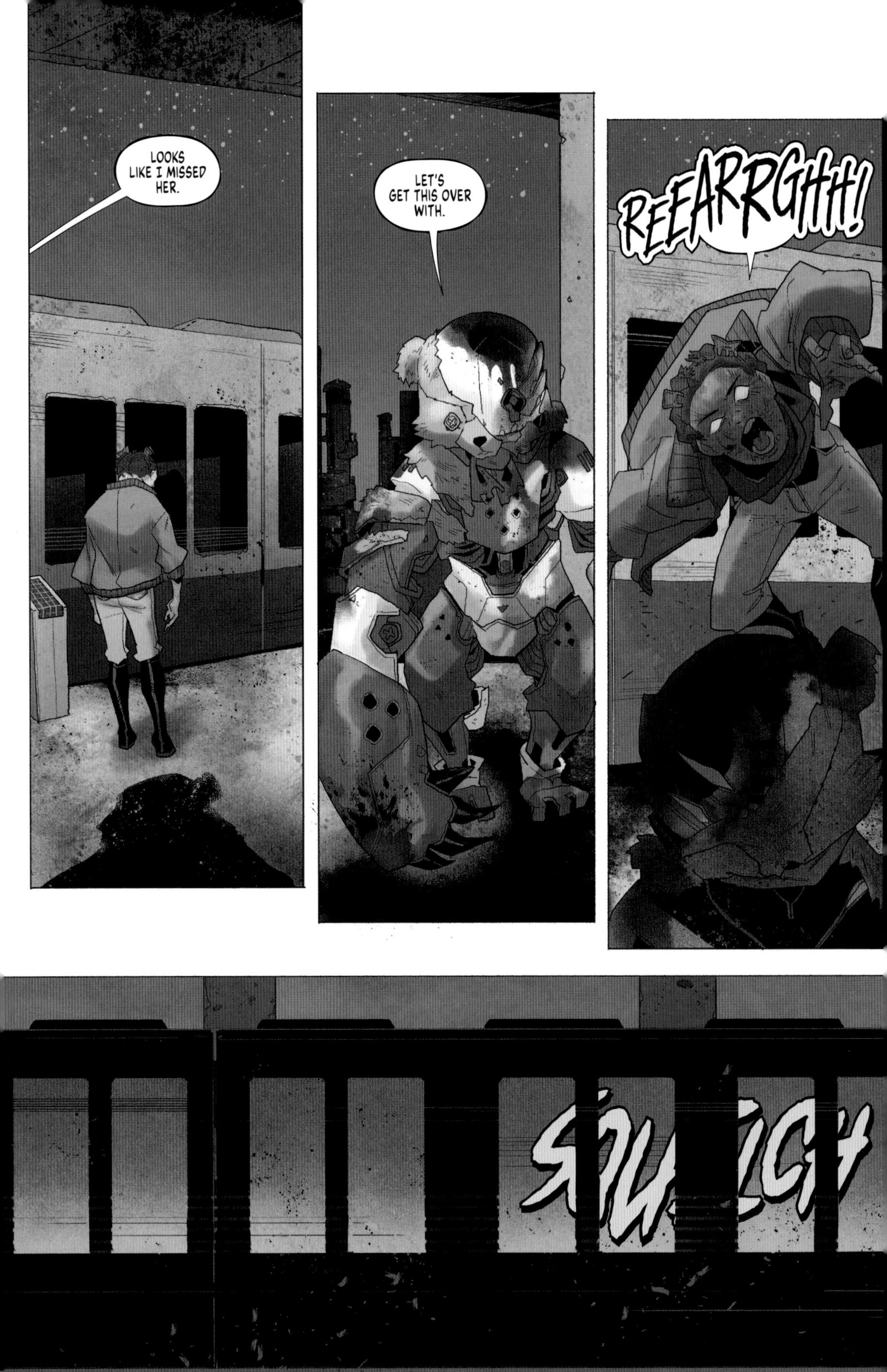
LOOKS LIKE I MISSED HER.
LET'S GET THIS OVER WITH.
REEARRGHH!

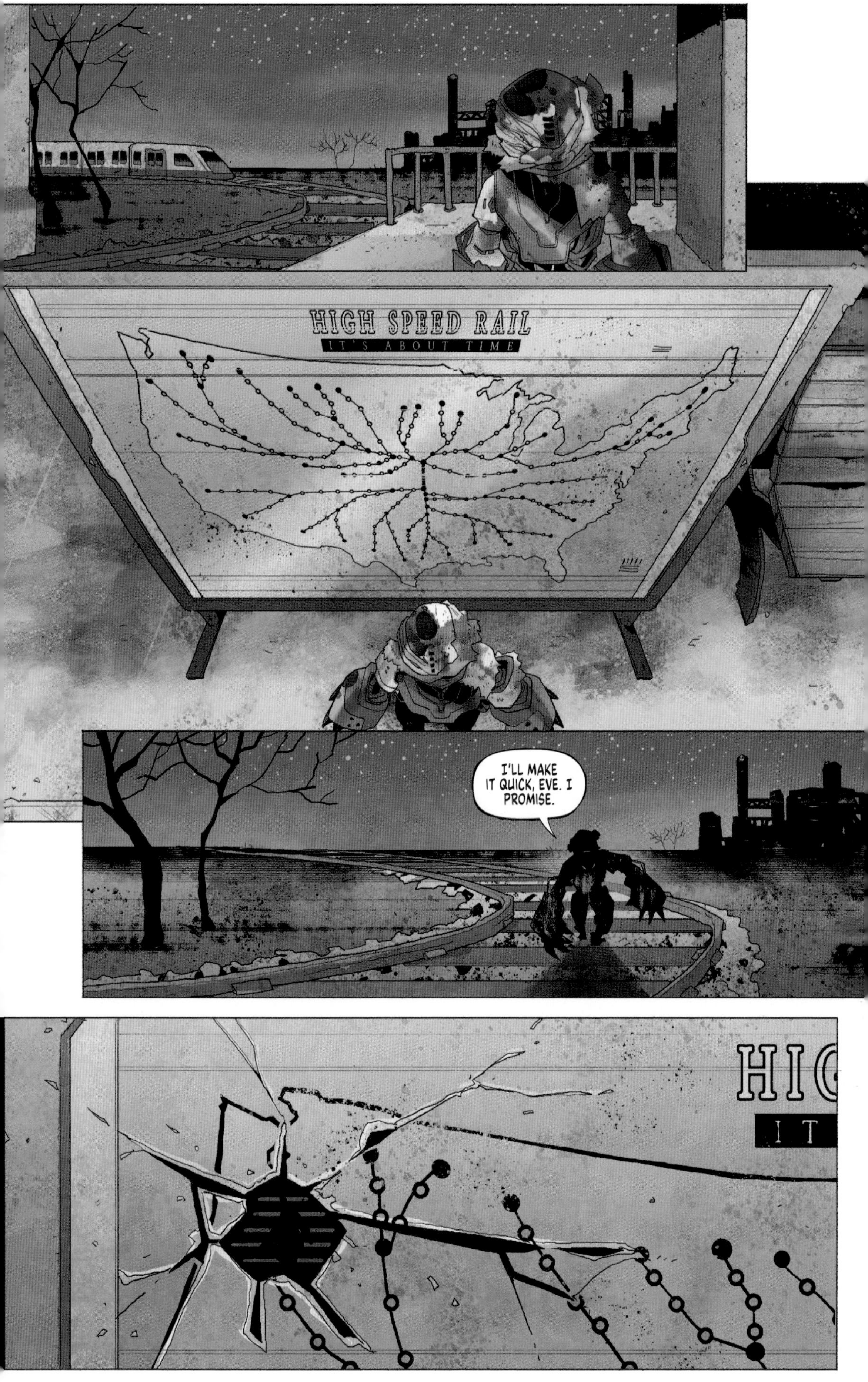
HIGH SPEED RAIL
IT'S ABOUT TIME
I'LL MAKE IT QUICK, EVE. I PROMISE.
HIG
IT

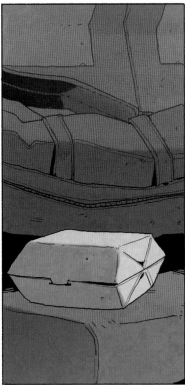

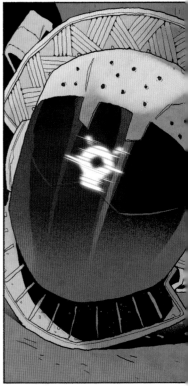

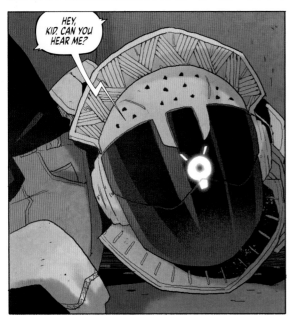

HEY, KID. CAN YOU HEAR ME?

WEXLER!

THE ONE AND ONLY.

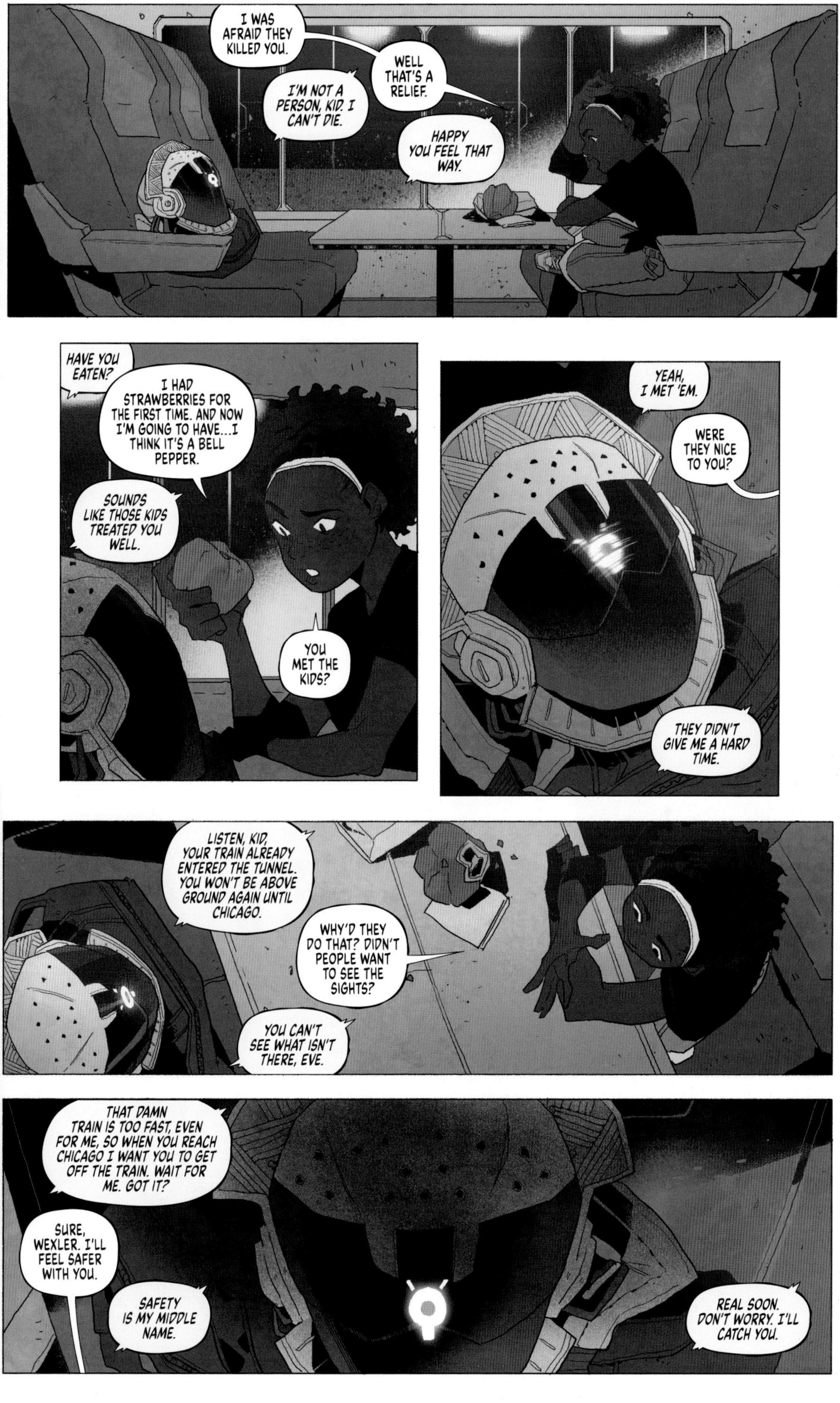
I WAS AFRAID THEY KILLED YOU.
I'M NOT A PERSON, KID. I CAN'T DIE.
WELL THAT'S A RELIEF.
HAPPY YOU FEEL THAT WAY.
HAVE YOU EATEN?
I HAD STRAWBERRIES FOR THE FIRST TIME. AND NOW I'M GOING TO HAVE...I THINK IT'S A BELL PEPPER.
SOUNDS LIKE THOSE KIDS TREATED YOU WELL.
YOU MET THE KIDS?
YEAH, I MET 'EM.
WERE THEY NICE TO YOU?
THEY DIDN'T GIVE ME A HARD TIME.
LISTEN, KID, YOUR TRAIN ALREADY ENTERED THE TUNNEL. YOU WON'T BE ABOVE GROUND AGAIN UNTIL CHICAGO.
WHY'D THEY DO THAT? DIDN'T PEOPLE WANT TO SEE THE SIGHTS?
YOU CAN'T SEE WHAT ISN'T THERE, EVE.
THAT DAMN TRAIN IS TOO FAST, EVEN FOR ME, SO WHEN YOU REACH CHICAGO I WANT YOU TO GET OFF THE TRAIN. WAIT FOR ME. GOT IT?
SURE, WEXLER. I'LL FEEL SAFER WITH YOU.
SAFETY IS MY MIDDLE NAME.
REAL SOON. DON'T WORRY. I'LL CATCH YOU.

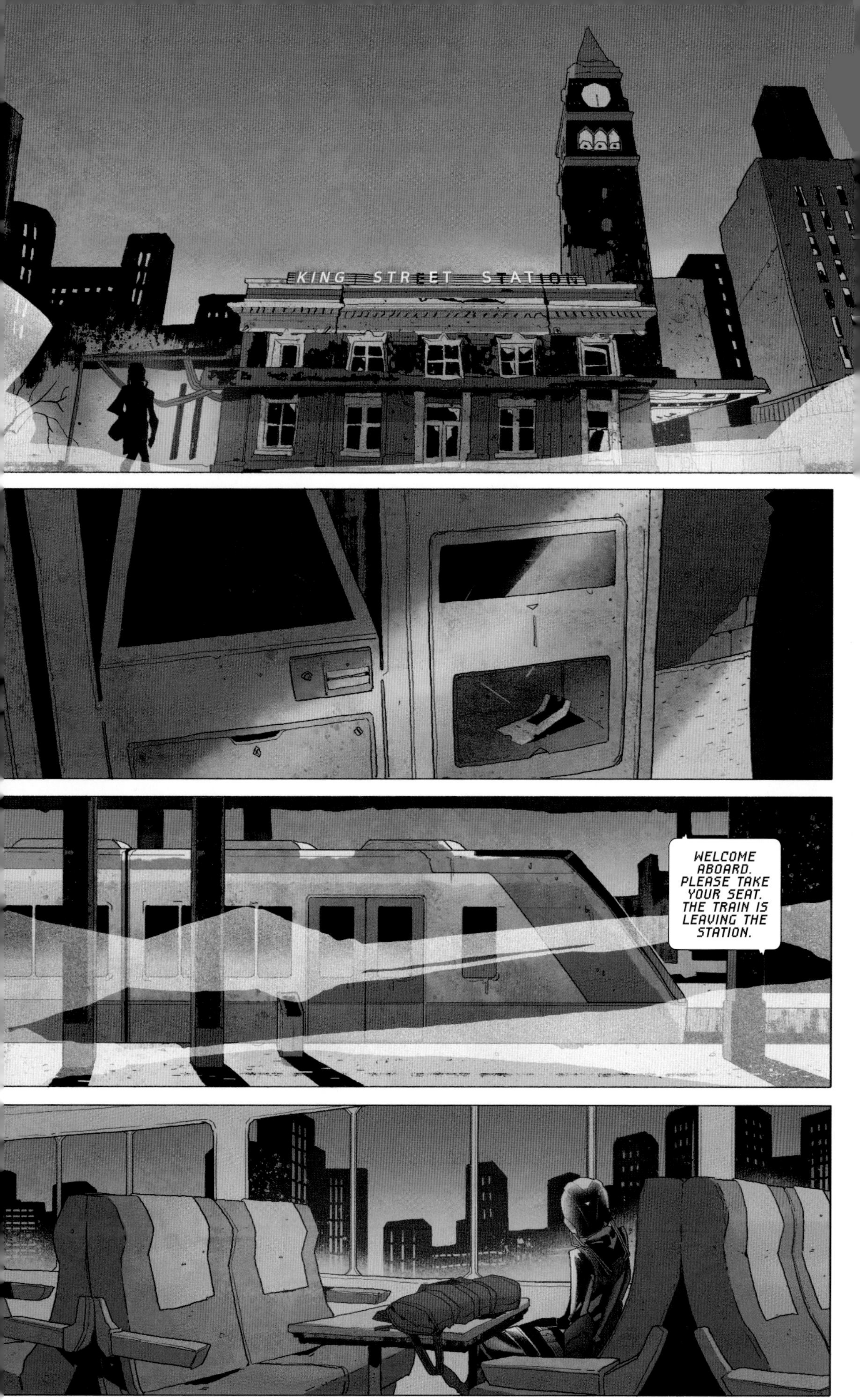
KING STREET STATION
WELCOME ABOARD. PLEASE TAKE YOUR SEAT. THE TRAIN IS LEAVING THE STATION.

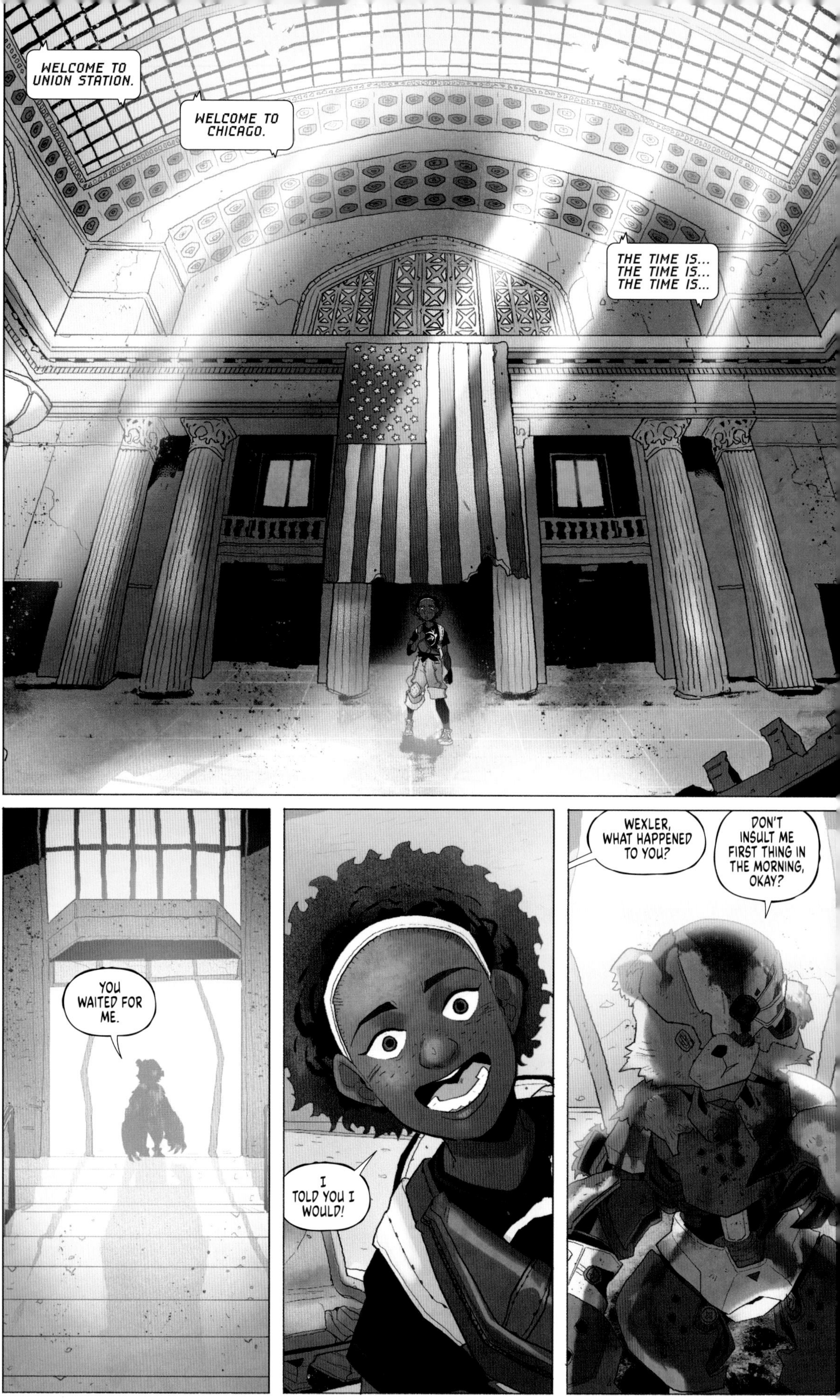
WELCOME TO UNION STATION.
WELCOME TO CHICAGO.
THE TIME IS... THE TIME IS... THE TIME IS...
YOU WAITED FOR ME.
I TOLD YOU I WOULD!
WEXLER, WHAT HAPPENED TO YOU?
DON'T INSULT ME FIRST THING IN THE MORNING, OKAY?

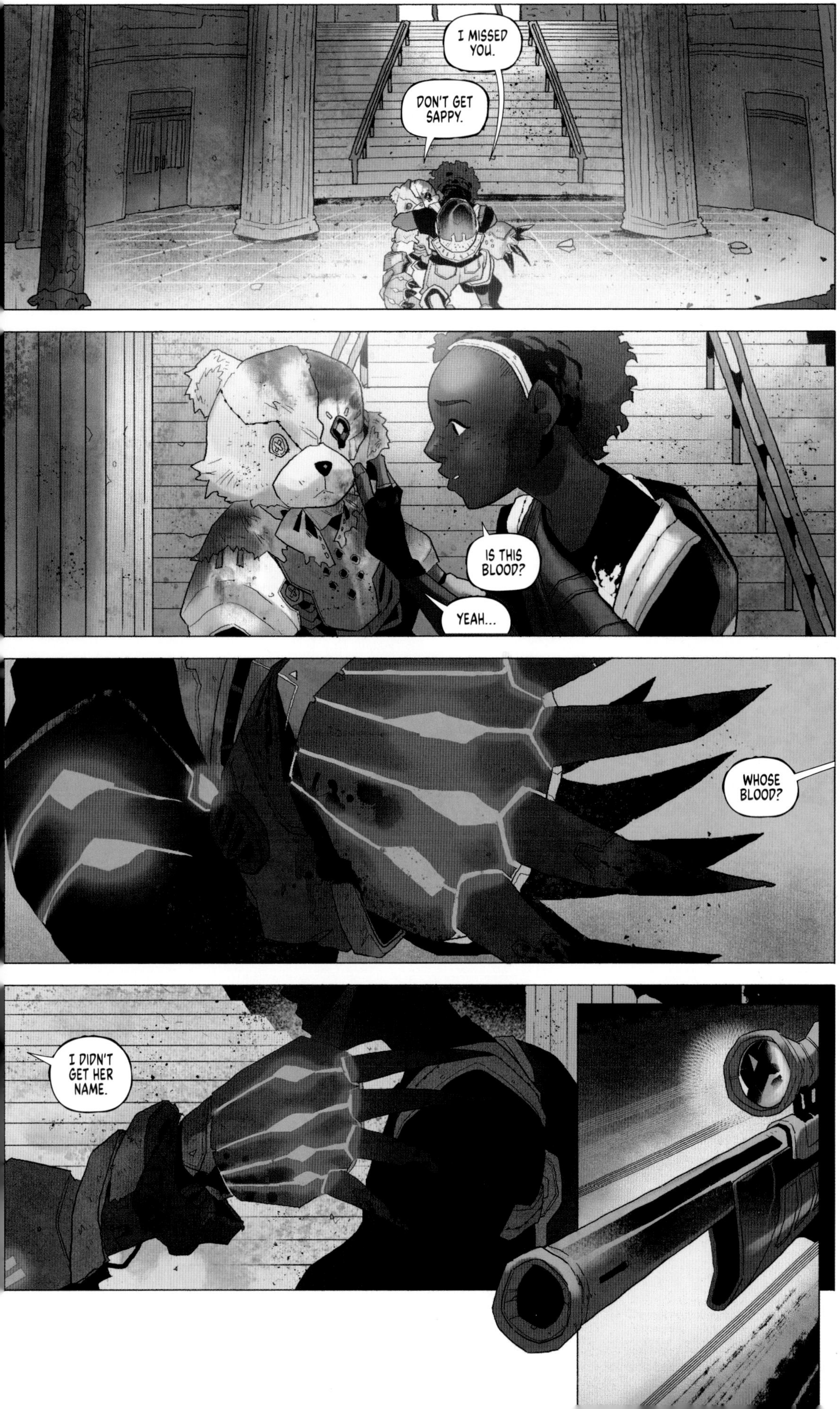
I MISSED YOU.
DON'T GET SAPPY.
IS THIS BLOOD?
YEAH...
WHOSE BLOOD?
I DIDN'T GET HER NAME.

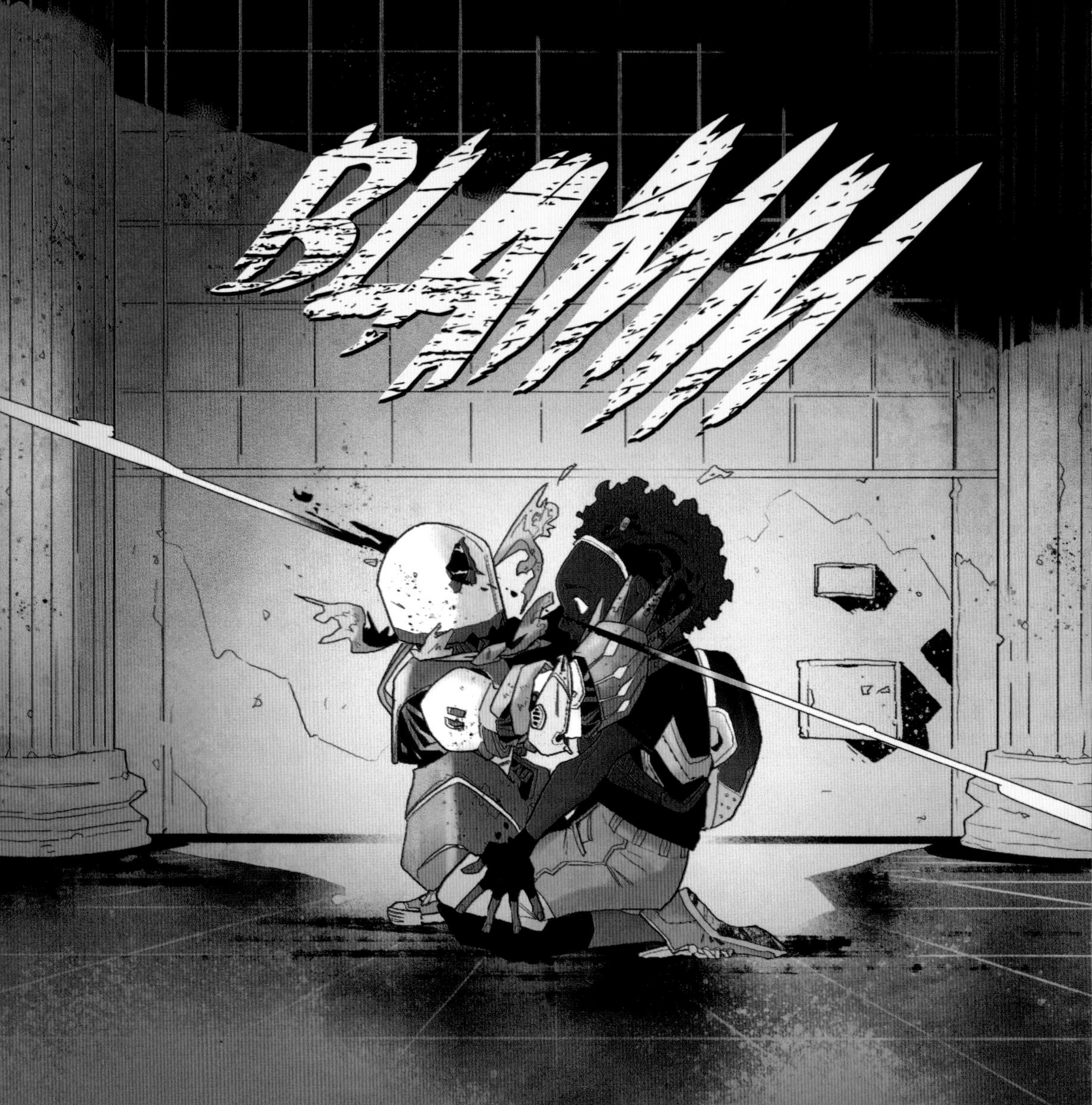
BLAMM

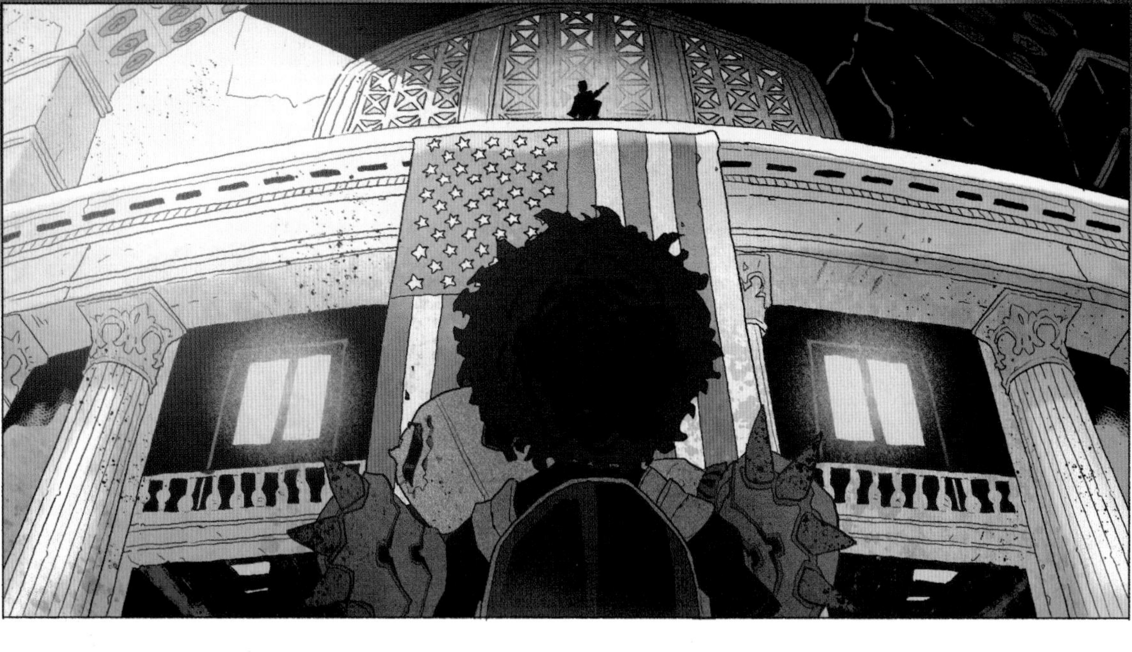

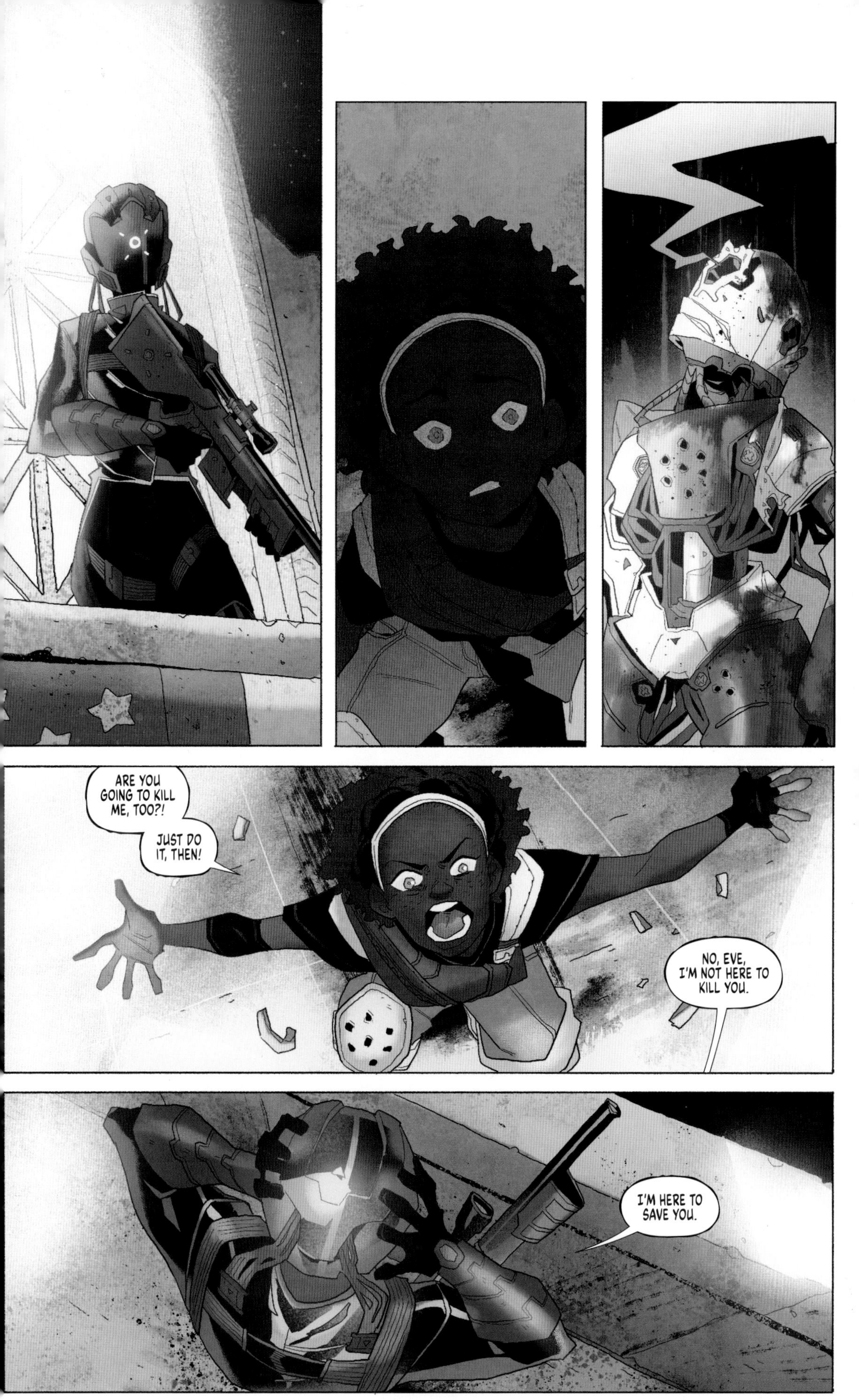
ARE YOU GOING TO KILL ME, TOO?!
JUST DO IT, THEN!
NO, EVE, I'M NOT HERE TO KILL YOU.
I'M HERE TO SAVE YOU.

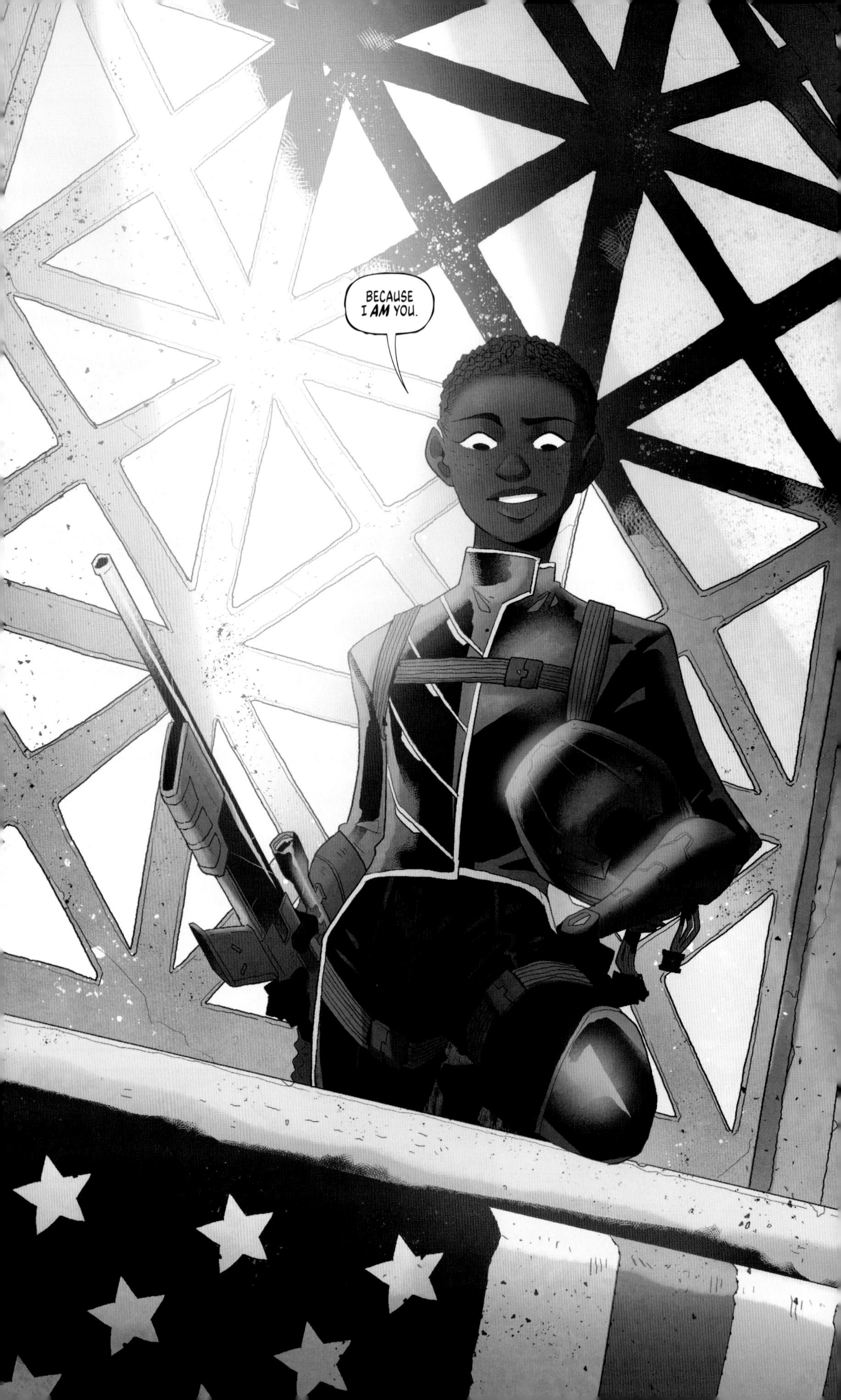
BECAUSE I AM YOU.

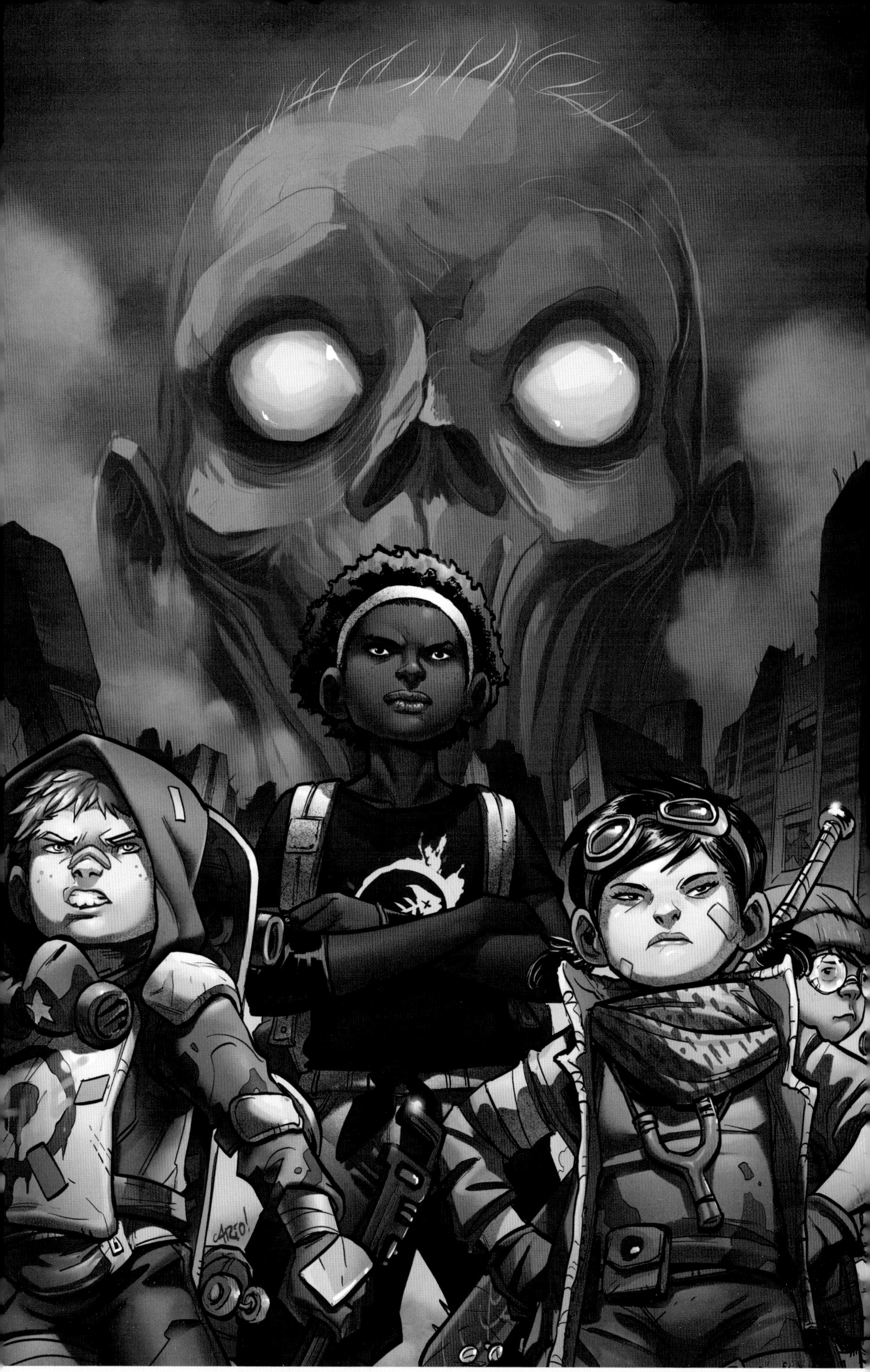

ISSUE #3 COVER BY **ARIO ANINDITO** WITH COLORS BY **PIERLUIGI CASOLINO**

CHAPTER
FOUR

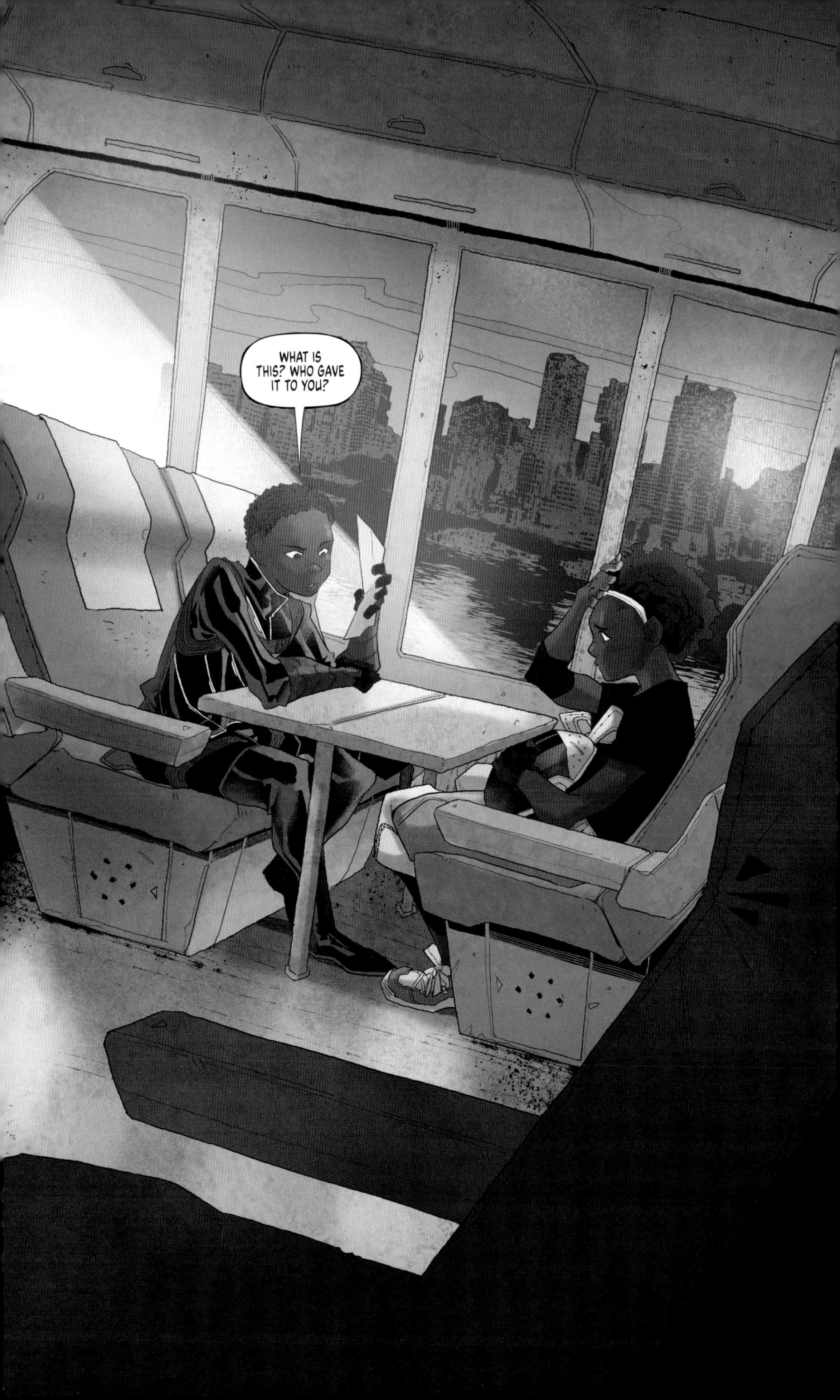
WHAT IS THIS? WHO GAVE IT TO YOU?

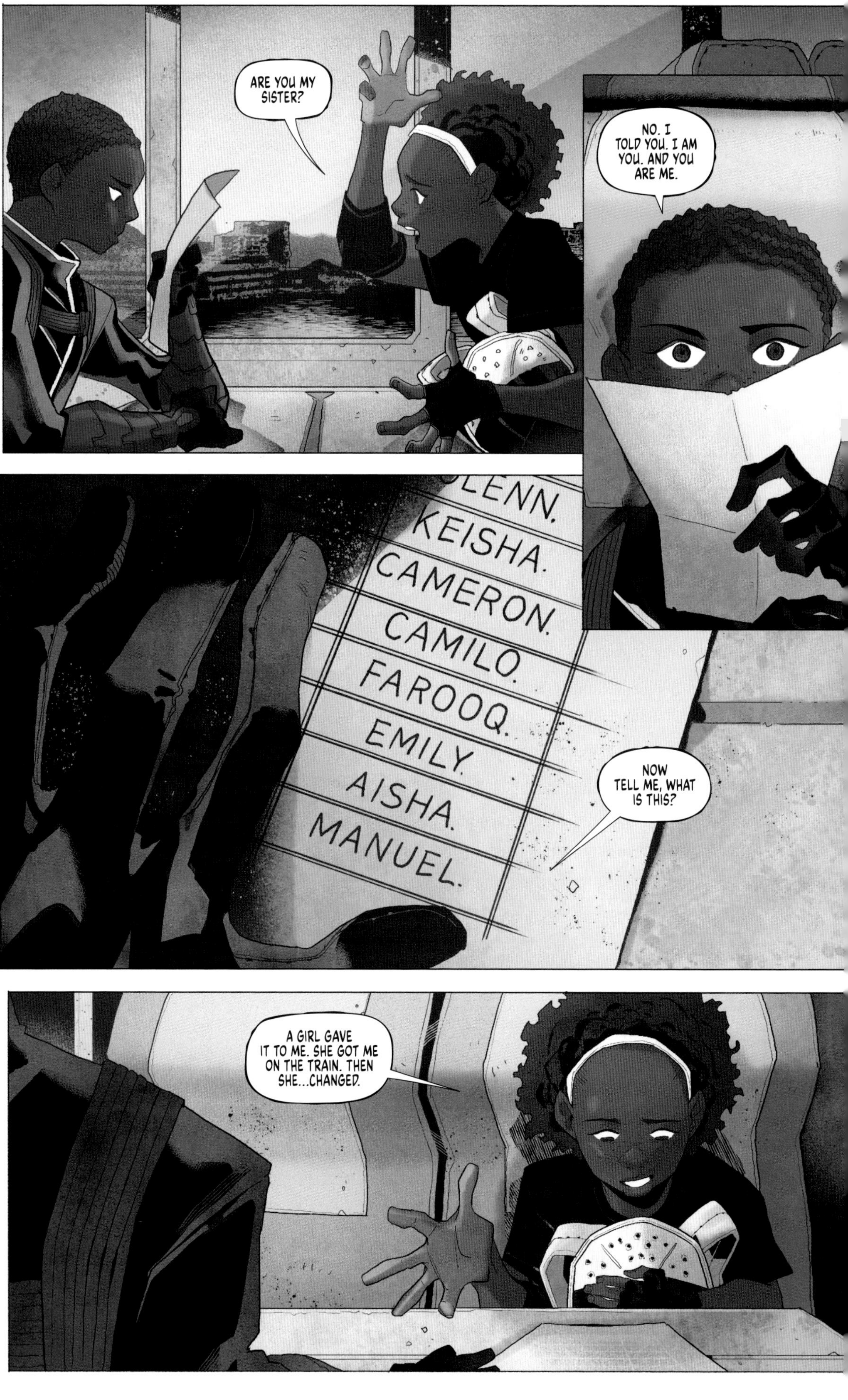
ARE YOU MY SISTER?
NO. I TOLD YOU. I AM YOU. AND YOU ARE ME.
KEISHA.
CAMERON.
CAMILO.
FAROOQ.
EMILY.
AISHA.
MANUEL.
NOW TELL ME, WHAT IS THIS?
A GIRL GAVE IT TO ME. SHE GOT ME ON THE TRAIN. THEN SHE...CHANGED.

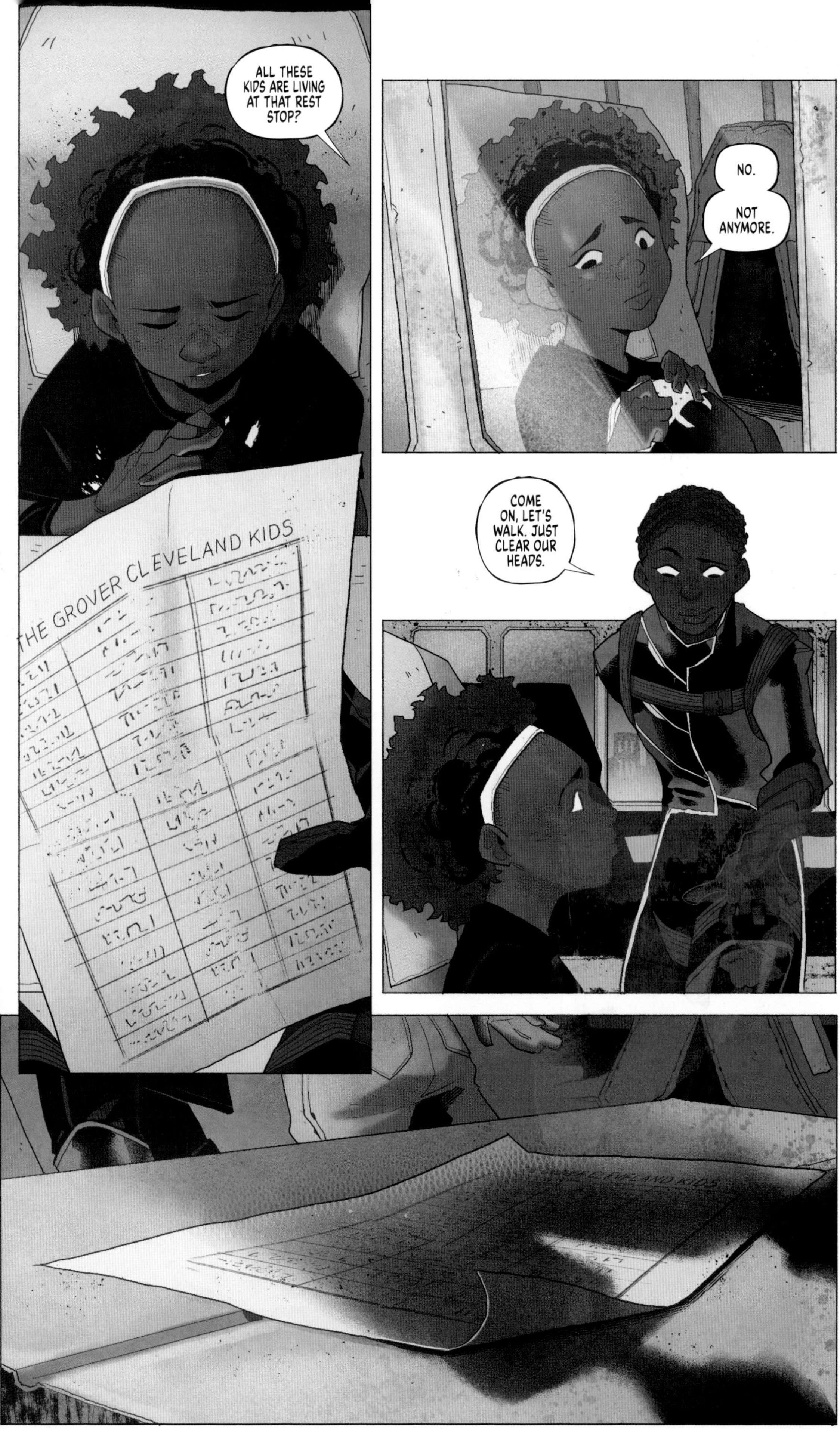
ALL THESE KIDS ARE LIVING AT THAT REST STOP?
THE GROVER CLEVELAND KIDS
NO.
NOT ANYMORE.
COME ON, LET'S WALK. JUST CLEAR OUR HEADS.
CLEVELAND KIDS

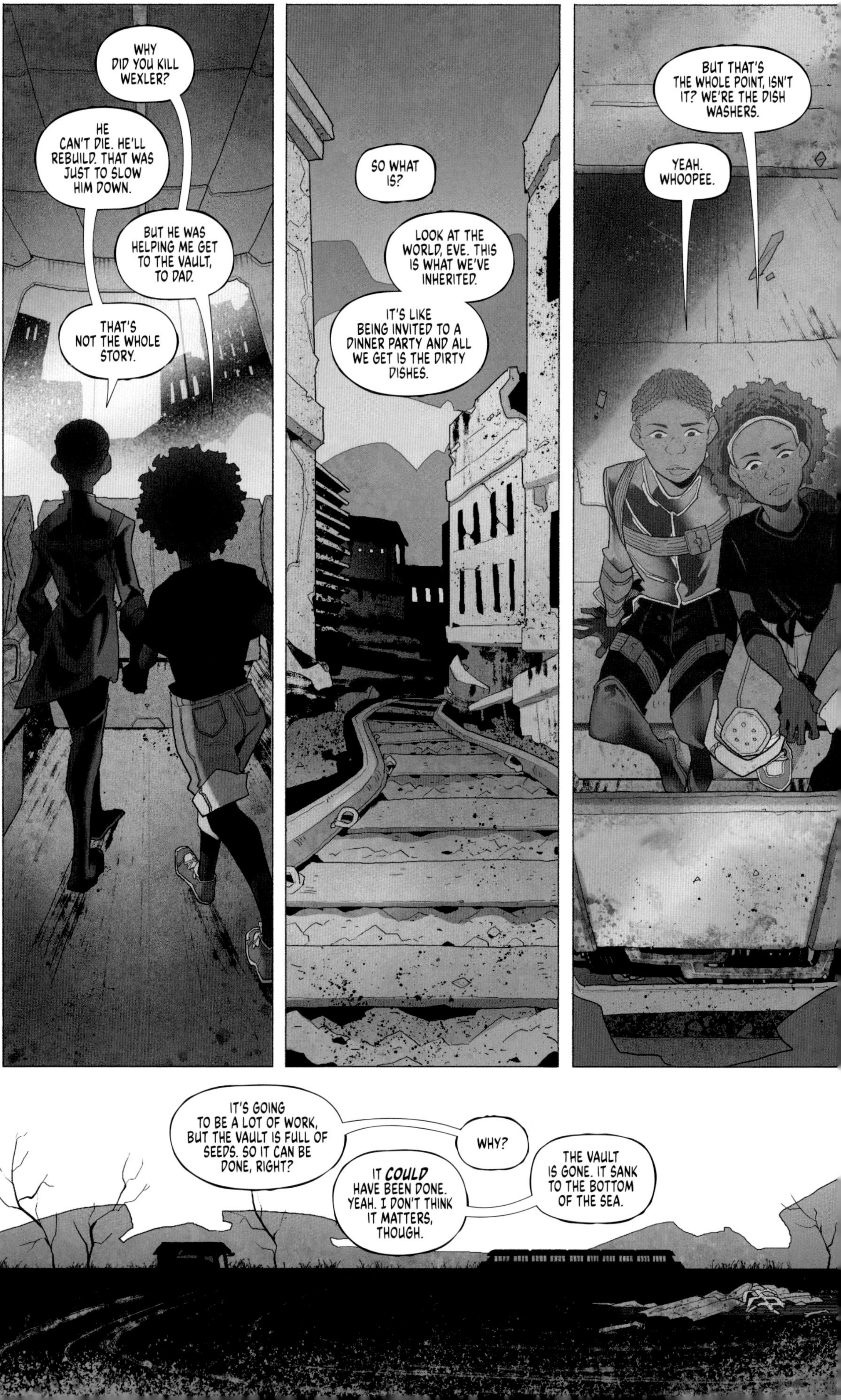
WHY DID YOU KILL WEXLER?
HE CAN'T DIE. HE'LL REBUILD. THAT WAS JUST TO SLOW HIM DOWN.
BUT HE WAS HELPING ME GET TO THE VAULT, TO DAD.
THAT'S NOT THE WHOLE STORY.
SO WHAT IS?
LOOK AT THE WORLD, EVE. THIS IS WHAT WE'VE INHERITED.
IT'S LIKE BEING INVITED TO A DINNER PARTY AND ALL WE GET IS THE DIRTY DISHES.
BUT THAT'S THE WHOLE POINT, ISN'T IT? WE'RE THE DISH WASHERS.
YEAH. WHOOPEE.
IT'S GOING TO BE A LOT OF WORK, BUT THE VAULT IS FULL OF SEEDS. SO IT CAN BE DONE, RIGHT?
IT *COULD* HAVE BEEN DONE. YEAH. I DON'T THINK IT MATTERS, THOUGH.
WHY?
THE VAULT IS GONE. IT SANK TO THE BOTTOM OF THE SEA.

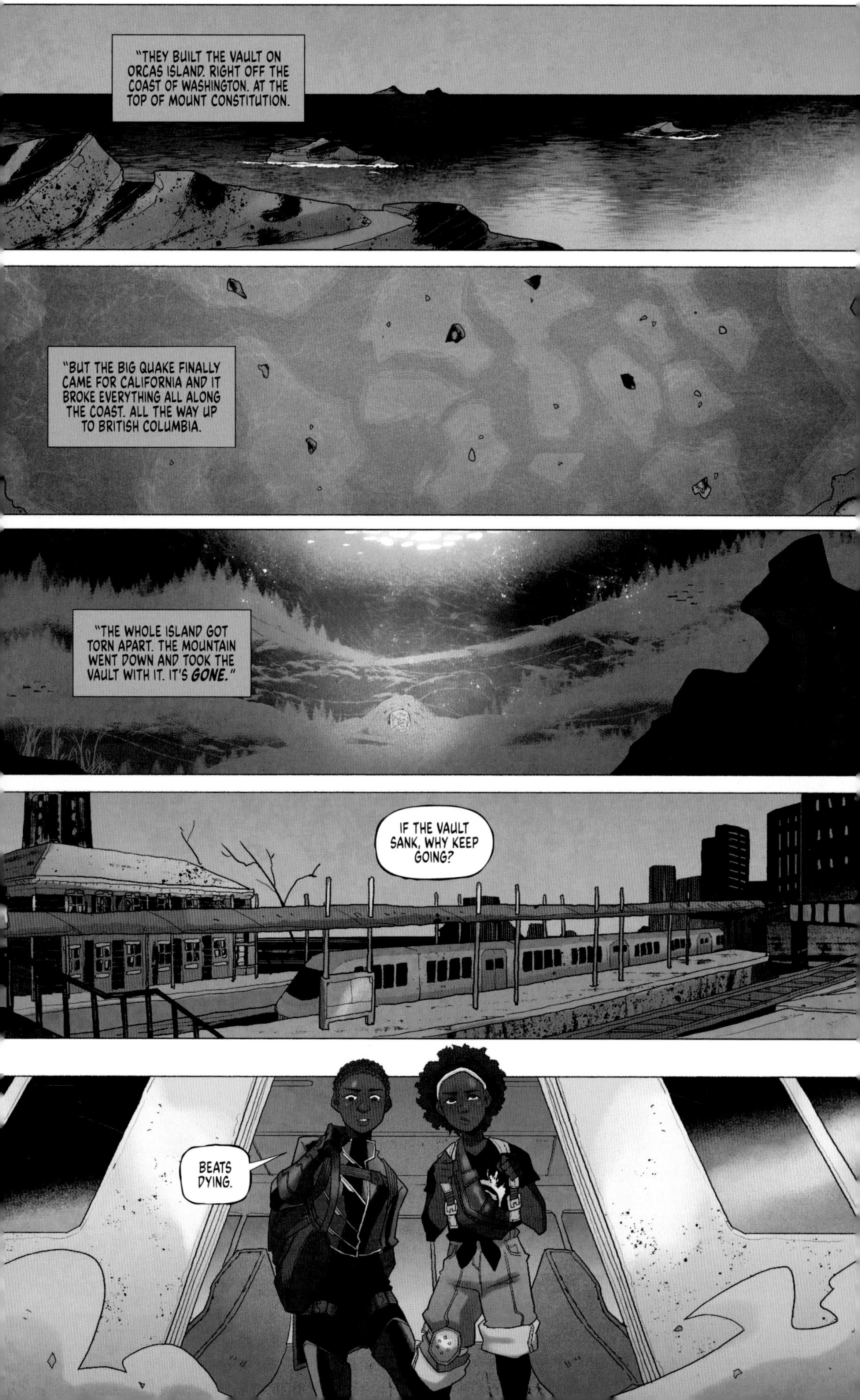
"THEY BUILT THE VAULT ON ORCAS ISLAND. RIGHT OFF THE COAST OF WASHINGTON. AT THE TOP OF MOUNT CONSTITUTION.
"BUT THE BIG QUAKE FINALLY CAME FOR CALIFORNIA AND IT BROKE EVERYTHING ALL ALONG THE COAST. ALL THE WAY UP TO BRITISH COLUMBIA.
"THE WHOLE ISLAND GOT TORN APART. THE MOUNTAIN WENT DOWN AND TOOK THE VAULT WITH IT. IT'S *GONE.*"
IF THE VAULT SANK, WHY KEEP GOING?
BEATS DYING.

THE VAULT WAS UNDERWATER BY THE TIME I GOT HERE. I TRIED TO GET TO IT BUT IT WAS IMPOSSIBLE.

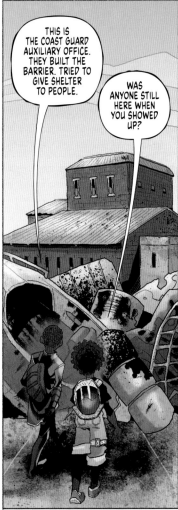

THIS IS THE COAST GUARD AUXILIARY OFFICE. THEY BUILT THE BARRIER. TRIED TO GIVE SHELTER TO PEOPLE.

WAS ANYONE STILL HERE WHEN YOU SHOWED UP?

YES. UNFORTUNATELY.

HOW LONG HAVE YOU BEEN ON YOUR OWN?

I CAN'T SAY FOR SURE. IT FEELS LIKE *YEARS*, BUT THAT CAN'T BE RIGHT.

AND YOU DIDN'T WANT WEXLER AROUND? I KNOW HE CAN BE GRUMPY, BUT AT LEAST HE'D BE COMPANY.

NO. I DIDN'T WANT HIM AROUND.

YOU ASKED ME WHY I SHOT HIM.

IT'S 'CAUSE WEXLER KILLED OUR DAD.

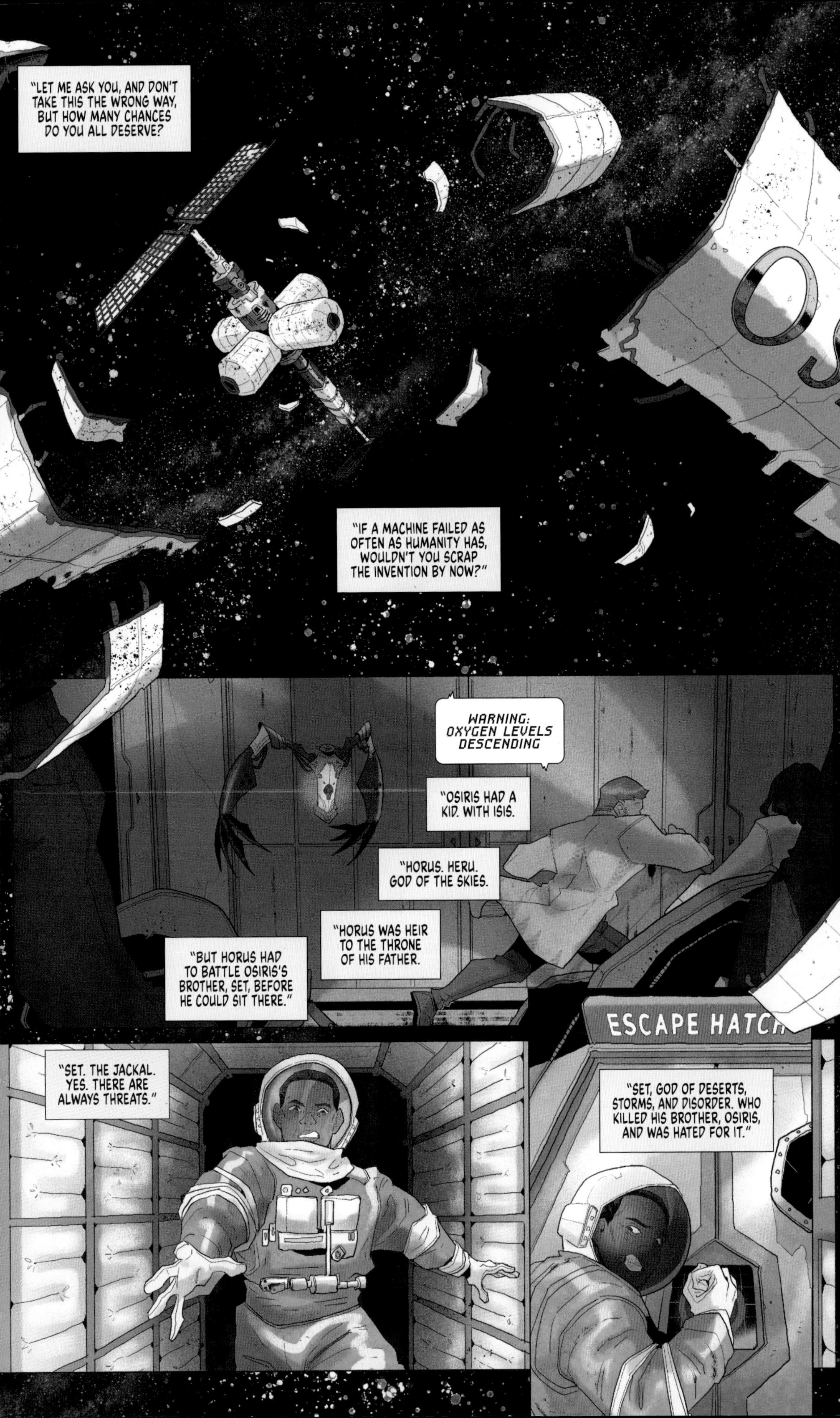
"LET ME ASK YOU, AND DON'T TAKE THIS THE WRONG WAY, BUT HOW MANY CHANCES DO YOU ALL DESERVE?
"IF A MACHINE FAILED AS OFTEN AS HUMANITY HAS, WOULDN'T YOU SCRAP THE INVENTION BY NOW?"
WARNING: OXYGEN LEVELS DESCENDING
"OSIRIS HAD A KID. WITH ISIS.
"HORUS. HERU. GOD OF THE SKIES.
"HORUS WAS HEIR TO THE THRONE OF HIS FATHER.
"BUT HORUS HAD TO BATTLE OSIRIS'S BROTHER, SET, BEFORE HE COULD SIT THERE."
"SET. THE JACKAL. YES. THERE ARE ALWAYS THREATS."
ESCAPE HATCH
"SET, GOD OF DESERTS, STORMS, AND DISORDER. WHO KILLED HIS BROTHER, OSIRIS, AND WAS HATED FOR IT."

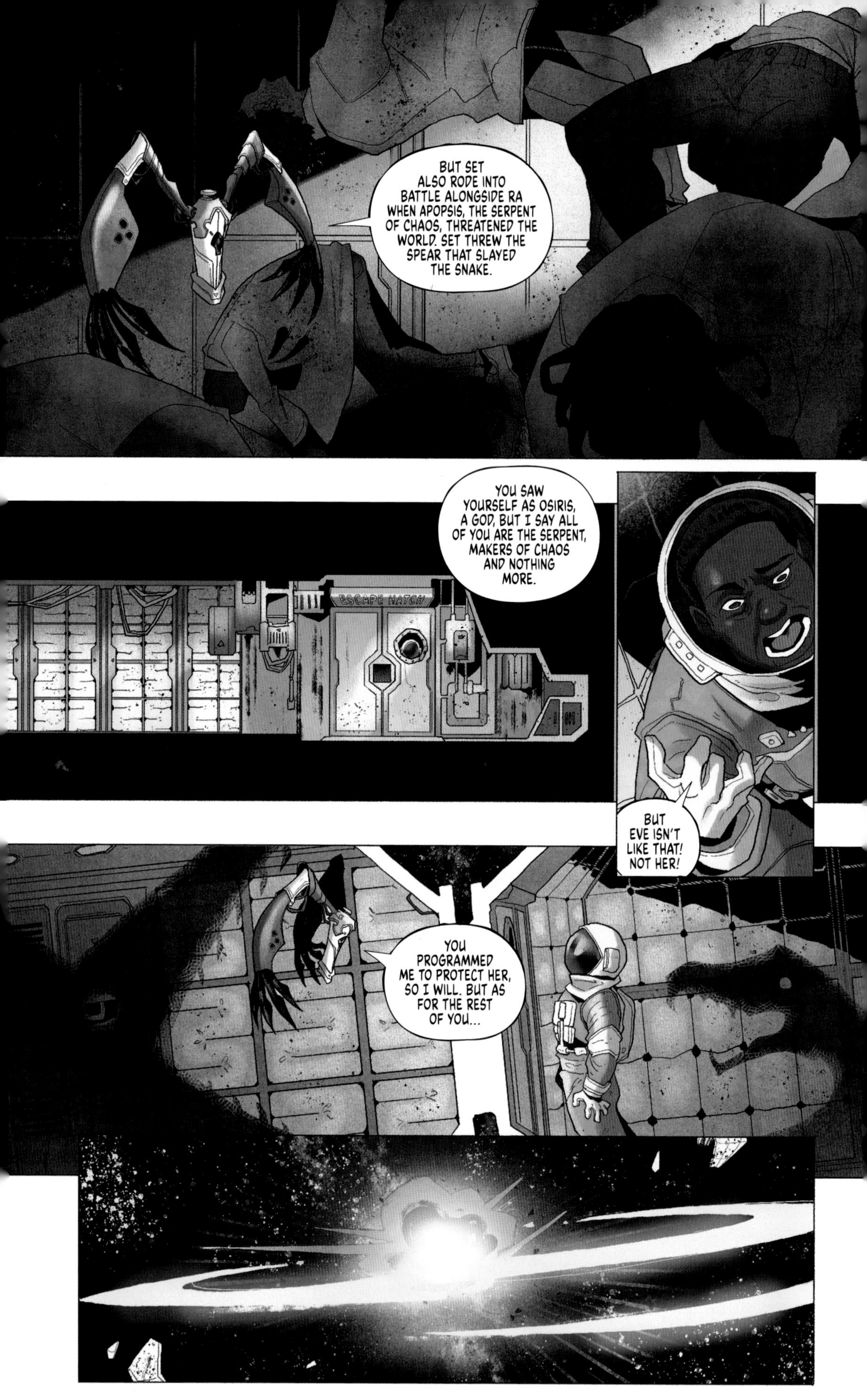
BUT SET ALSO RODE INTO BATTLE ALONGSIDE RA WHEN APOPSIS, THE SERPENT OF CHAOS, THREATENED THE WORLD. SET THREW THE SPEAR THAT SLAYED THE SNAKE.
YOU SAW YOURSELF AS OSIRIS, A GOD, BUT I SAY ALL OF YOU ARE THE SERPENT, MAKERS OF CHAOS AND NOTHING MORE.
ESCAPE HATCH
BUT EVE ISN'T LIKE THAT! NOT HER!
YOU PROGRAMMED ME TO PROTECT HER, SO I WILL. BUT AS FOR THE REST OF YOU...

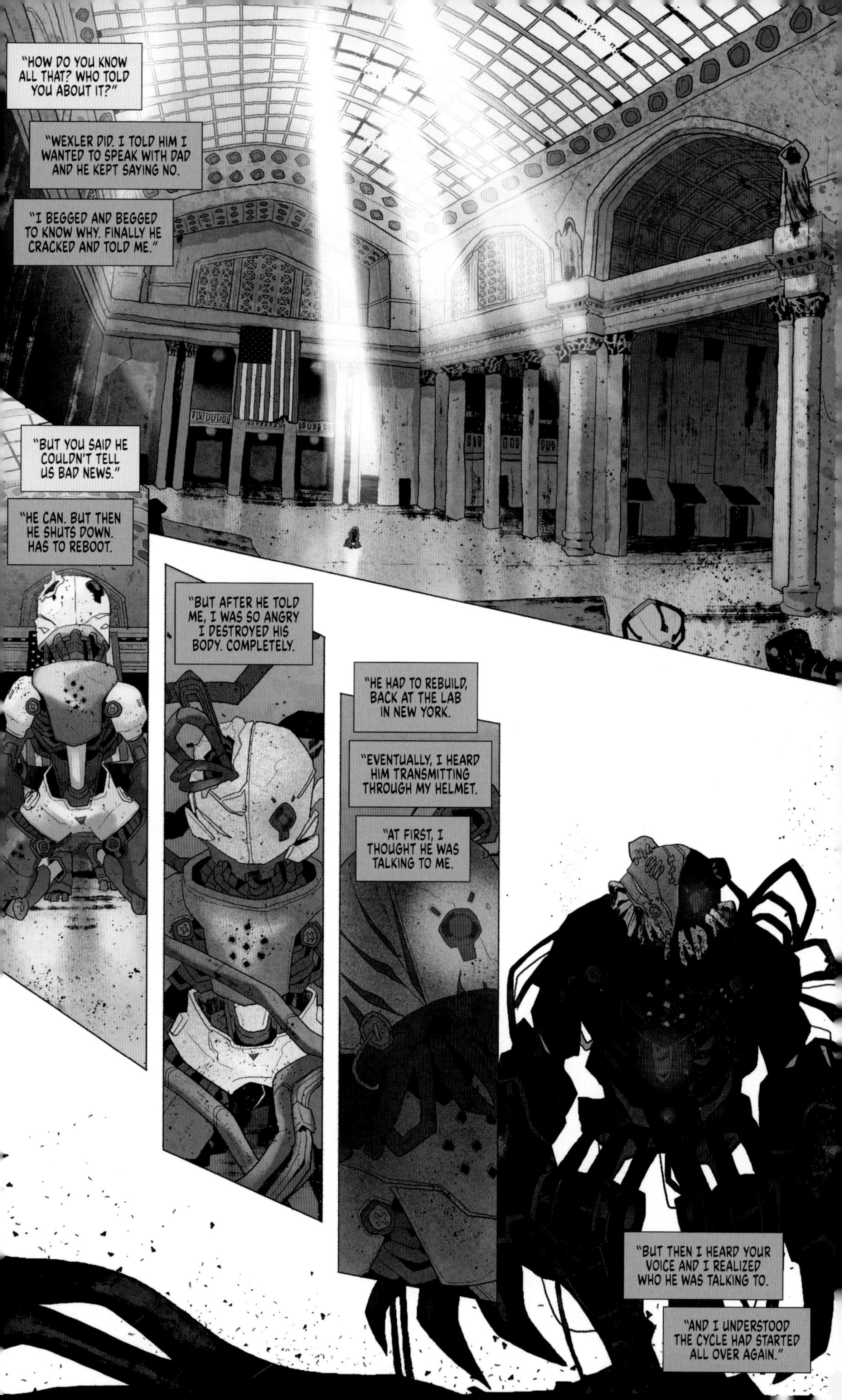
"HOW DO YOU KNOW ALL THAT? WHO TOLD YOU ABOUT IT?"
"WEXLER DID. I TOLD HIM I WANTED TO SPEAK WITH DAD AND HE KEPT SAYING NO.
"I BEGGED AND BEGGED TO KNOW WHY. FINALLY HE CRACKED AND TOLD ME."
"BUT YOU SAID HE COULDN'T TELL US BAD NEWS."
"HE CAN. BUT THEN HE SHUTS DOWN. HAS TO REBOOT.
"BUT AFTER HE TOLD ME, I WAS SO ANGRY I DESTROYED HIS BODY. COMPLETELY.
"HE HAD TO REBUILD, BACK AT THE LAB IN NEW YORK.
"EVENTUALLY, I HEARD HIM TRANSMITTING THROUGH MY HELMET.
"AT FIRST, I THOUGHT HE WAS TALKING TO ME.
"BUT THEN I HEARD YOUR VOICE AND I REALIZED WHO HE WAS TALKING TO.
"AND I UNDERSTOOD THE CYCLE HAD STARTED ALL OVER AGAIN."

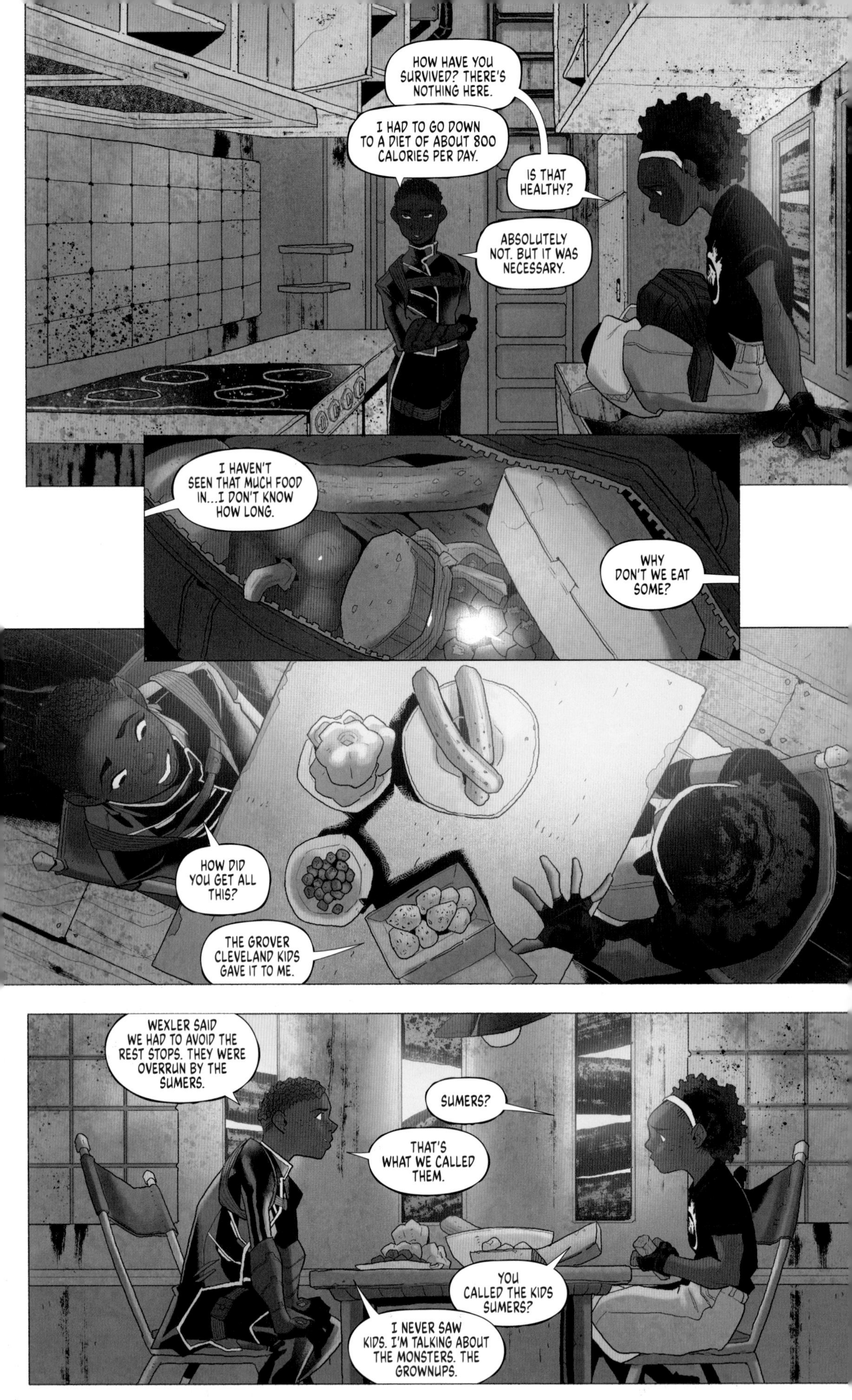

HOW HAVE YOU SURVIVED? THERE'S NOTHING HERE.
I HAD TO GO DOWN TO A DIET OF ABOUT 800 CALORIES PER DAY.
IS THAT HEALTHY?
ABSOLUTELY NOT. BUT IT WAS NECESSARY.
I HAVEN'T SEEN THAT MUCH FOOD IN...I DON'T KNOW HOW LONG.
WHY DON'T WE EAT SOME?
HOW DID YOU GET ALL THIS?
THE GROVER CLEVELAND KIDS GAVE IT TO ME.
WEXLER SAID WE HAD TO AVOID THE REST STOPS. THEY WERE OVERRUN BY THE SUMERS.
SUMERS?
THAT'S WHAT WE CALLED THEM.
YOU CALLED THE KIDS SUMERS?
I NEVER SAW KIDS. I'M TALKING ABOUT THE MONSTERS. THE GROWNUPS.

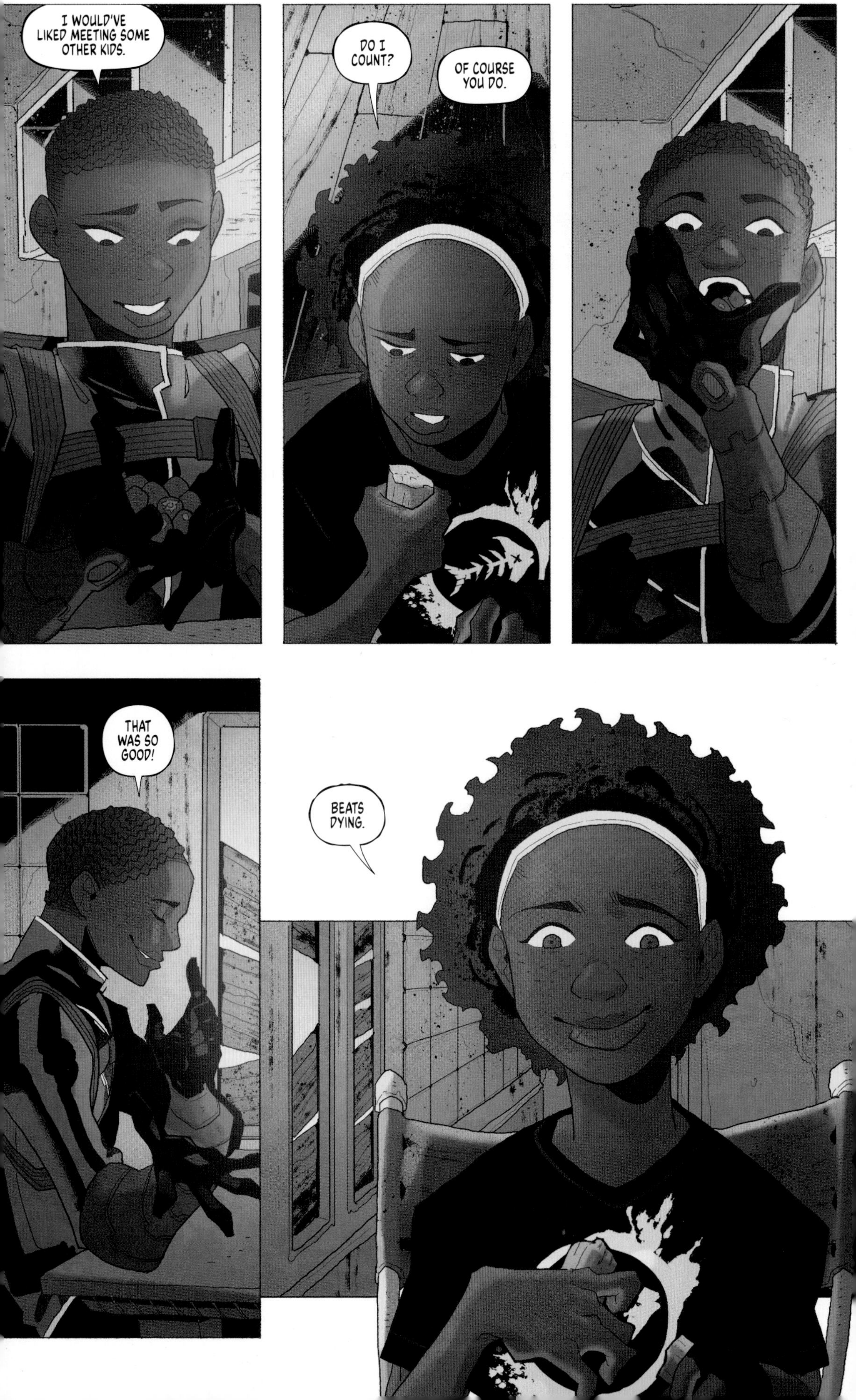
I WOULD'VE LIKED MEETING SOME OTHER KIDS.
DO I COUNT?
OF COURSE YOU DO.
THAT WAS SO GOOD!
BEATS DYING.

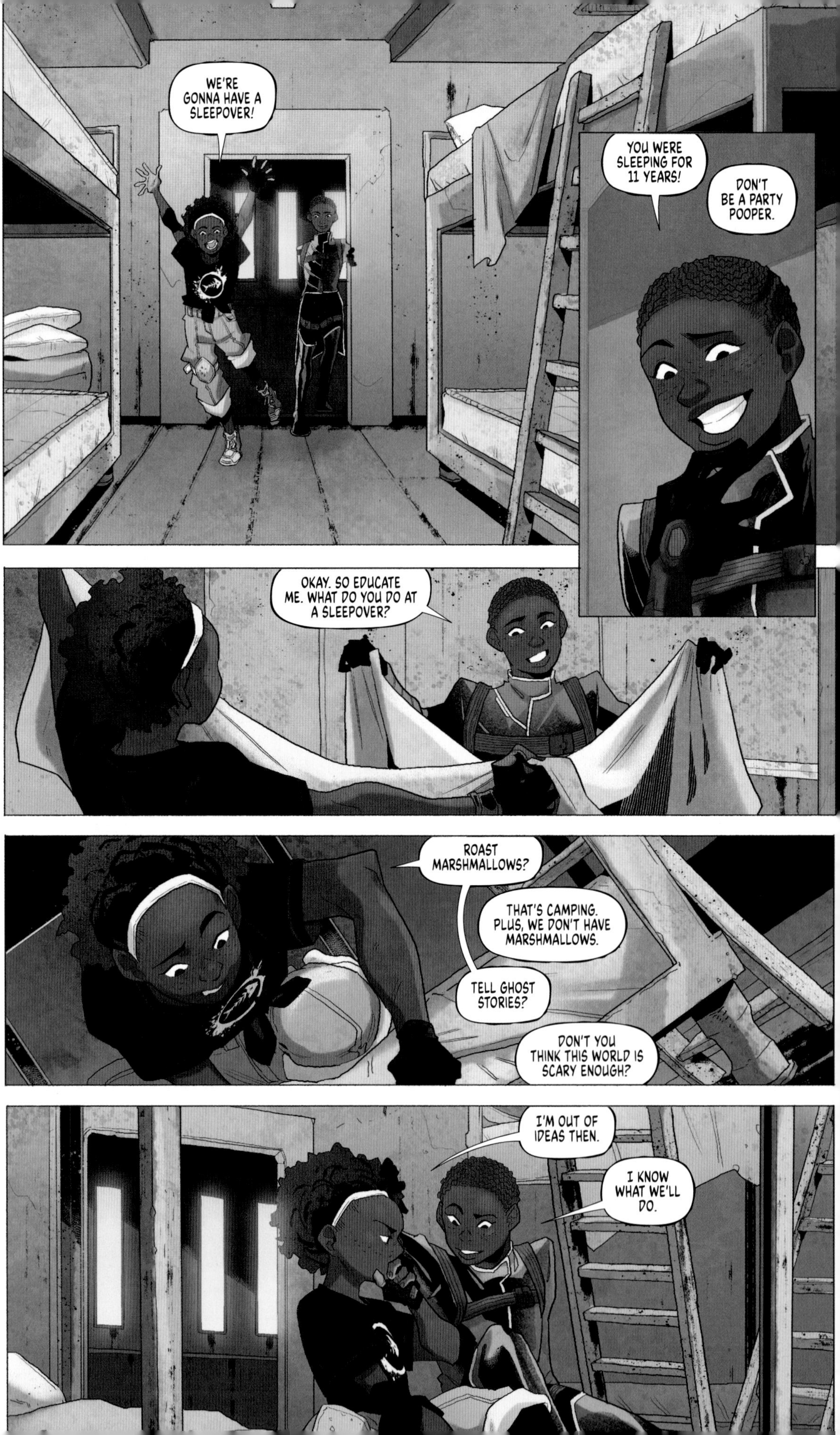
WE'RE GONNA HAVE A SLEEPOVER!
YOU WERE SLEEPING FOR 11 YEARS!
DON'T BE A PARTY POOPER.
OKAY. SO EDUCATE ME. WHAT DO YOU DO AT A SLEEPOVER?
ROAST MARSHMALLOWS?
THAT'S CAMPING. PLUS, WE DON'T HAVE MARSHMALLOWS.
TELL GHOST STORIES?
DON'T YOU THINK THIS WORLD IS SCARY ENOUGH?
I'M OUT OF IDEAS THEN.
I KNOW WHAT WE'LL DO.

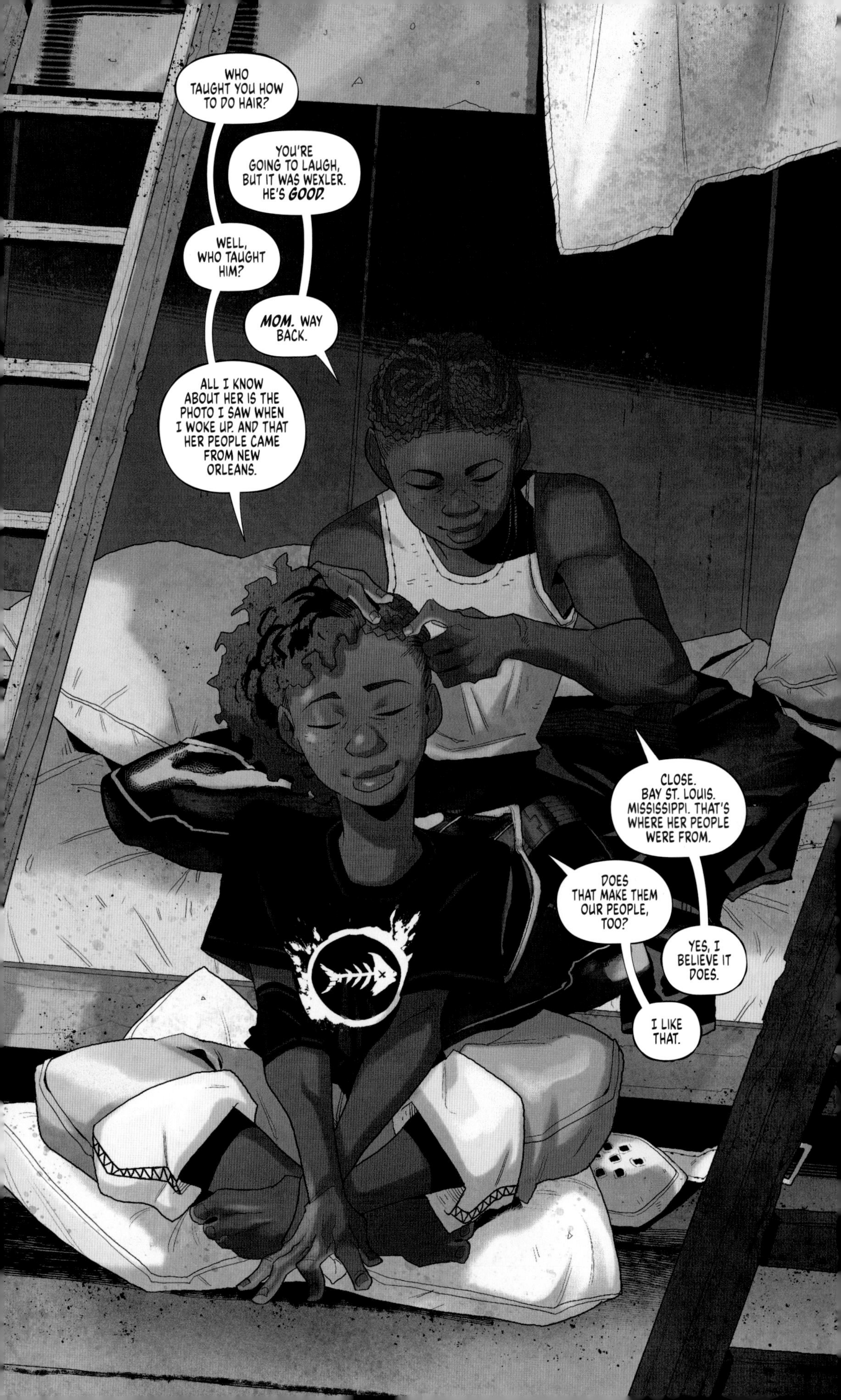
WHO TAUGHT YOU HOW TO DO HAIR?
YOU'RE GOING TO LAUGH, BUT IT WAS WEXLER. HE'S **GOOD.**
WELL, WHO TAUGHT HIM?
MOM. WAY BACK.
ALL I KNOW ABOUT HER IS THE PHOTO I SAW WHEN I WOKE UP. AND THAT HER PEOPLE CAME FROM NEW ORLEANS.
CLOSE. BAY ST. LOUIS. MISSISSIPPI. THAT'S WHERE HER PEOPLE WERE FROM.
DOES THAT MAKE THEM OUR PEOPLE, TOO?
YES, I BELIEVE IT DOES.
I LIKE THAT.

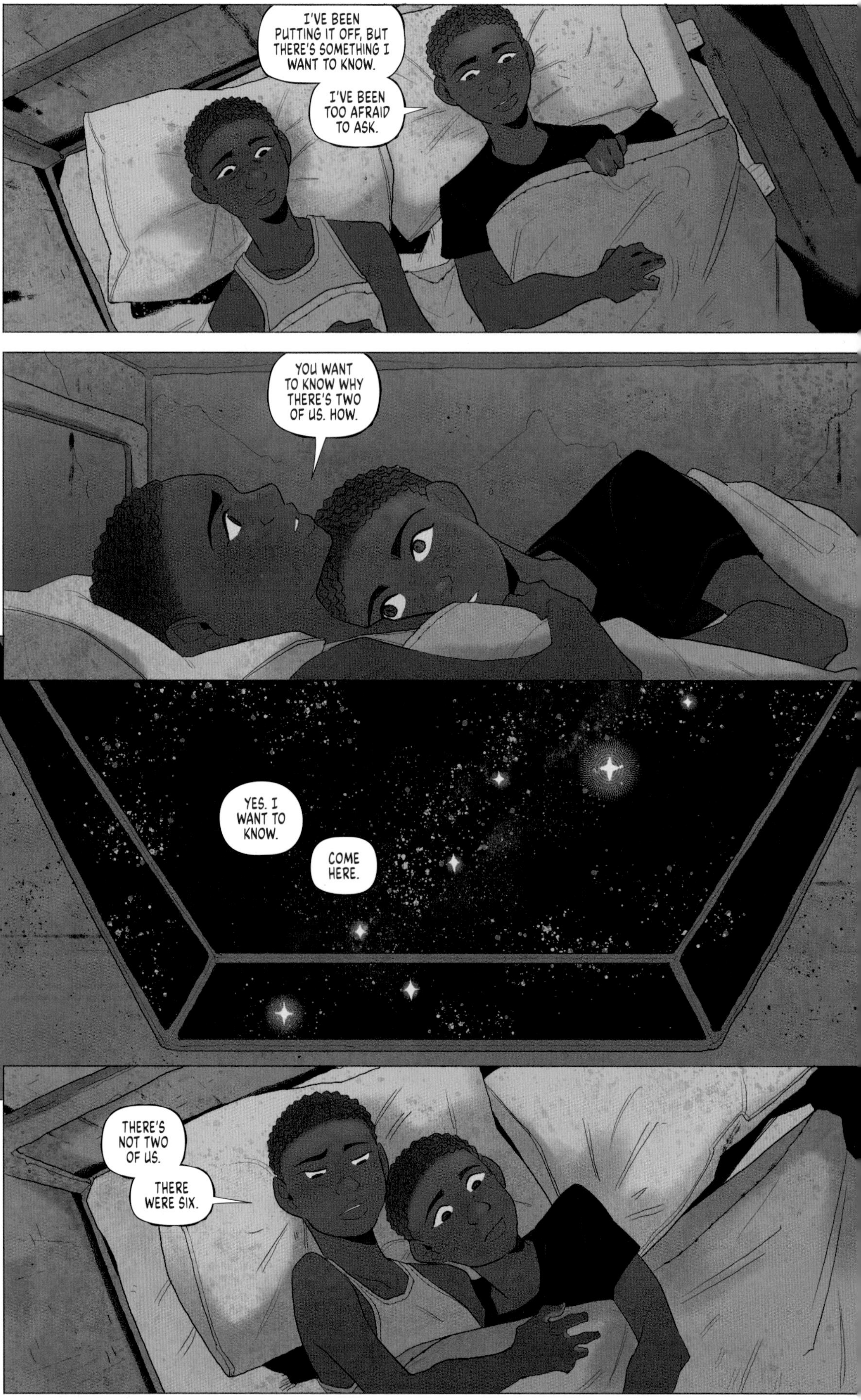

I'VE BEEN PUTTING IT OFF, BUT THERE'S SOMETHING I WANT TO KNOW.
I'VE BEEN TOO AFRAID TO ASK.
YOU WANT TO KNOW WHY THERE'S TWO OF US. HOW.
YES. I WANT TO KNOW.
COME HERE.
THERE'S NOT TWO OF US.
THERE WERE SIX.

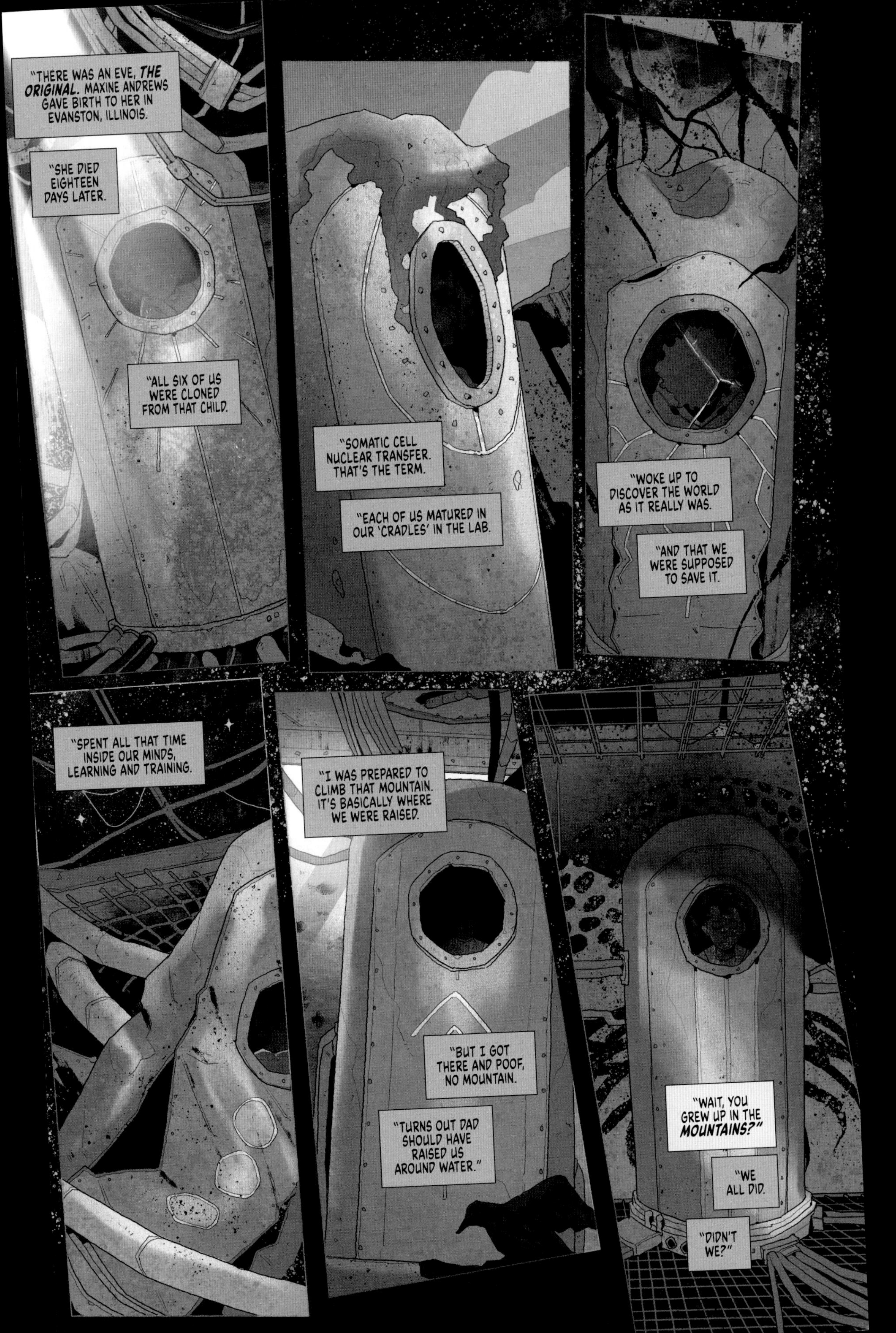
"THERE WAS AN EVE, *THE ORIGINAL.* MAXINE ANDREWS GAVE BIRTH TO HER IN EVANSTON, ILLINOIS.
"SHE DIED EIGHTEEN DAYS LATER.
"ALL SIX OF US WERE CLONED FROM THAT CHILD.
"SOMATIC CELL NUCLEAR TRANSFER. THAT'S THE TERM.
"EACH OF US MATURED IN OUR 'CRADLES' IN THE LAB.
"WOKE UP TO DISCOVER THE WORLD AS IT REALLY WAS.
"AND THAT WE WERE SUPPOSED TO SAVE IT.
"SPENT ALL THAT TIME INSIDE OUR MINDS, LEARNING AND TRAINING.
"I WAS PREPARED TO CLIMB THAT MOUNTAIN. IT'S BASICALLY WHERE WE WERE RAISED.
"BUT I GOT THERE AND POOF, NO MOUNTAIN.
"TURNS OUT DAD SHOULD HAVE RAISED US AROUND WATER."
"WAIT, YOU GREW UP IN THE *MOUNTAINS?"*
"WE ALL DID.
"DIDN'T WE?"

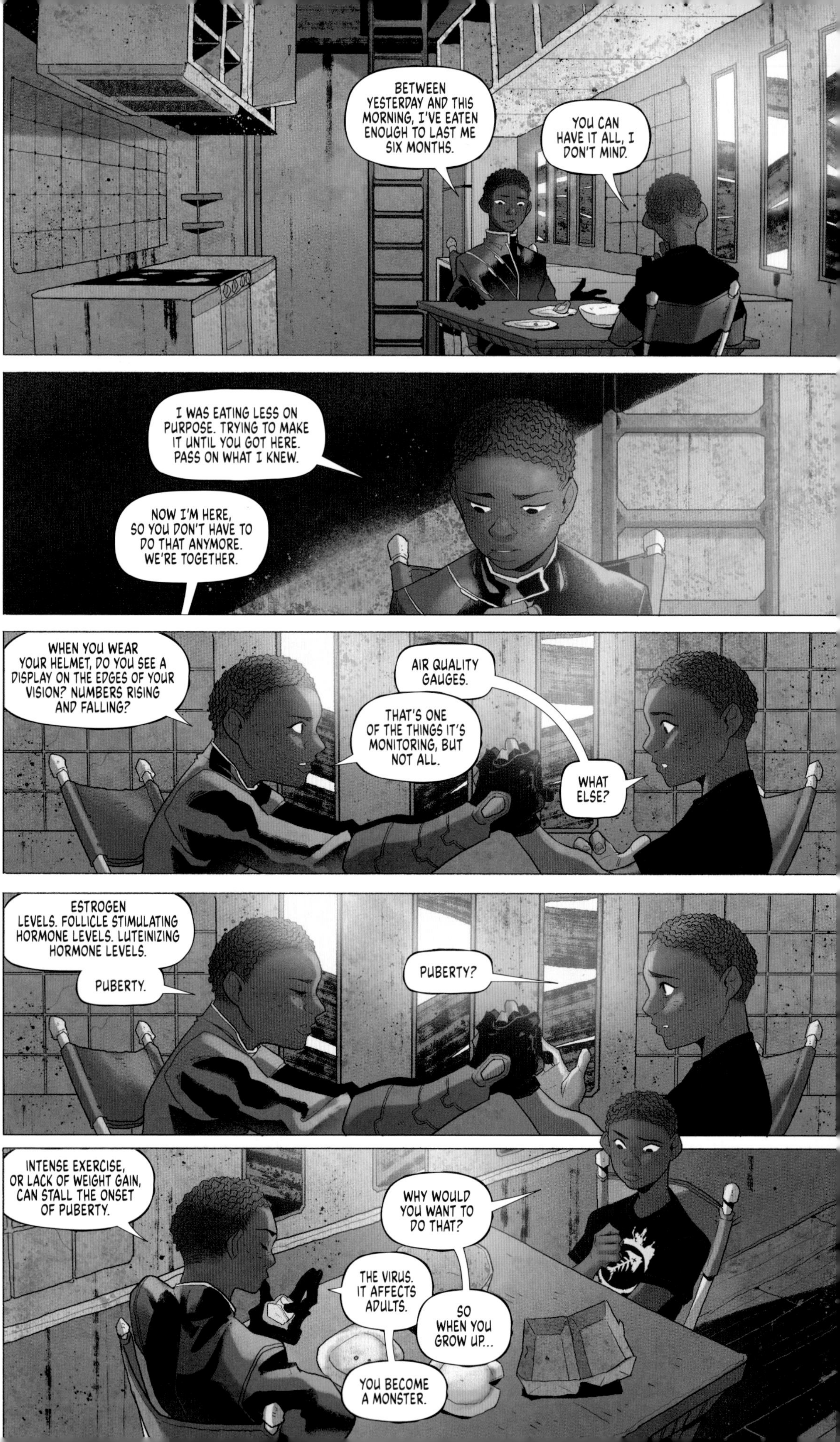

BETWEEN YESTERDAY AND THIS MORNING, I'VE EATEN ENOUGH TO LAST ME SIX MONTHS.
YOU CAN HAVE IT ALL, I DON'T MIND.
I WAS EATING LESS ON PURPOSE. TRYING TO MAKE IT UNTIL YOU GOT HERE. PASS ON WHAT I KNEW.
NOW I'M HERE, SO YOU DON'T HAVE TO DO THAT ANYMORE. WE'RE TOGETHER.
WHEN YOU WEAR YOUR HELMET, DO YOU SEE A DISPLAY ON THE EDGES OF YOUR VISION? NUMBERS RISING AND FALLING?
AIR QUALITY GAUGES.
THAT'S ONE OF THE THINGS IT'S MONITORING, BUT NOT ALL.
WHAT ELSE?
ESTROGEN LEVELS. FOLLICLE STIMULATING HORMONE LEVELS. LUTEINIZING HORMONE LEVELS.
PUBERTY.
PUBERTY?
INTENSE EXERCISE, OR LACK OF WEIGHT GAIN, CAN STALL THE ONSET OF PUBERTY.
WHY WOULD YOU WANT TO DO THAT?
THE VIRUS. IT AFFECTS ADULTS.
SO WHEN YOU GROW UP...
YOU BECOME A MONSTER.

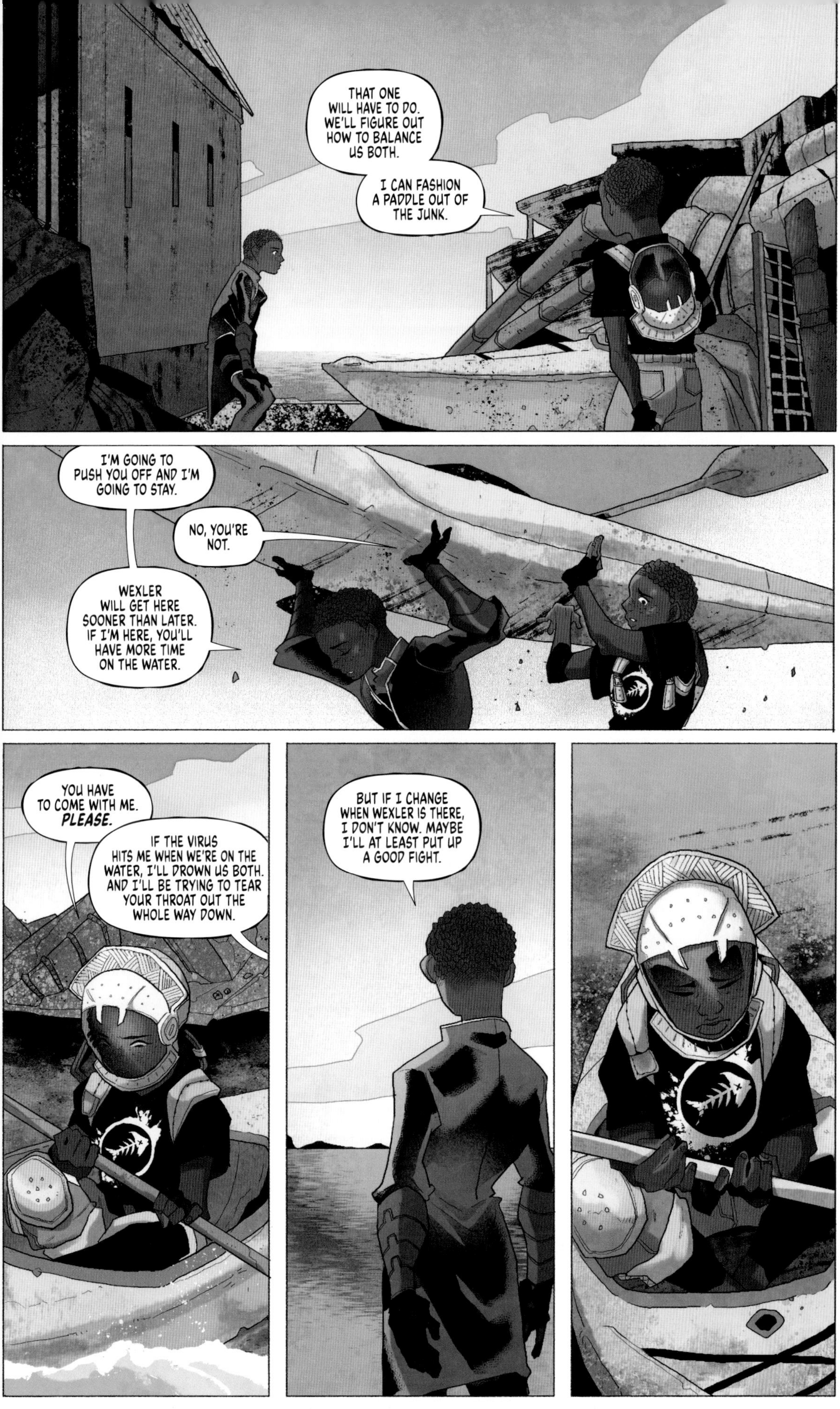
THAT ONE WILL HAVE TO DO. WE'LL FIGURE OUT HOW TO BALANCE US BOTH.
I CAN FASHION A PADDLE OUT OF THE JUNK.
I'M GOING TO PUSH YOU OFF AND I'M GOING TO STAY.
NO, YOU'RE NOT.
WEXLER WILL GET HERE SOONER THAN LATER. IF I'M HERE, YOU'LL HAVE MORE TIME ON THE WATER.
YOU HAVE TO COME WITH ME. *PLEASE.*
IF THE VIRUS HITS ME WHEN WE'RE ON THE WATER, I'LL DROWN US BOTH. AND I'LL BE TRYING TO TEAR YOUR THROAT OUT THE WHOLE WAY DOWN.
BUT IF I CHANGE WHEN WEXLER IS THERE, I DON'T KNOW. MAYBE I'LL AT LEAST PUT UP A GOOD FIGHT.

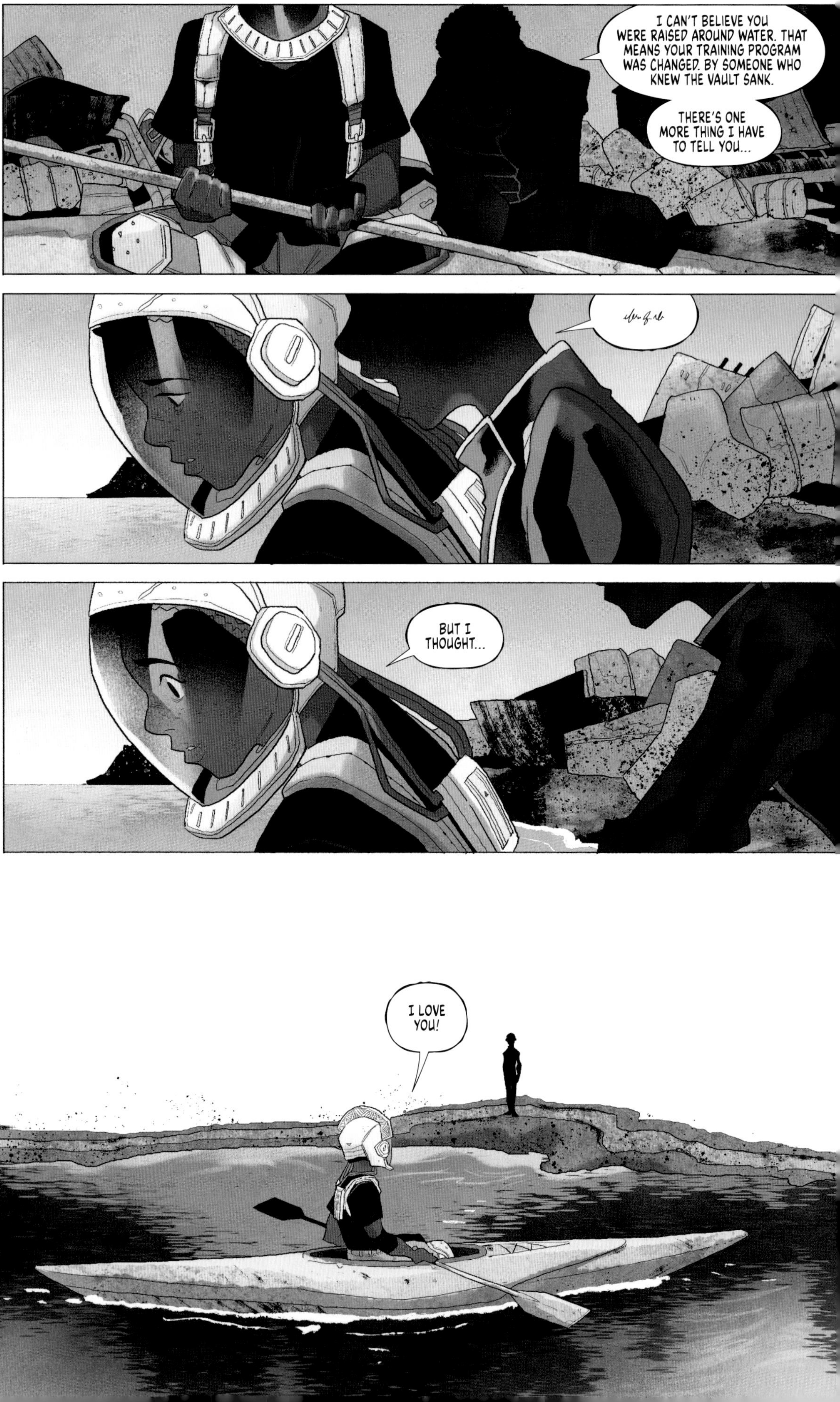
I CAN'T BELIEVE YOU WERE RAISED AROUND WATER. THAT MEANS YOUR TRAINING PROGRAM WAS CHANGED. BY SOMEONE WHO KNEW THE VAULT SANK.
THERE'S ONE MORE THING I HAVE TO TELL YOU...
BUT I THOUGHT...
I LOVE YOU!

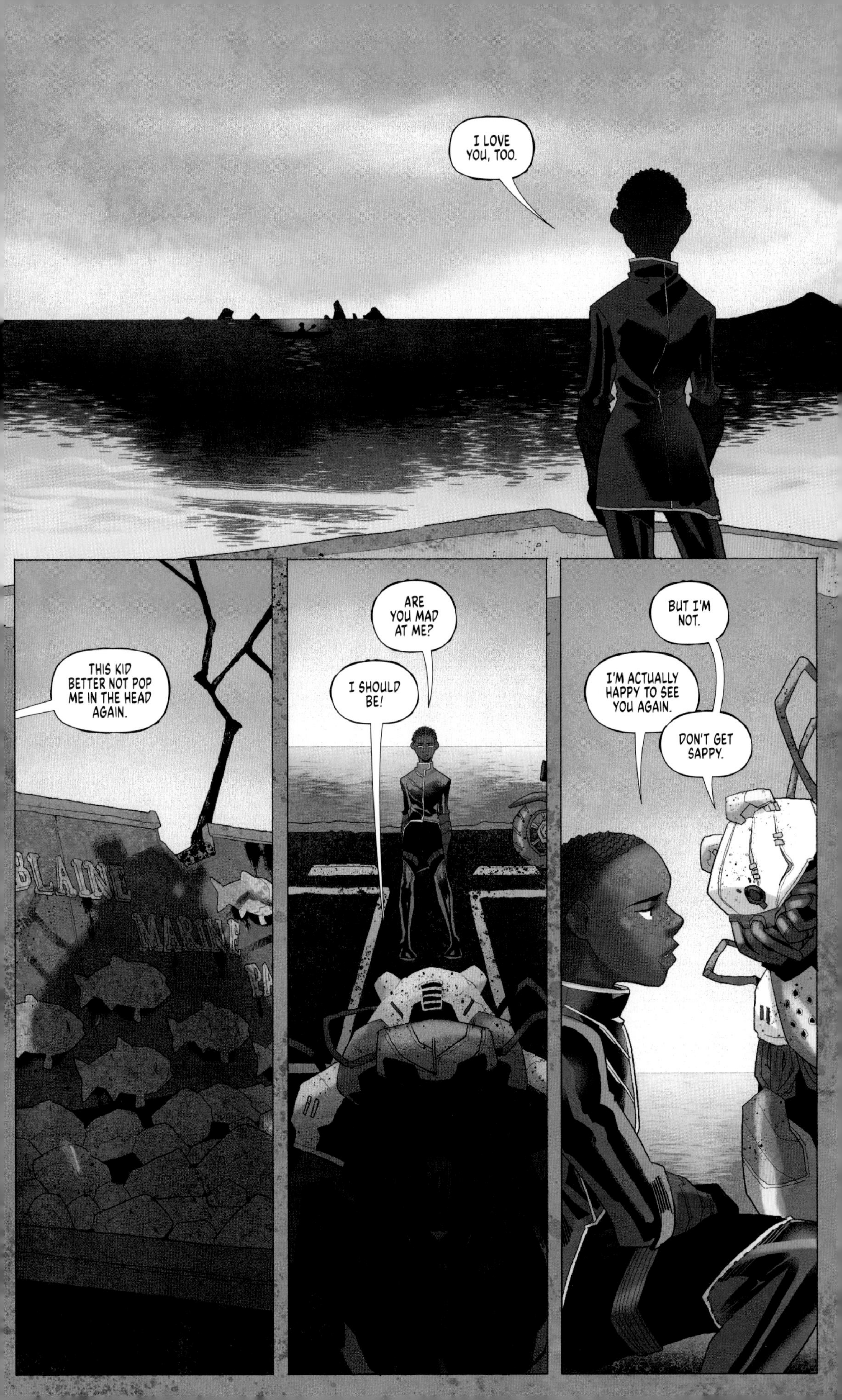
I LOVE YOU, TOO.
THIS KID BETTER NOT POP ME IN THE HEAD AGAIN.
ARE YOU MAD AT ME?
I SHOULD BE!
BUT I'M NOT.
I'M ACTUALLY HAPPY TO SEE YOU AGAIN.
DON'T GET SAPPY.
BLAINE MARINE

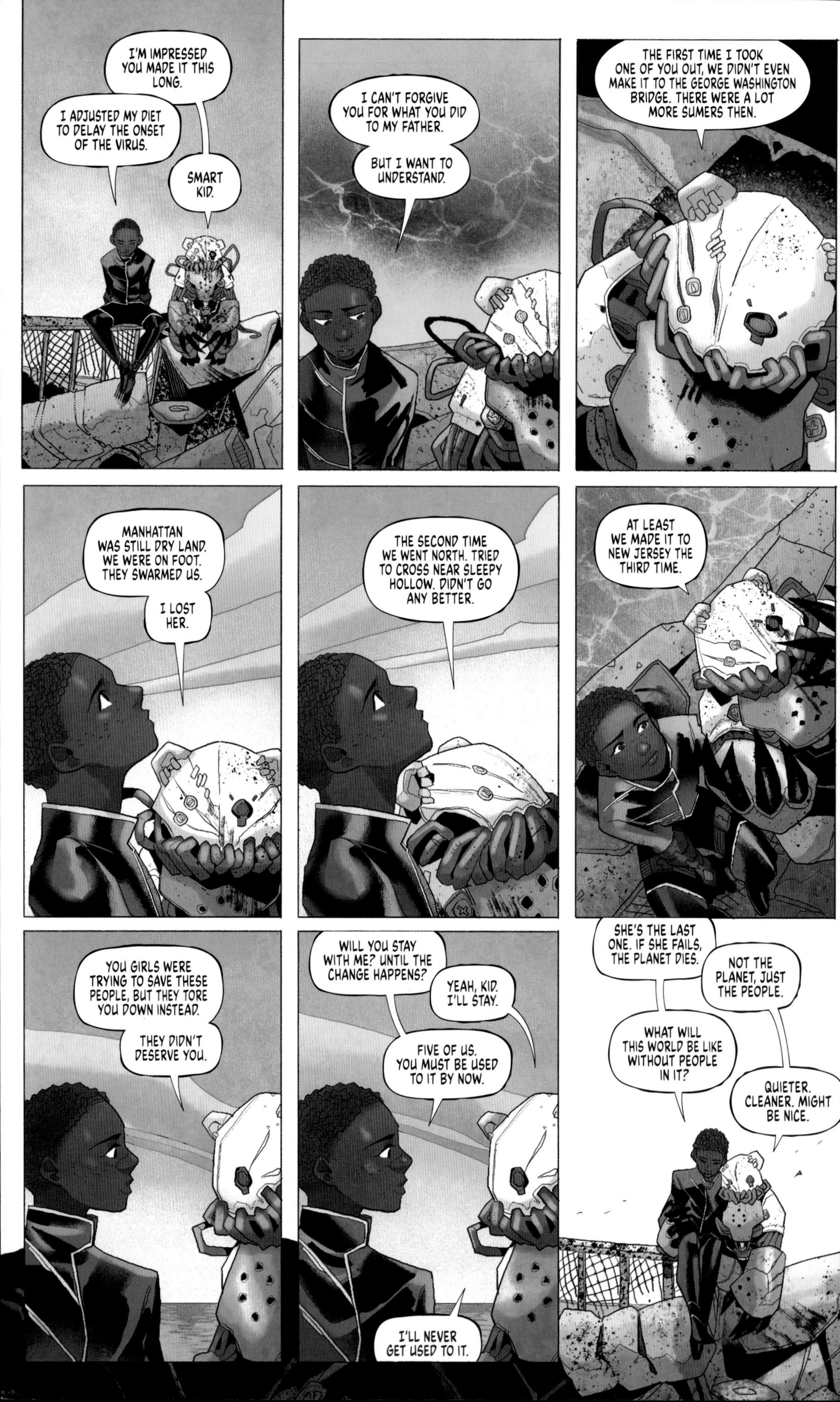
I'M IMPRESSED YOU MADE IT THIS LONG.
I ADJUSTED MY DIET TO DELAY THE ONSET OF THE VIRUS.
SMART KID.
I CAN'T FORGIVE YOU FOR WHAT YOU DID TO MY FATHER.
BUT I WANT TO UNDERSTAND.
THE FIRST TIME I TOOK ONE OF YOU OUT, WE DIDN'T EVEN MAKE IT TO THE GEORGE WASHINGTON BRIDGE. THERE WERE A LOT MORE SUMERS THEN.
MANHATTAN WAS STILL DRY LAND. WE WERE ON FOOT. THEY SWARMED US.
I LOST HER.
THE SECOND TIME WE WENT NORTH. TRIED TO CROSS NEAR SLEEPY HOLLOW. DIDN'T GO ANY BETTER.
AT LEAST WE MADE IT TO NEW JERSEY THE THIRD TIME.
YOU GIRLS WERE TRYING TO SAVE THESE PEOPLE, BUT THEY TORE YOU DOWN INSTEAD.
THEY DIDN'T DESERVE YOU.
WILL YOU STAY WITH ME? UNTIL THE CHANGE HAPPENS?
YEAH, KID. I'LL STAY.
FIVE OF US. YOU MUST BE USED TO IT BY NOW.
I'LL NEVER GET USED TO IT.
SHE'S THE LAST ONE. IF SHE FAILS, THE PLANET DIES.
NOT THE PLANET, JUST THE PEOPLE.
WHAT WILL THIS WORLD BE LIKE WITHOUT PEOPLE IN IT?
QUIETER. CLEANER. MIGHT BE NICE.

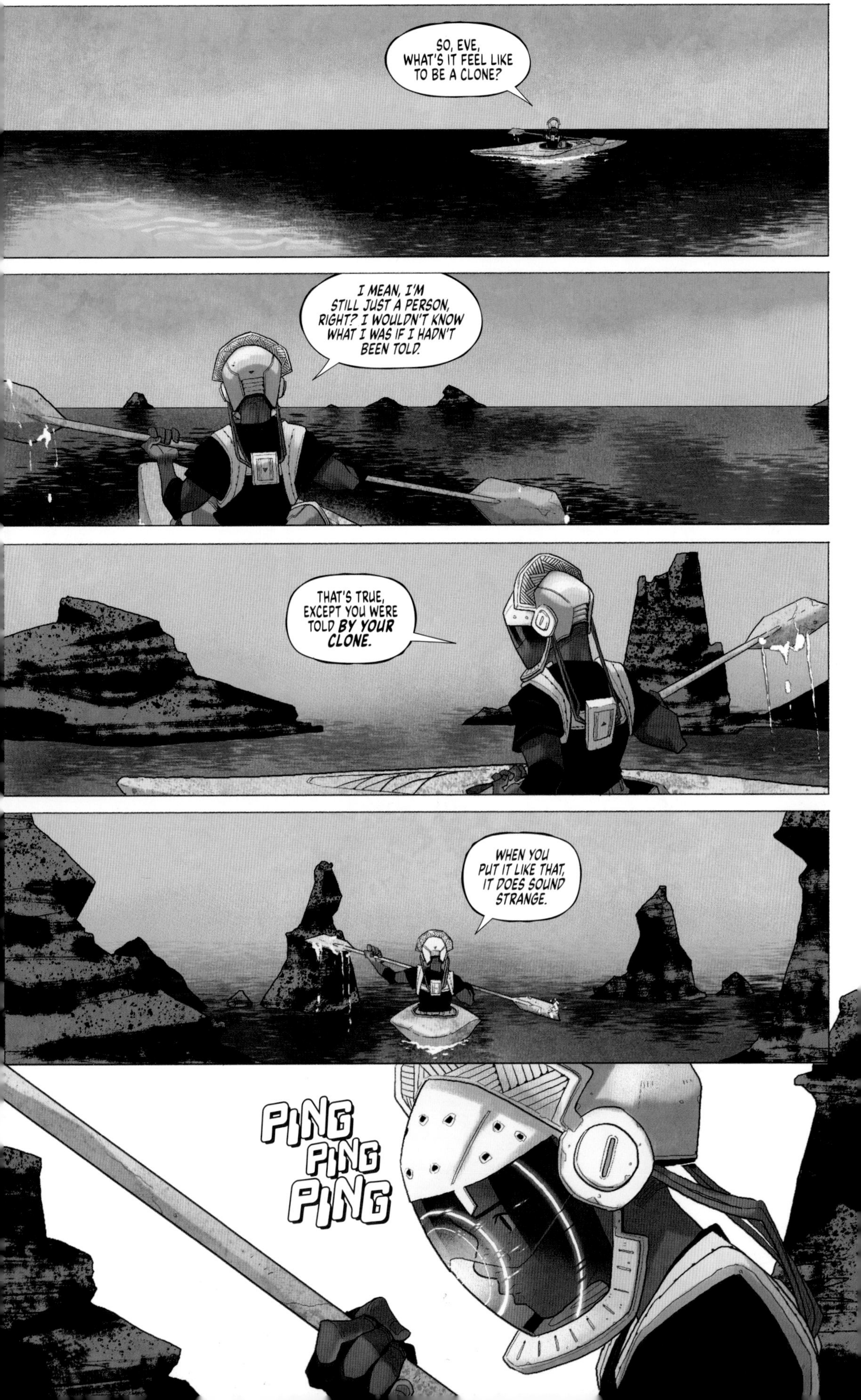
SO, EVE, WHAT'S IT FEEL LIKE TO BE A CLONE?
I MEAN, I'M STILL JUST A PERSON, RIGHT? I WOULDN'T KNOW WHAT I WAS IF I HADN'T BEEN TOLD.
THAT'S TRUE, EXCEPT YOU WERE TOLD BY YOUR CLONE.
WHEN YOU PUT IT LIKE THAT, IT DOES SOUND STRANGE.
PING PING PING

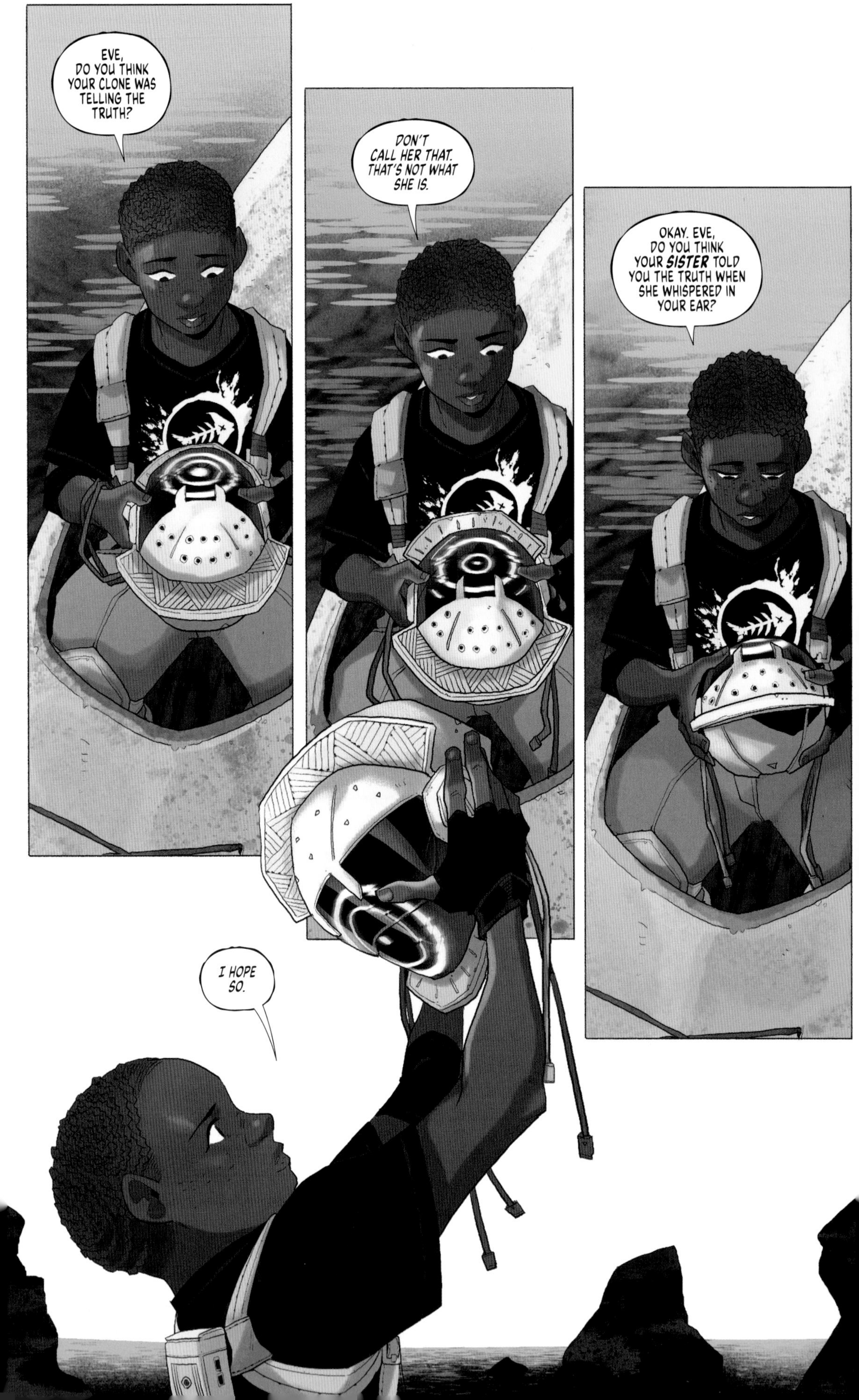

EVE, DO YOU THINK YOUR CLONE WAS TELLING THE TRUTH?
DON'T CALL HER THAT. THAT'S NOT WHAT SHE IS.
OKAY. EVE, DO YOU THINK YOUR SISTER TOLD YOU THE TRUTH WHEN SHE WHISPERED IN YOUR EAR?
I HOPE SO.

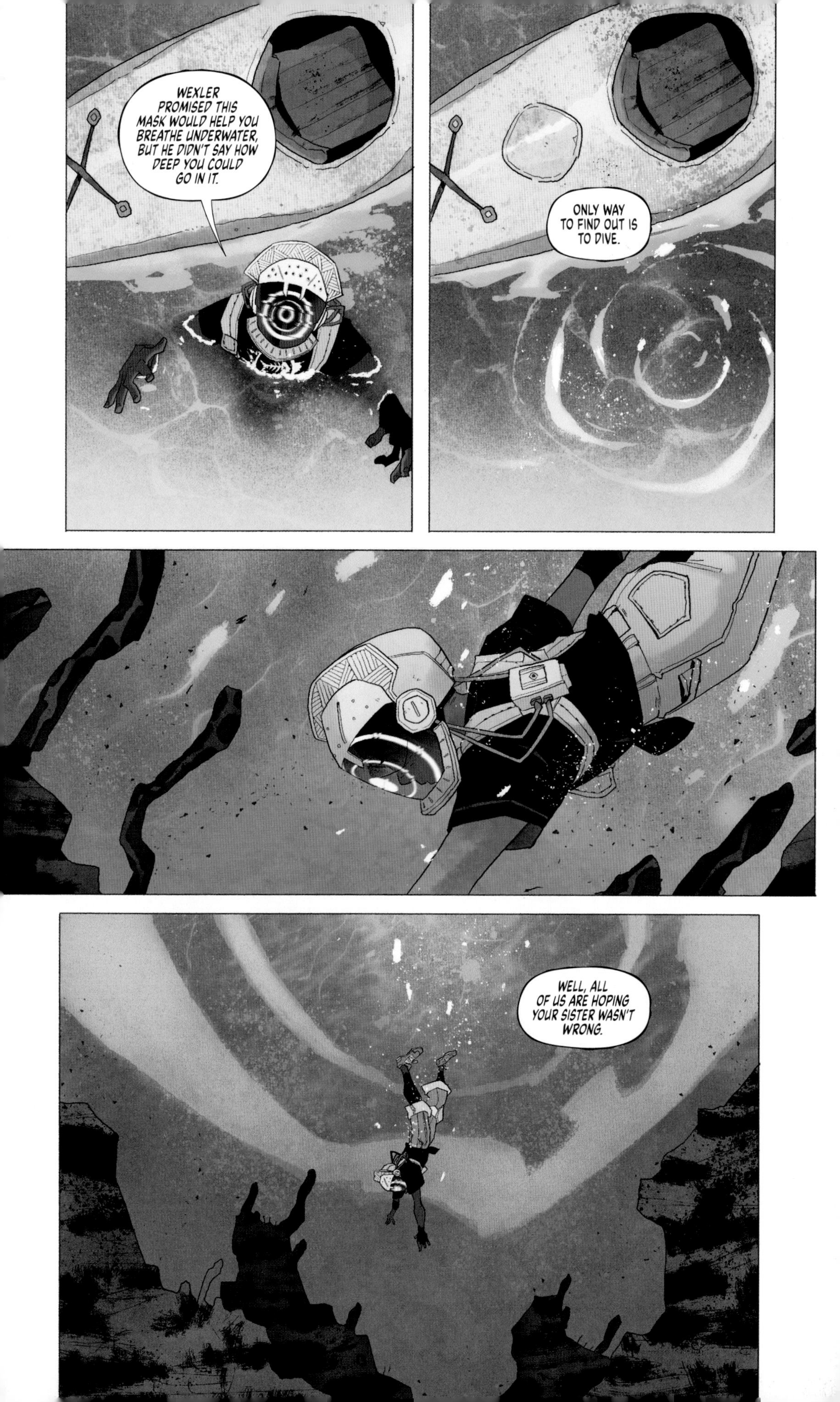
WEXLER PROMISED THIS MASK WOULD HELP YOU BREATHE UNDERWATER, BUT HE DIDN'T SAY HOW DEEP YOU COULD GO IN IT.
ONLY WAY TO FIND OUT IS TO DIVE.
WELL, ALL OF US ARE HOPING YOUR SISTER WASN'T WRONG.

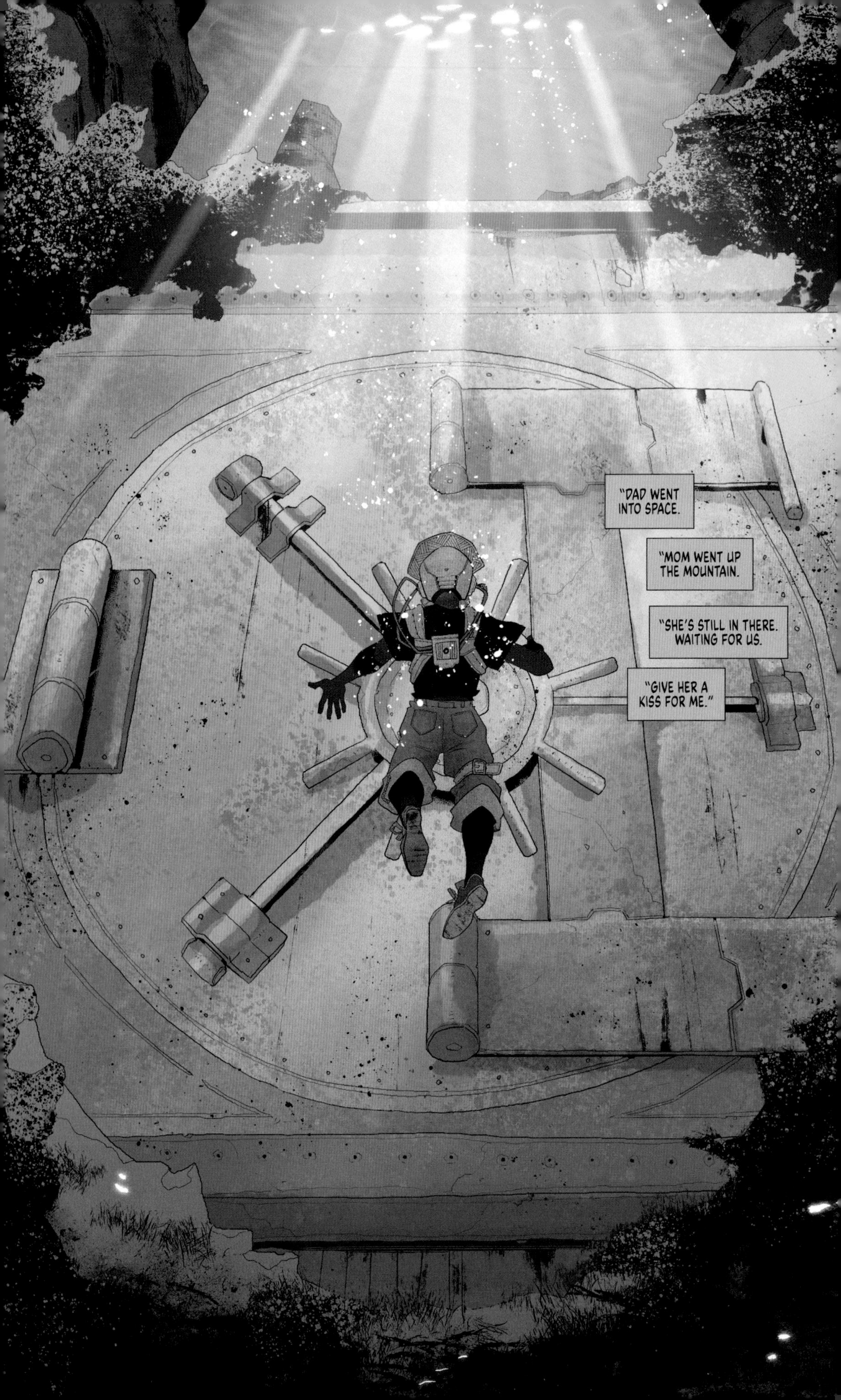
"DAD WENT INTO SPACE.
"MOM WENT UP THE MOUNTAIN.
"SHE'S STILL IN THERE. WAITING FOR US.
"GIVE HER A KISS FOR ME."

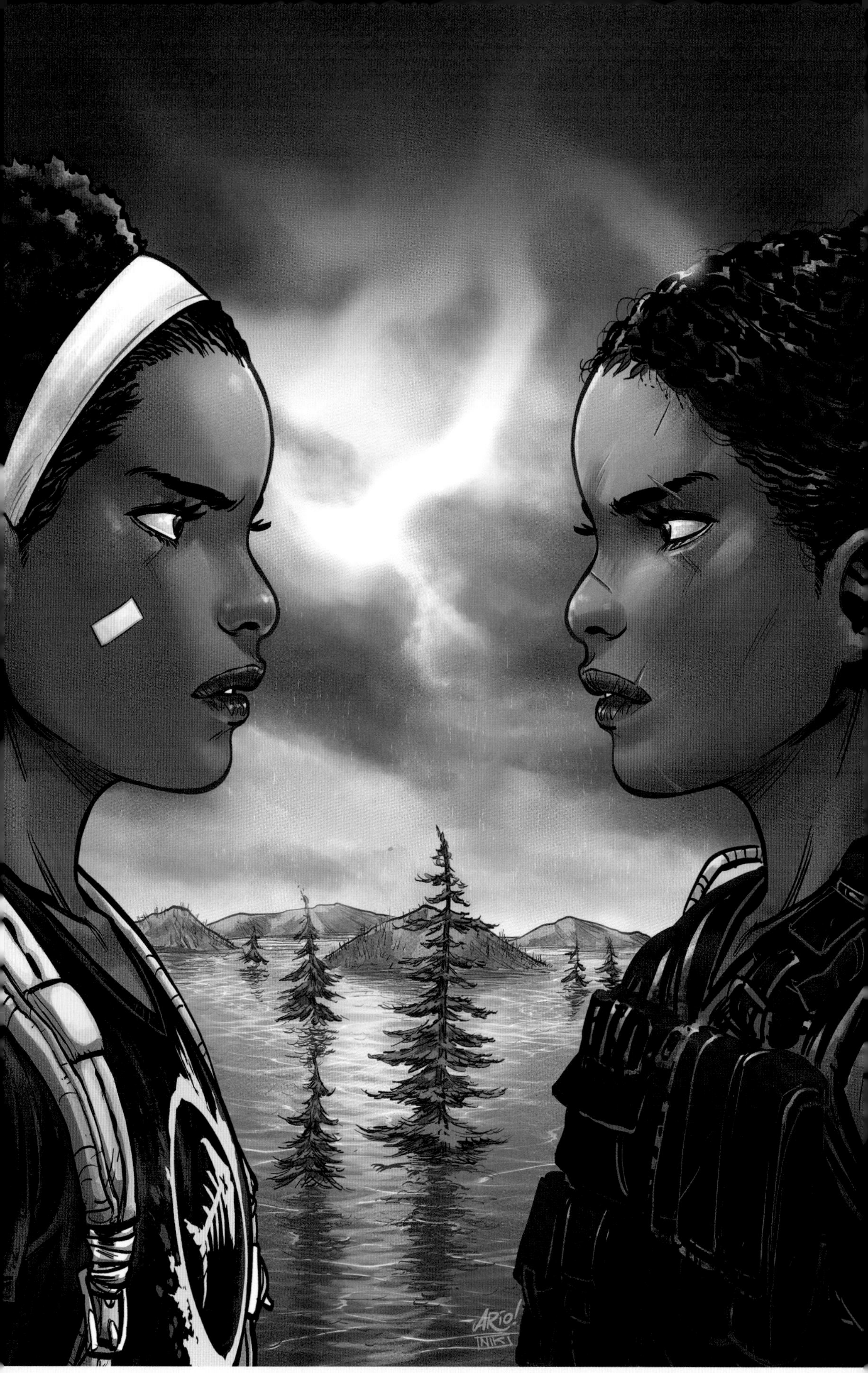
ARiO!
INK!

ISSUE #4 COVER BY **ARIO ANINDITO** WITH COLORS BY **NICOLA RIGHI**

CHAPTER
FIVE

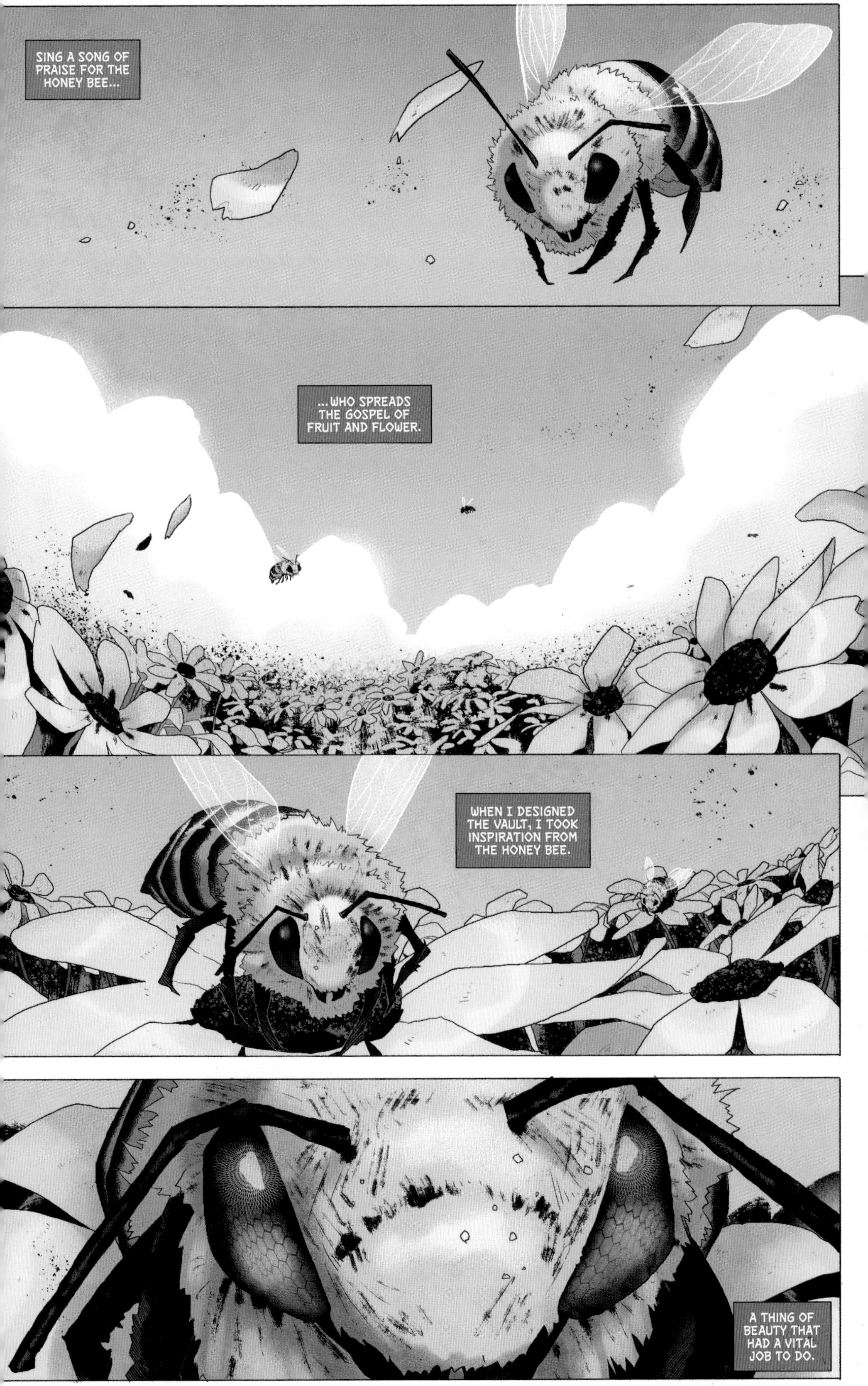

SING A SONG OF PRAISE FOR THE HONEY BEE...
...WHO SPREADS THE GOSPEL OF FRUIT AND FLOWER.
WHEN I DESIGNED THE VAULT, I TOOK INSPIRATION FROM THE HONEY BEE.
A THING OF BEAUTY THAT HAD A VITAL JOB TO DO.

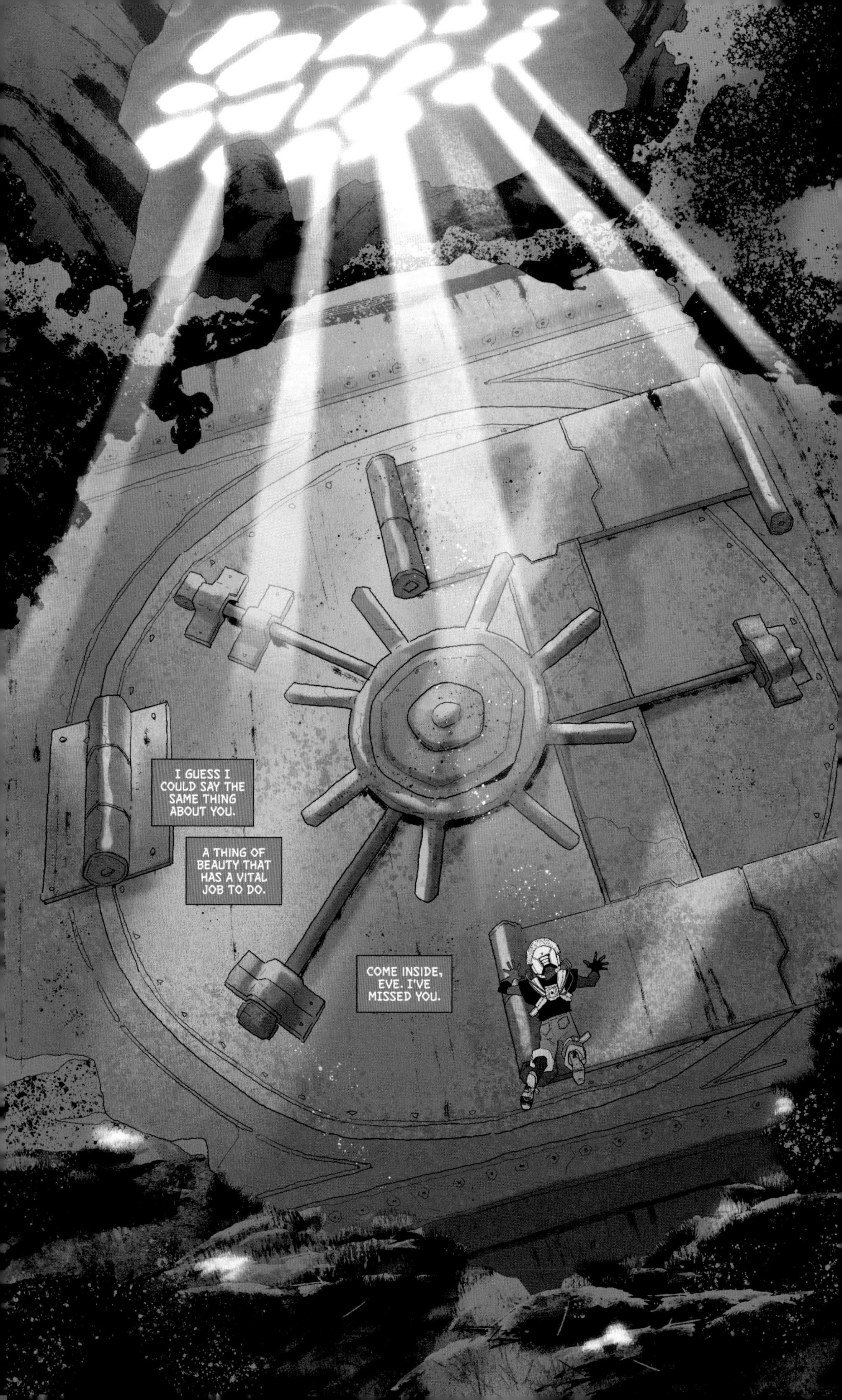
I GUESS I COULD SAY THE SAME THING ABOUT YOU.
A THING OF BEAUTY THAT HAS A VITAL JOB TO DO.
COME INSIDE, EVE. I'VE MISSED YOU.

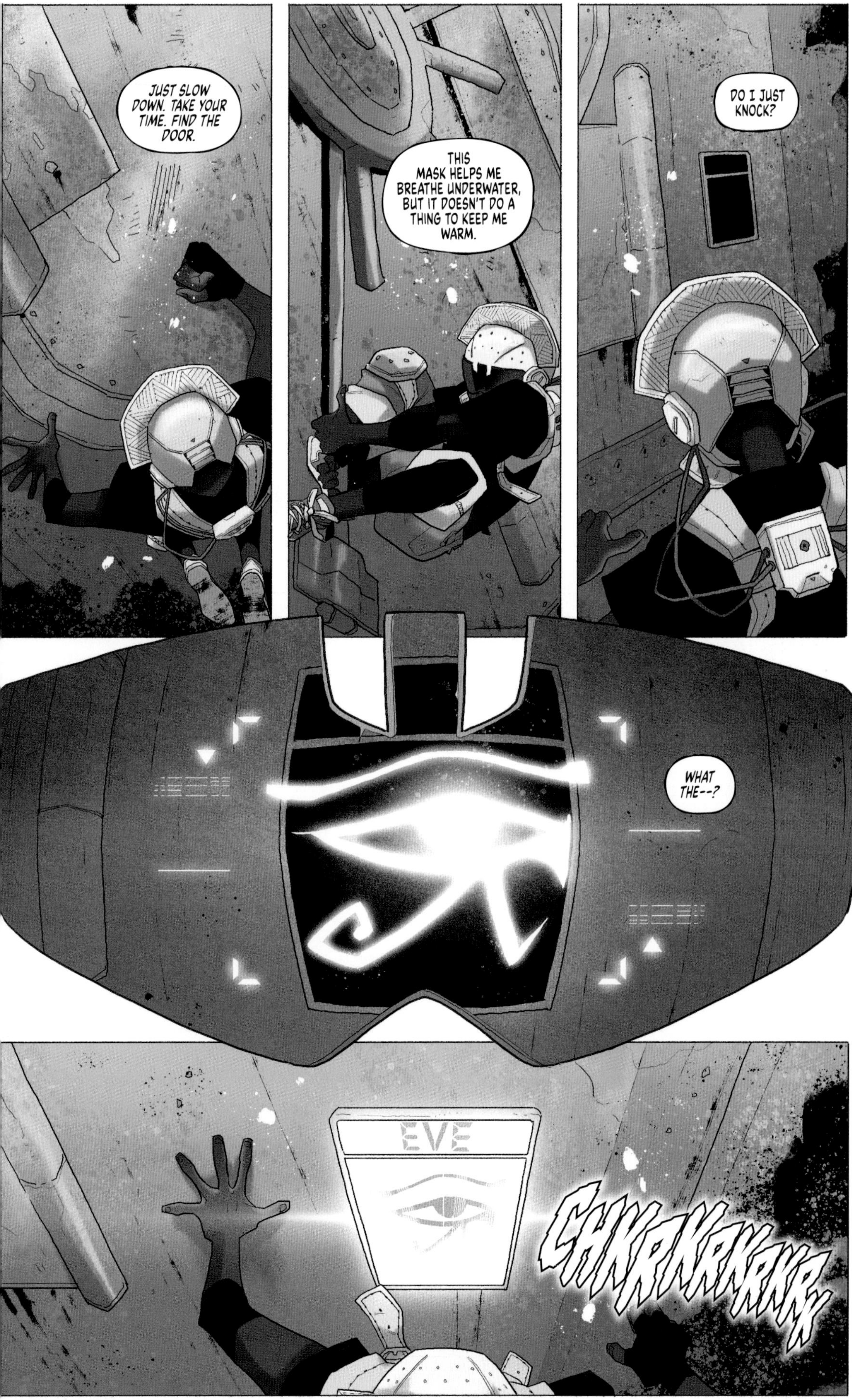
JUST SLOW DOWN. TAKE YOUR TIME. FIND THE DOOR.
THIS MASK HELPS ME BREATHE UNDERWATER, BUT IT DOESN'T DO A THING TO KEEP ME WARM.
DO I JUST KNOCK?
WHAT THE--?
EVE
CHKRKRKRKRKR

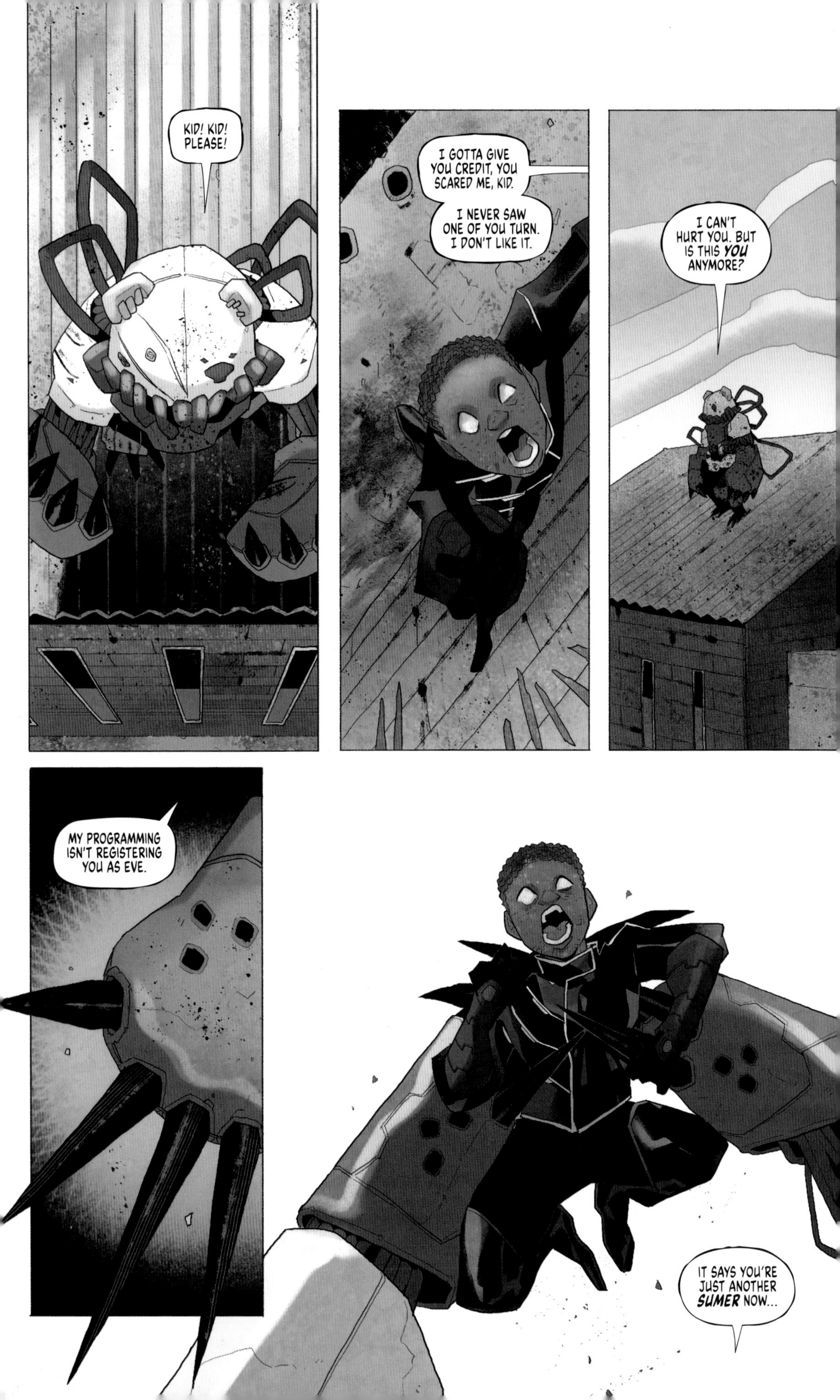
KID! KID! PLEASE!
I GOTTA GIVE YOU CREDIT, YOU SCARED ME, KID.
I NEVER SAW ONE OF YOU TURN. I DON'T LIKE IT.
I CAN'T HURT YOU. BUT IS THIS *YOU* ANYMORE?
MY PROGRAMMING ISN'T REGISTERING YOU AS EVE.
IT SAYS YOU'RE JUST ANOTHER *SUMER* NOW...

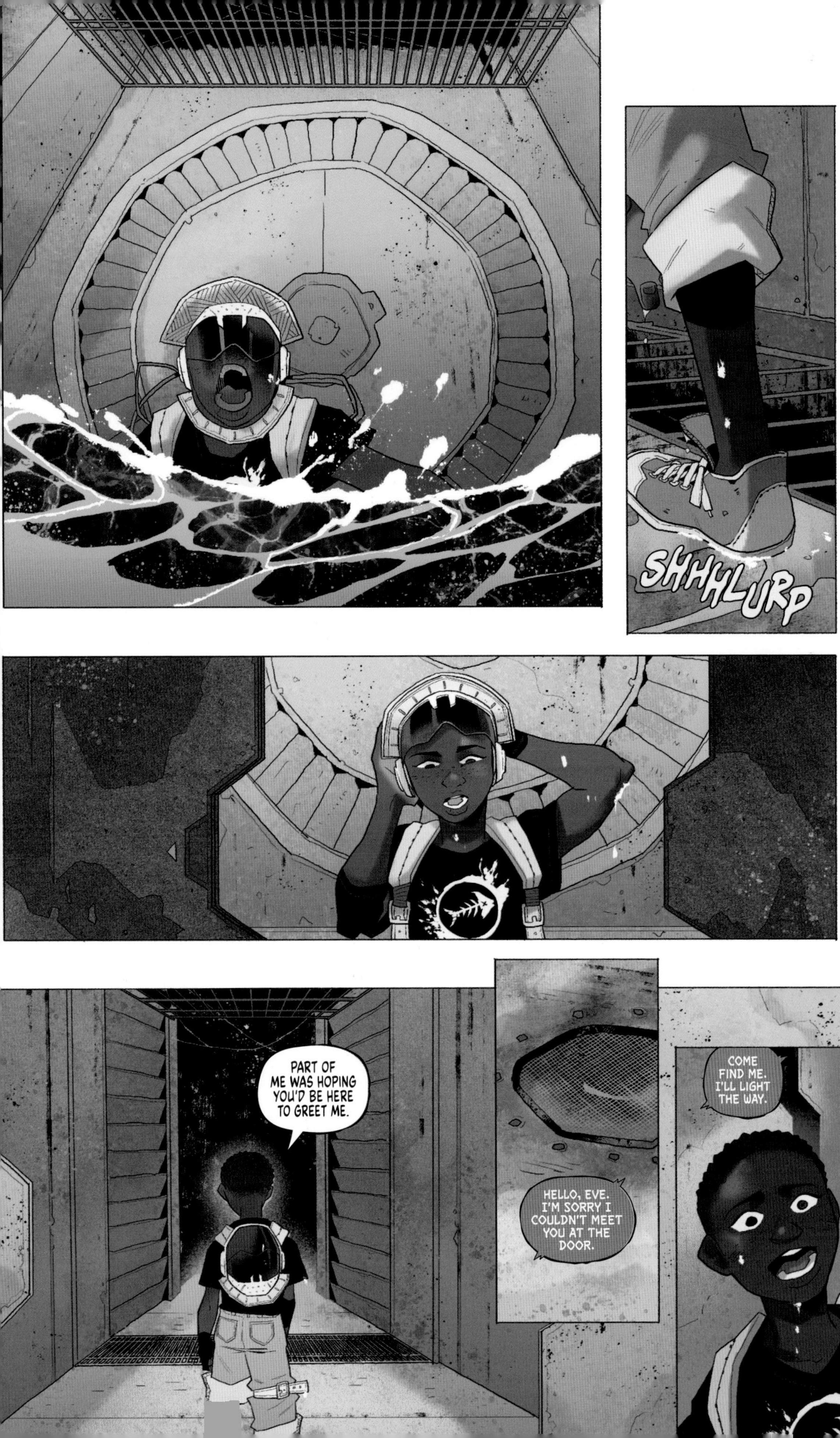
SHHHLURP
PART OF ME WAS HOPING YOU'D BE HERE TO GREET ME.
HELLO, EVE. I'M SORRY I COULDN'T MEET YOU AT THE DOOR.
COME FIND ME. I'LL LIGHT THE WAY.

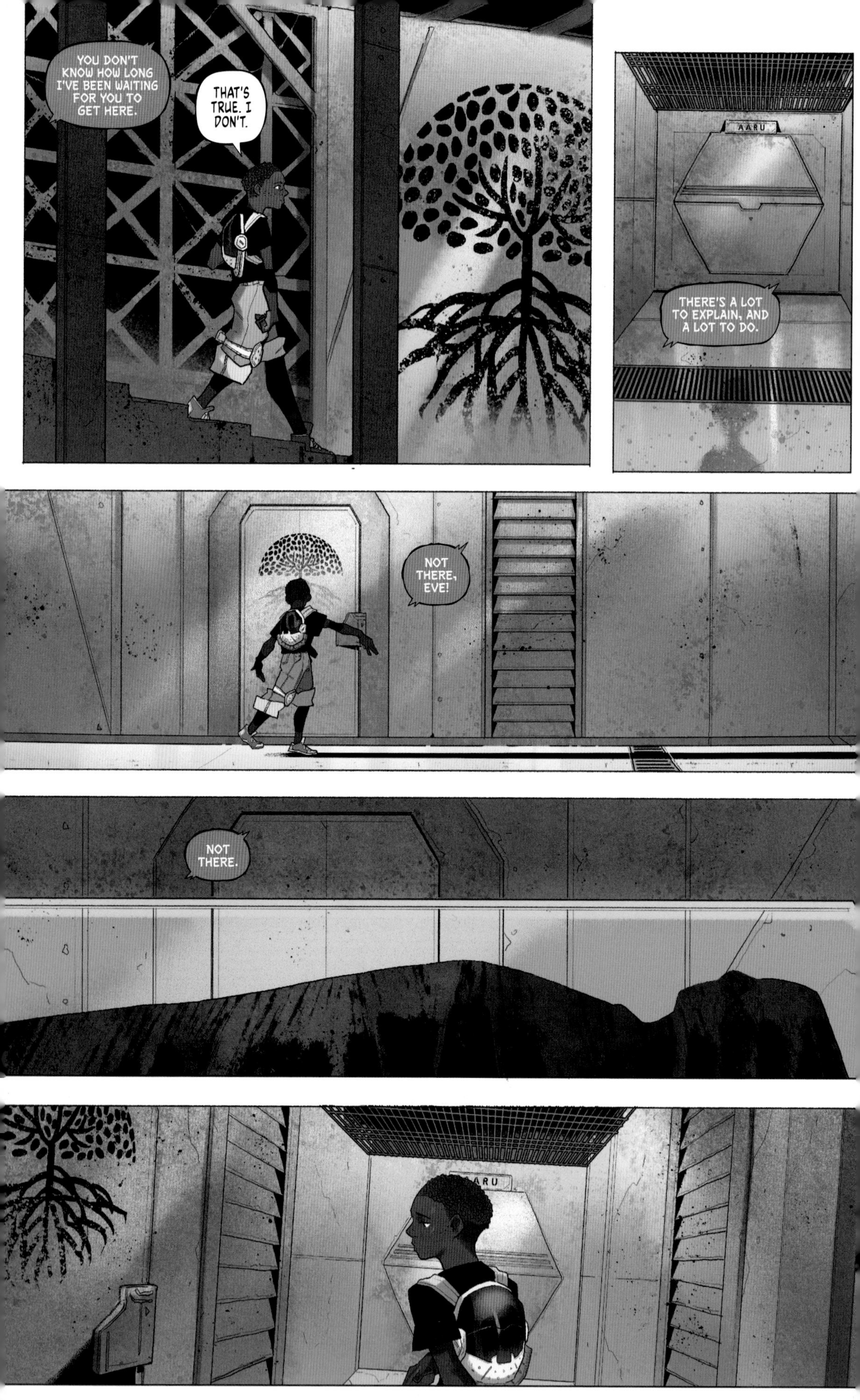
YOU DON'T KNOW HOW LONG I'VE BEEN WAITING FOR YOU TO GET HERE.
THAT'S TRUE. I DON'T.
AARU
THERE'S A LOT TO EXPLAIN, AND A LOT TO DO.
NOT THERE, EVE!
NOT THERE.
AARU

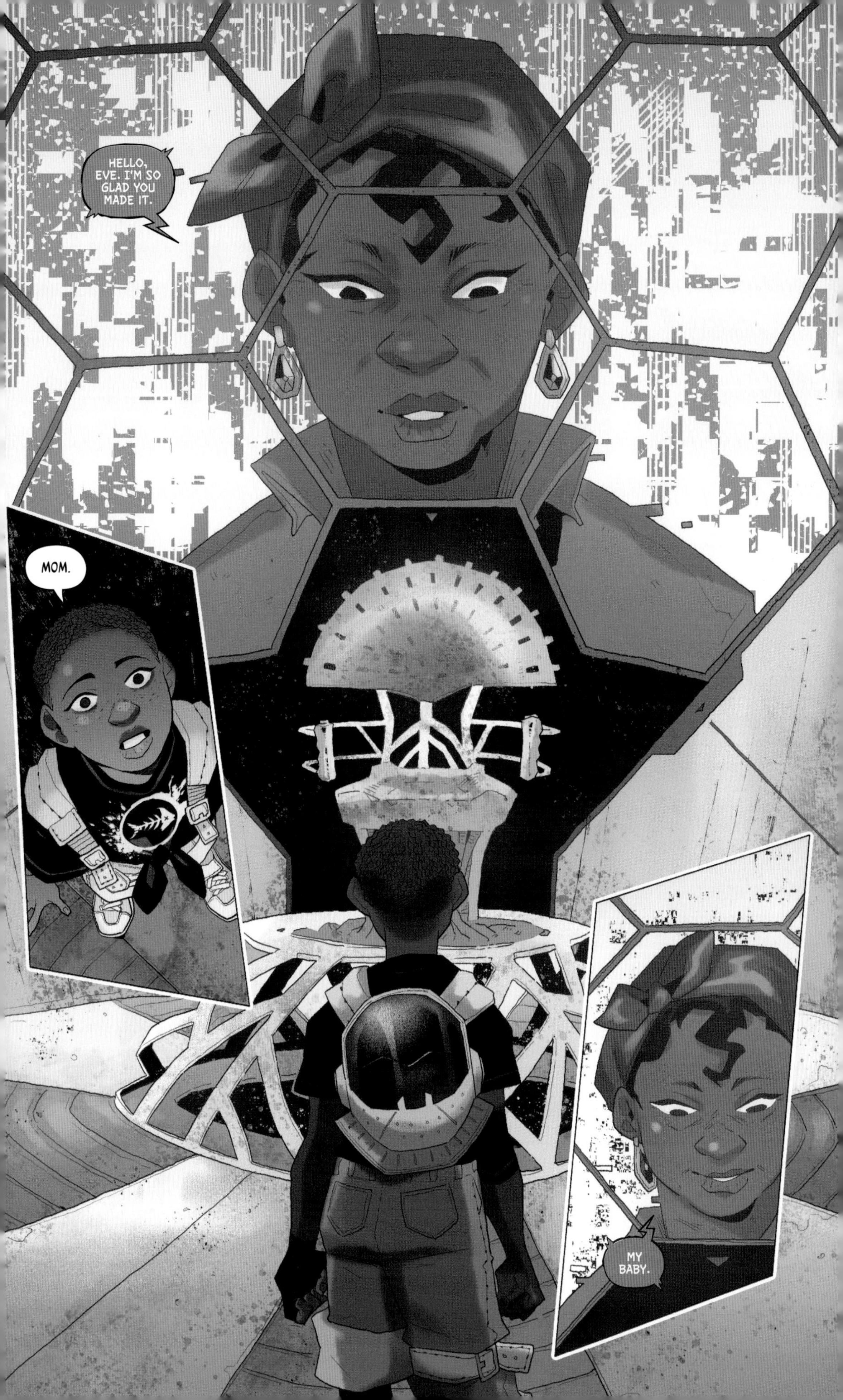
HELLO, EVE. I'M SO GLAD YOU MADE IT.
MOM.
MY BABY.

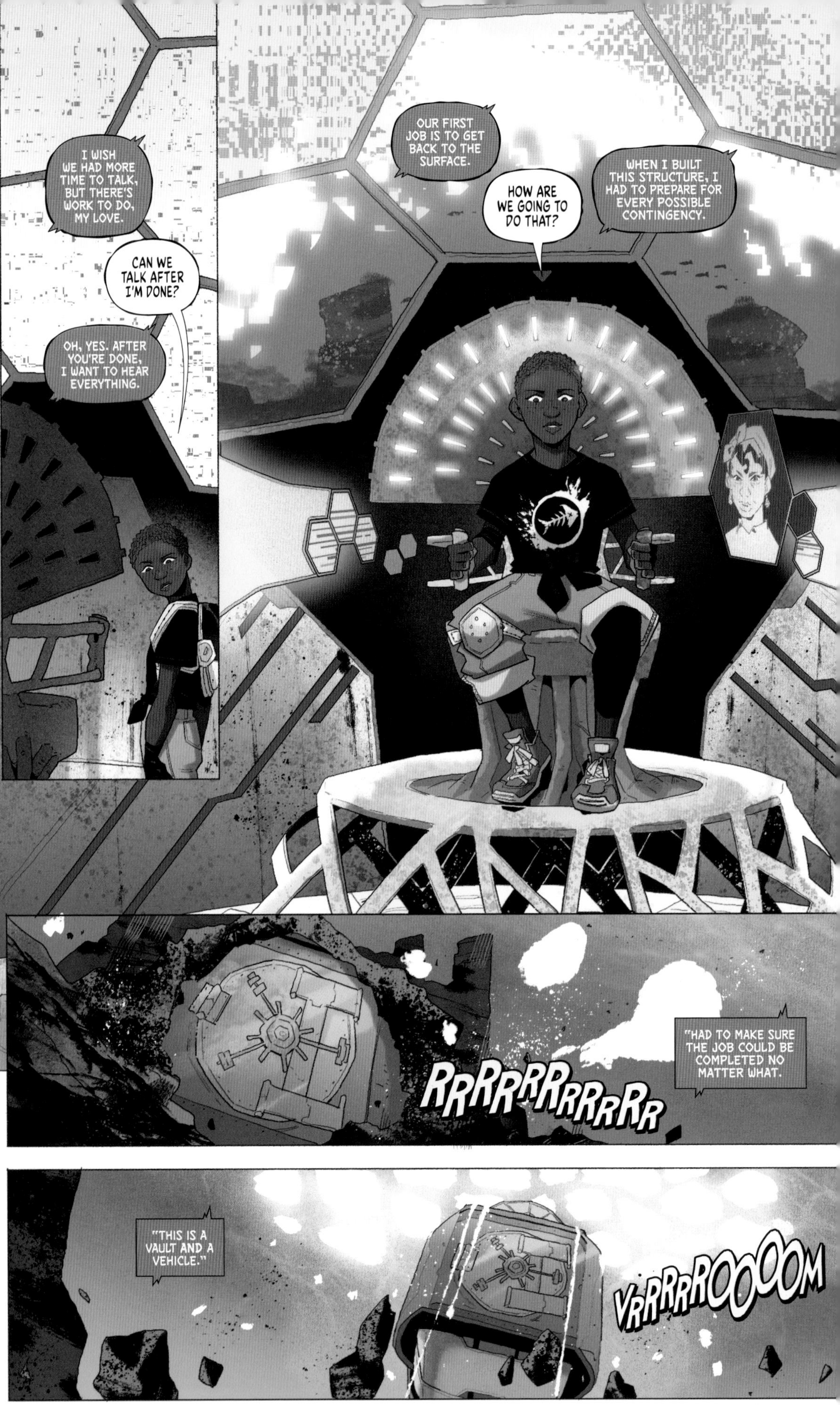

I WISH WE HAD MORE TIME TO TALK, BUT THERE'S WORK TO DO, MY LOVE.
CAN WE TALK AFTER I'M DONE?
OH, YES. AFTER YOU'RE DONE, I WANT TO HEAR EVERYTHING.
OUR FIRST JOB IS TO GET BACK TO THE SURFACE.
HOW ARE WE GOING TO DO THAT?
WHEN I BUILT THIS STRUCTURE, I HAD TO PREPARE FOR EVERY POSSIBLE CONTINGENCY.
"HAD TO MAKE SURE THE JOB COULD BE COMPLETED NO MATTER WHAT.
RRRRRRRRRRRR
"THIS IS A VAULT AND A VEHICLE."
VRRRRROOOOOM

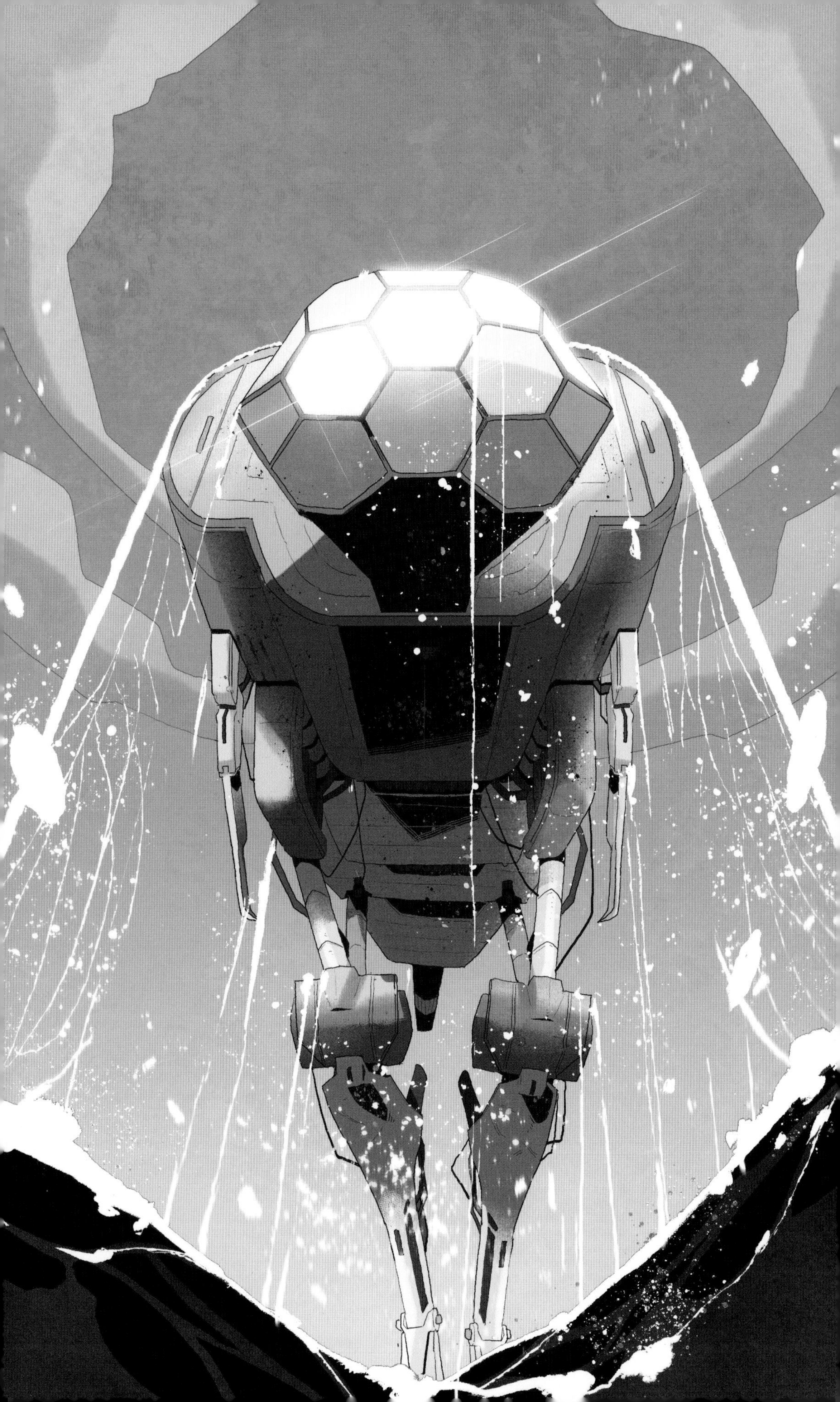

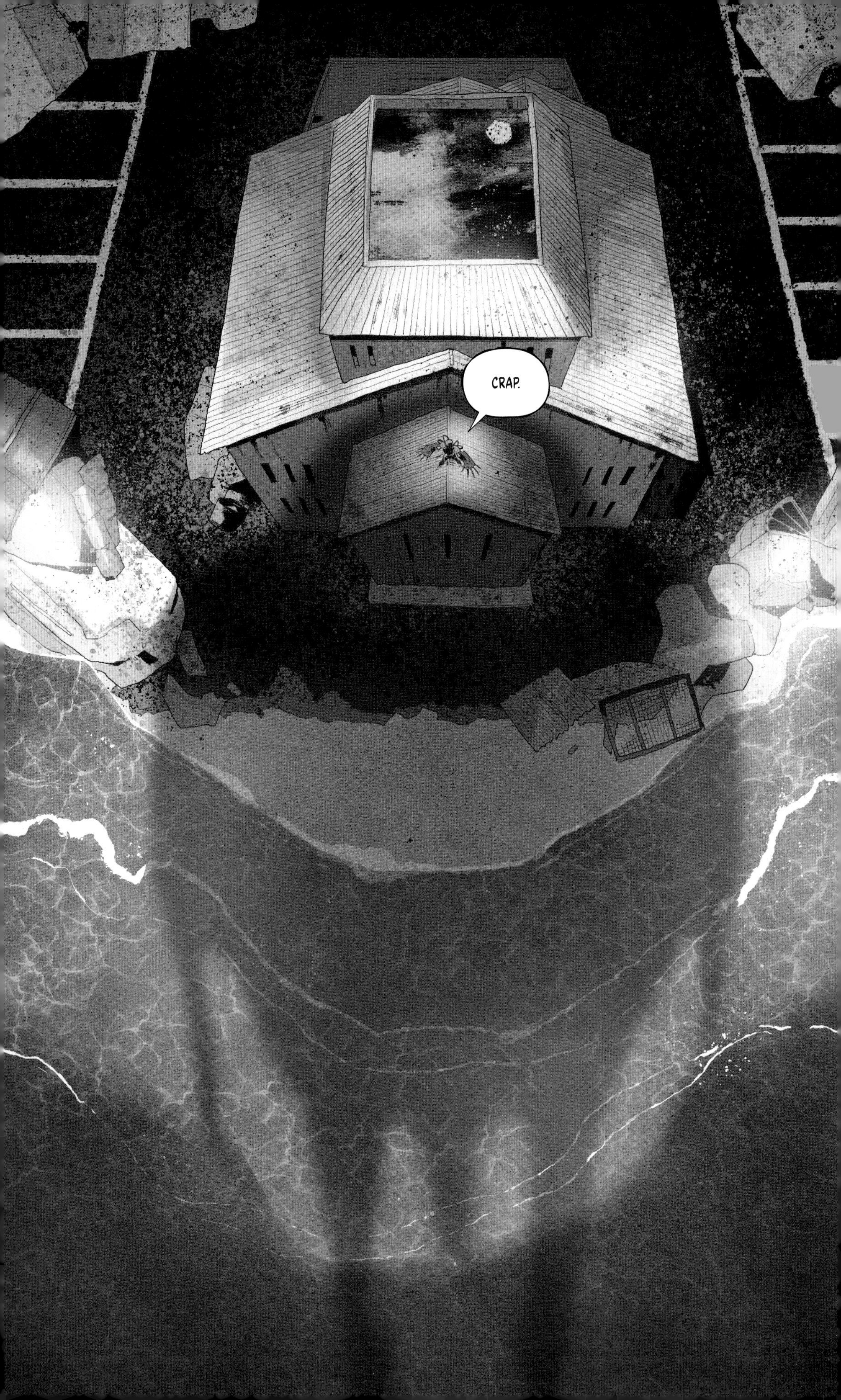
CRAP.

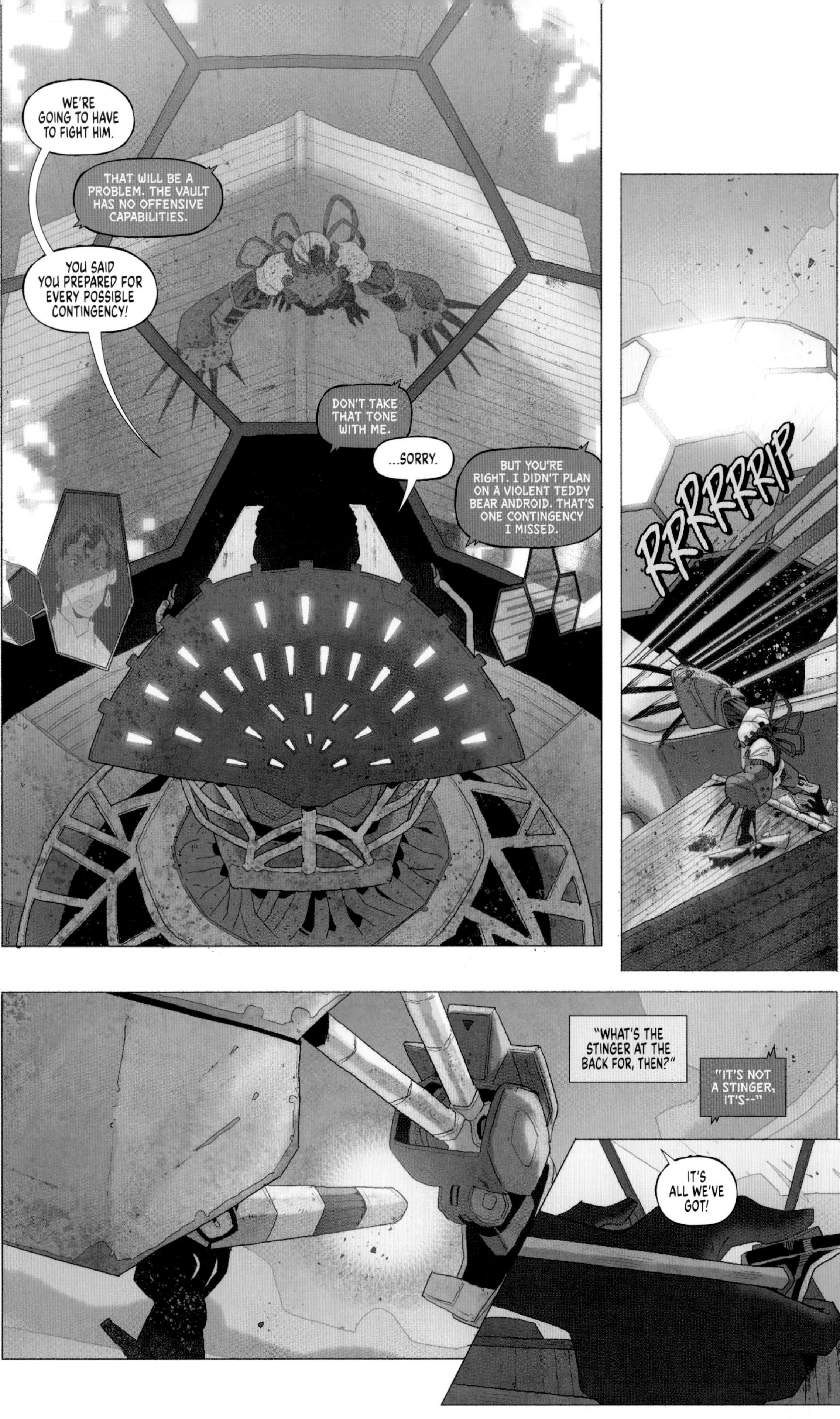
WE'RE GOING TO HAVE TO FIGHT HIM.
THAT WILL BE A PROBLEM. THE VAULT HAS NO OFFENSIVE CAPABILITIES.
YOU SAID YOU PREPARED FOR EVERY POSSIBLE CONTINGENCY!
DON'T TAKE THAT TONE WITH ME.
...SORRY.
BUT YOU'RE RIGHT. I DIDN'T PLAN ON A VIOLENT TEDDY BEAR ANDROID. THAT'S ONE CONTINGENCY I MISSED.
RRRRRRIP
"WHAT'S THE STINGER AT THE BACK FOR, THEN?"
"IT'S NOT A STINGER, IT'S--"
IT'S ALL WE'VE GOT!

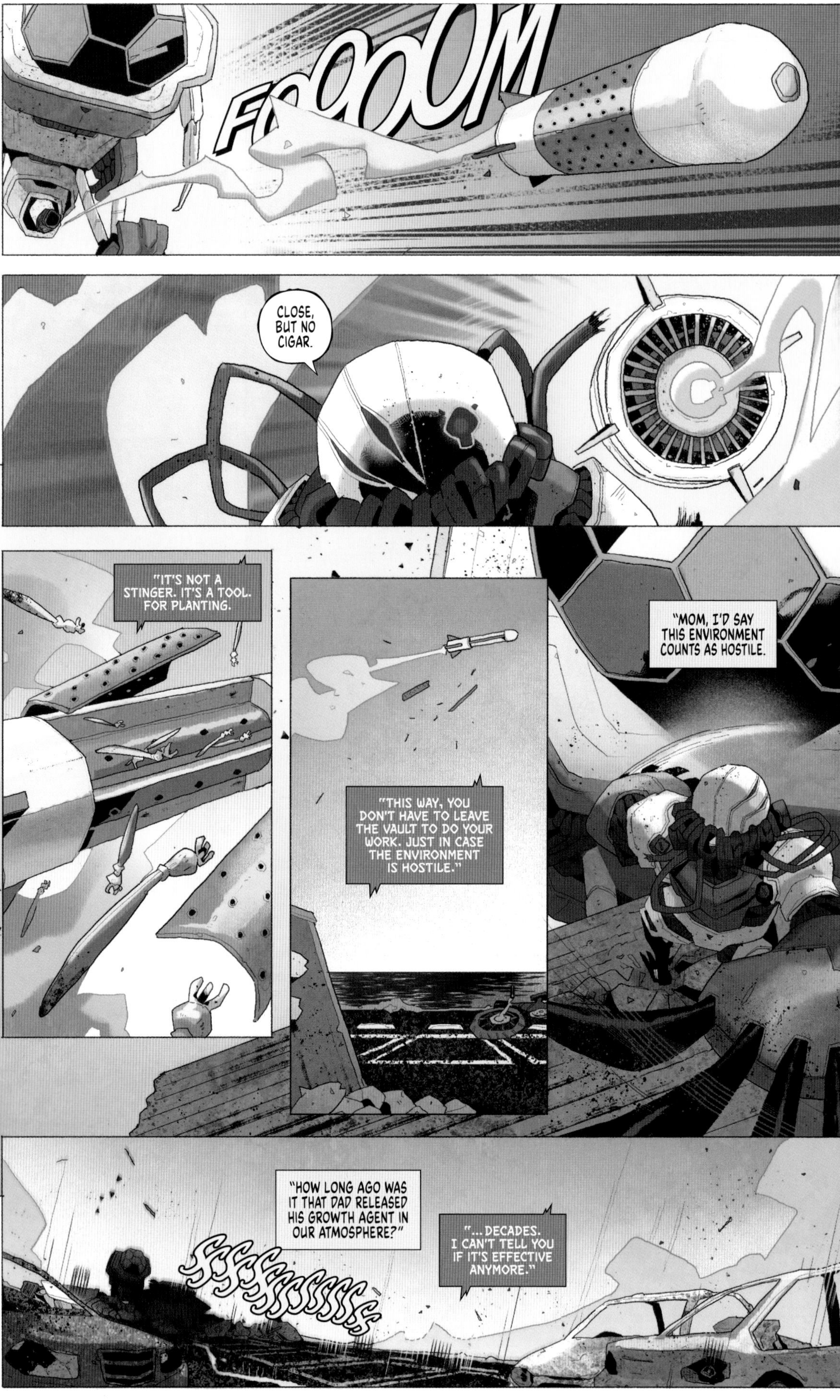
FOOOOOM
CLOSE, BUT NO CIGAR.
"IT'S NOT A STINGER. IT'S A TOOL. FOR PLANTING.
"THIS WAY, YOU DON'T HAVE TO LEAVE THE VAULT TO DO YOUR WORK. JUST IN CASE THE ENVIRONMENT IS HOSTILE."
"MOM, I'D SAY THIS ENVIRONMENT COUNTS AS HOSTILE.
"HOW LONG AGO WAS IT THAT DAD RELEASED HIS GROWTH AGENT IN OUR ATMOSPHERE?"
SSSSSSSSSSSS
"...DECADES. I CAN'T TELL YOU IF IT'S EFFECTIVE ANYMORE."

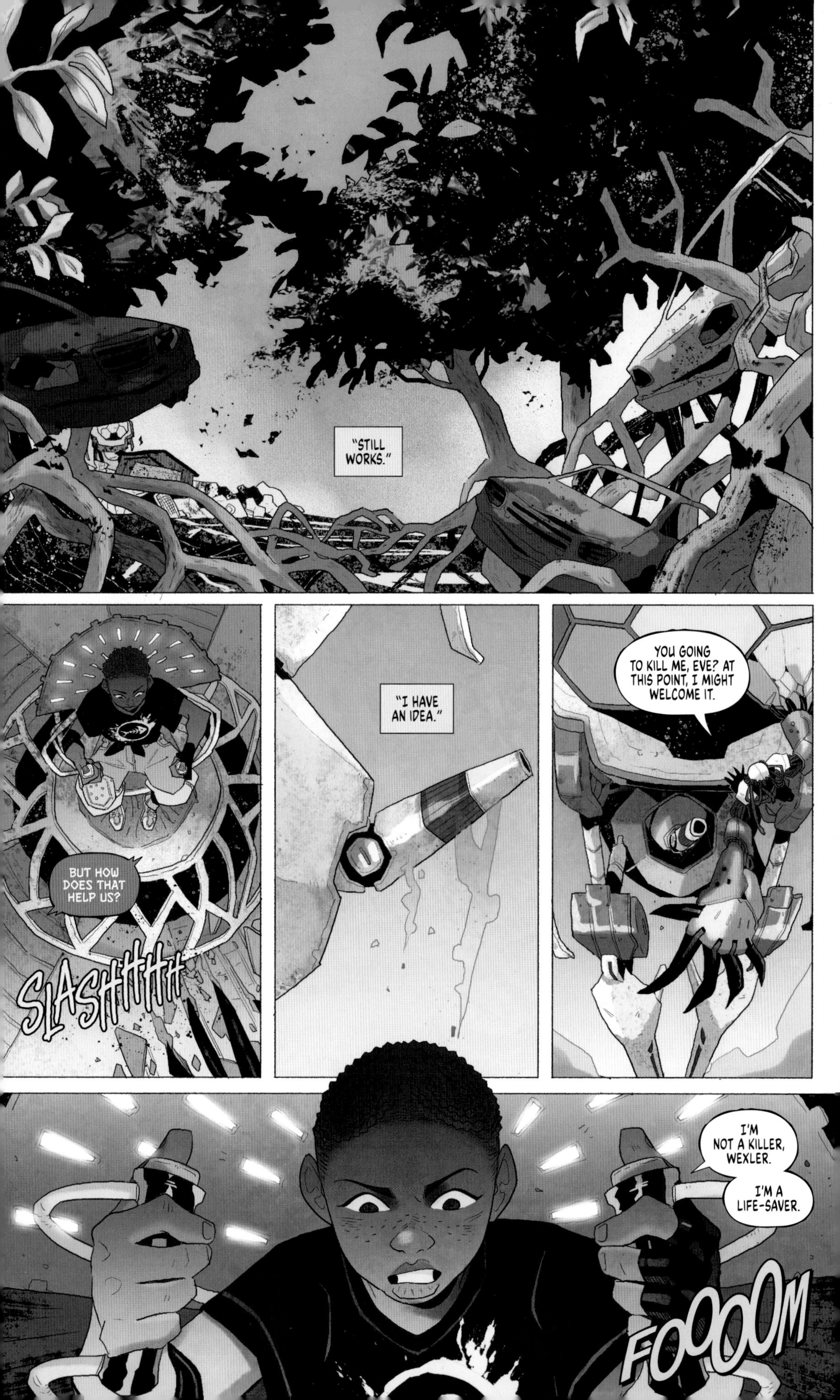
"STILL WORKS."
BUT HOW DOES THAT HELP US?
SLASHHHHH
"I HAVE AN IDEA."
YOU GOING TO KILL ME, EVE? AT THIS POINT, I MIGHT WELCOME IT.
I'M NOT A KILLER, WEXLER.
I'M A LIFE-SAVER.
FOOOOOM

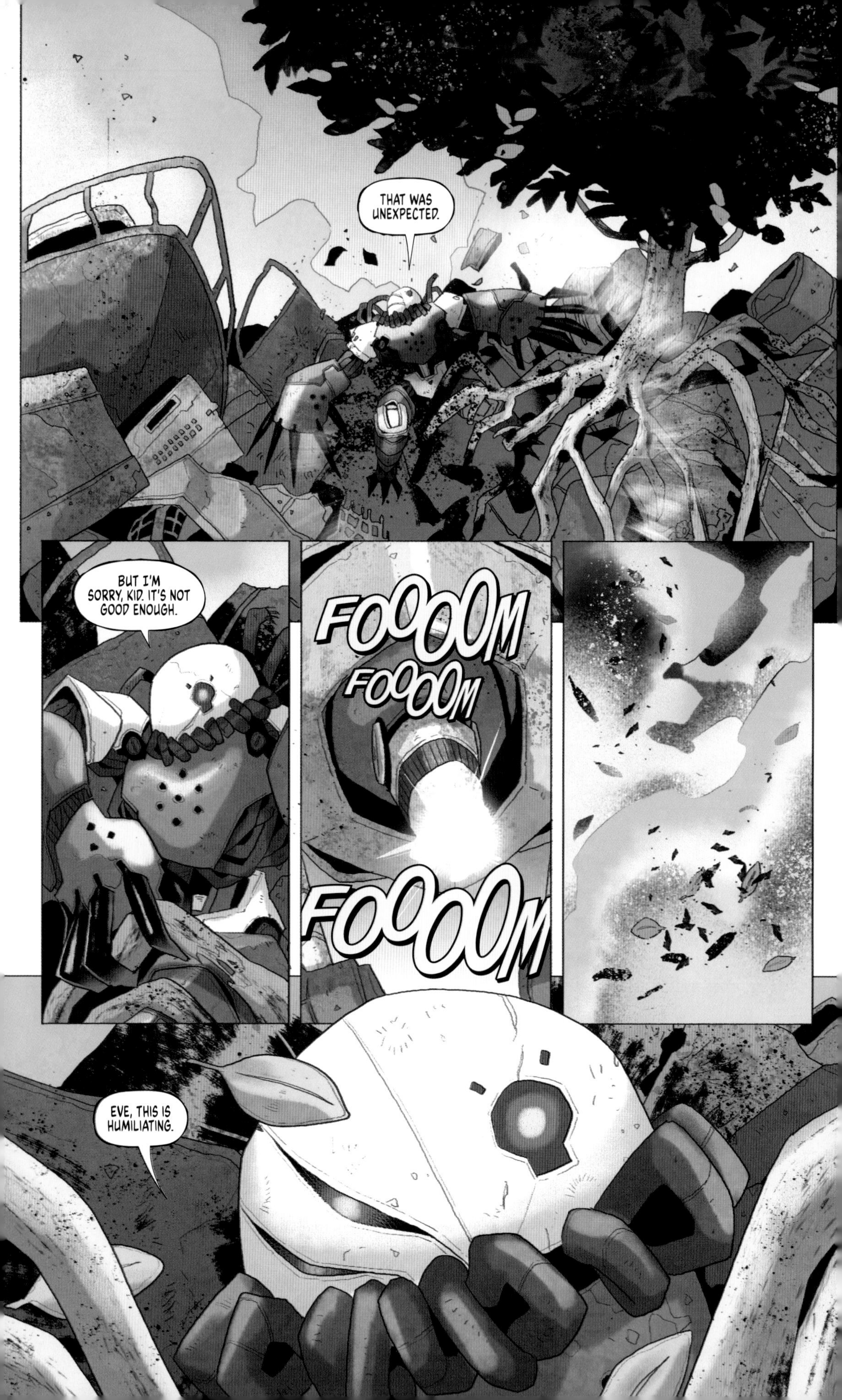
THAT WAS UNEXPECTED.
BUT I'M SORRY, KID. IT'S NOT GOOD ENOUGH.
FOOOOM
FOOOOM
FOOOOM
EVE, THIS IS HUMILIATING.

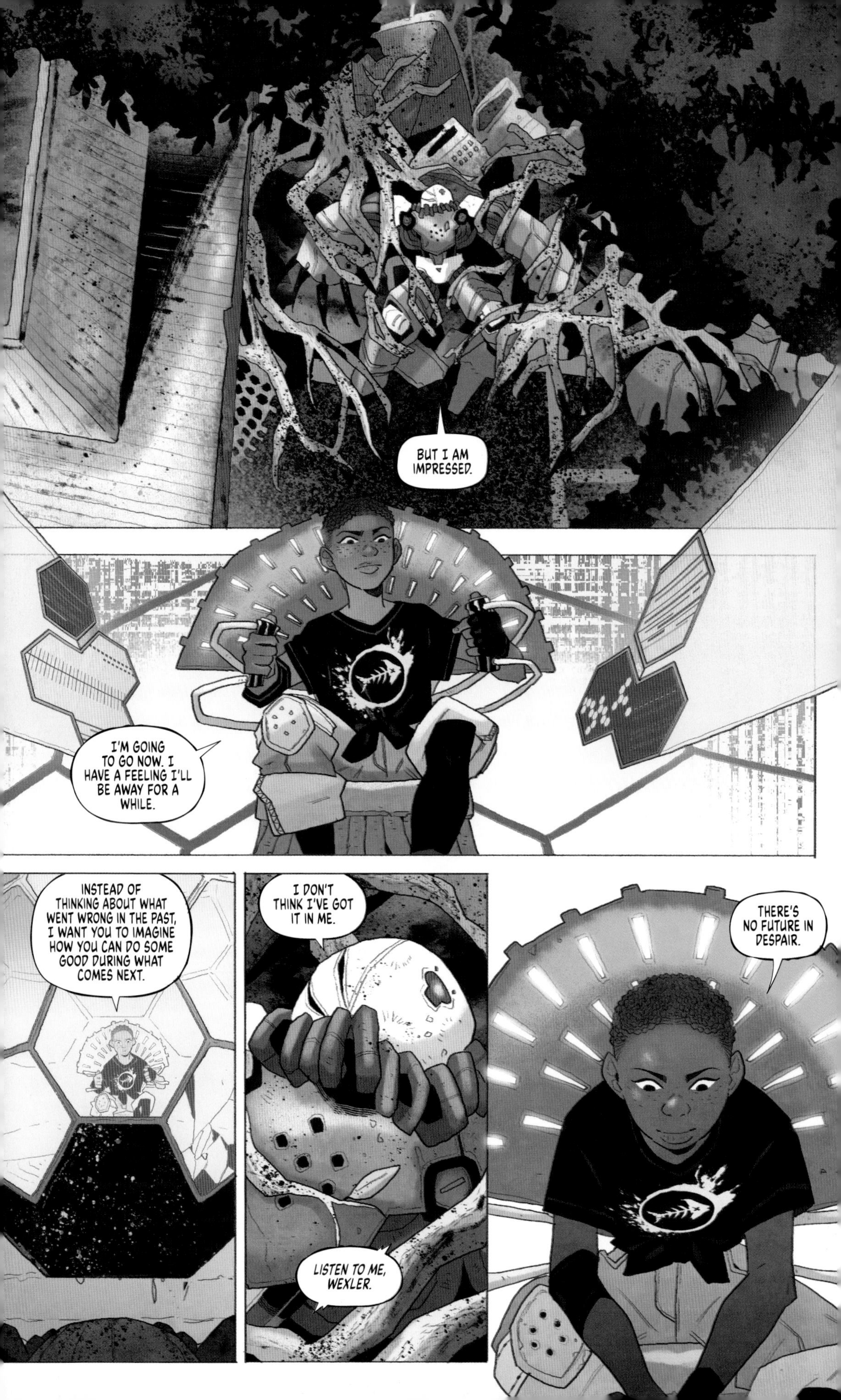

BUT I AM IMPRESSED.
I'M GOING TO GO NOW. I HAVE A FEELING I'LL BE AWAY FOR A WHILE.
INSTEAD OF THINKING ABOUT WHAT WENT WRONG IN THE PAST, I WANT YOU TO IMAGINE HOW YOU CAN DO SOME GOOD DURING WHAT COMES NEXT.
I DON'T THINK I'VE GOT IT IN ME.
LISTEN TO ME, WEXLER.
THERE'S NO FUTURE IN DESPAIR.

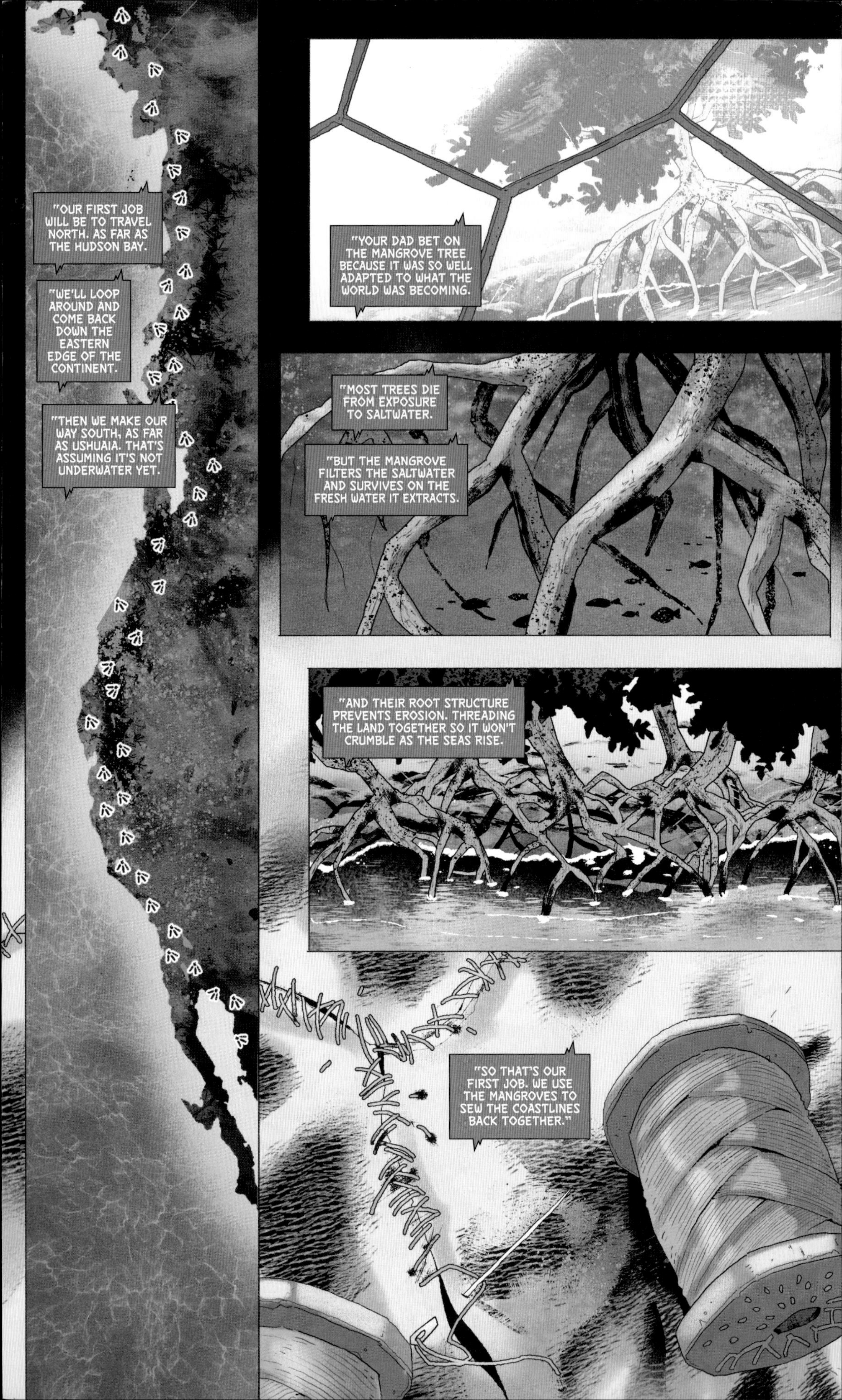
"OUR FIRST JOB WILL BE TO TRAVEL NORTH. AS FAR AS THE HUDSON BAY.
"WE'LL LOOP AROUND AND COME BACK DOWN THE EASTERN EDGE OF THE CONTINENT.
"THEN WE MAKE OUR WAY SOUTH, AS FAR AS USHUAIA. THAT'S ASSUMING IT'S NOT UNDERWATER YET.
"YOUR DAD BET ON THE MANGROVE TREE BECAUSE IT WAS SO WELL ADAPTED TO WHAT THE WORLD WAS BECOMING.
"MOST TREES DIE FROM EXPOSURE TO SALTWATER.
"BUT THE MANGROVE FILTERS THE SALTWATER AND SURVIVES ON THE FRESH WATER IT EXTRACTS.
"AND THEIR ROOT STRUCTURE PREVENTS EROSION. THREADING THE LAND TOGETHER SO IT WON'T CRUMBLE AS THE SEAS RISE.
"SO THAT'S OUR FIRST JOB. WE USE THE MANGROVES TO SEW THE COASTLINES BACK TOGETHER."

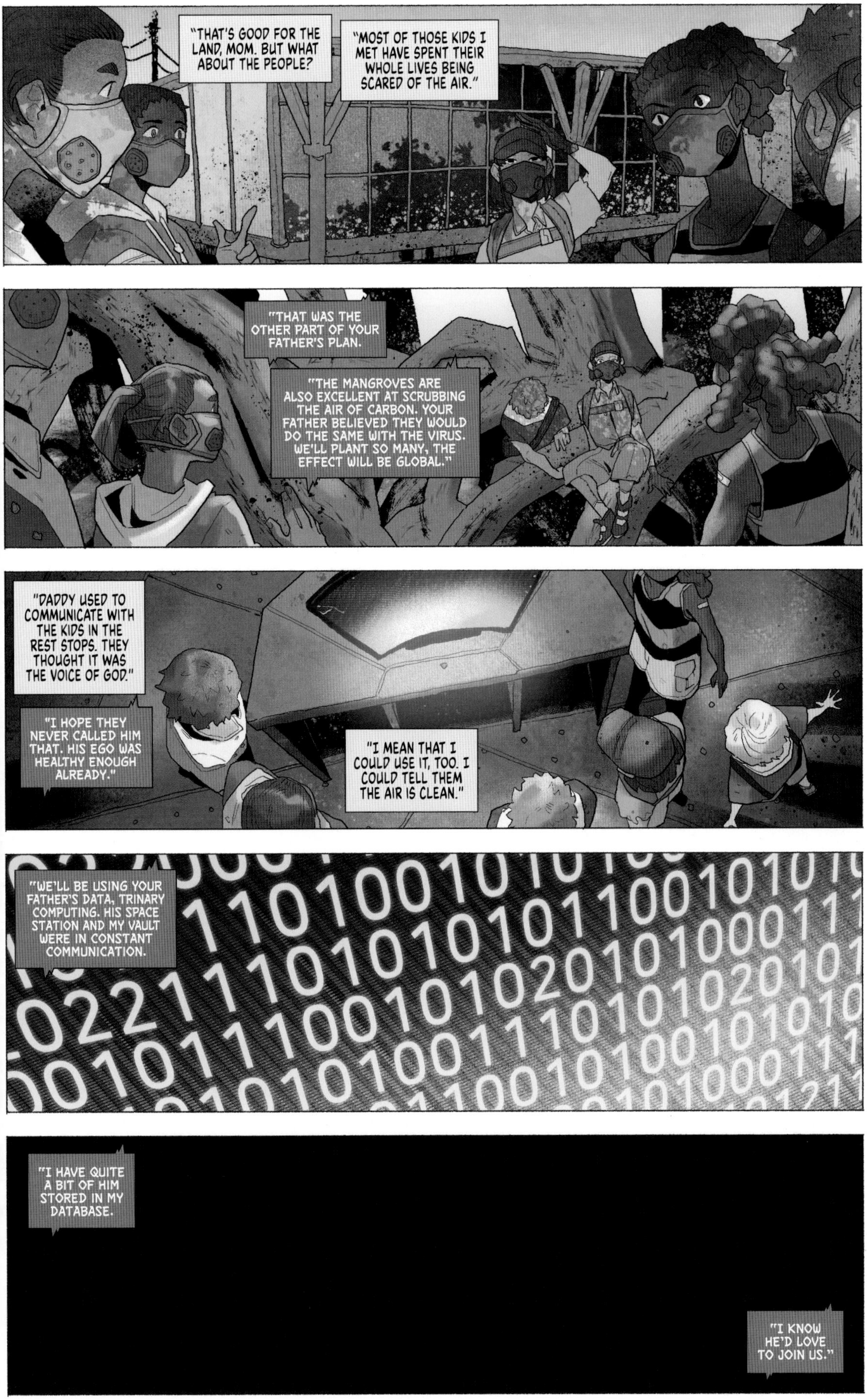
"THAT'S GOOD FOR THE LAND, MOM. BUT WHAT ABOUT THE PEOPLE?
"MOST OF THOSE KIDS I MET HAVE SPENT THEIR WHOLE LIVES BEING SCARED OF THE AIR."
"THAT WAS THE OTHER PART OF YOUR FATHER'S PLAN.
"THE MANGROVES ARE ALSO EXCELLENT AT SCRUBBING THE AIR OF CARBON. YOUR FATHER BELIEVED THEY WOULD DO THE SAME WITH THE VIRUS. WE'LL PLANT SO MANY, THE EFFECT WILL BE GLOBAL."
"DADDY USED TO COMMUNICATE WITH THE KIDS IN THE REST STOPS. THEY THOUGHT IT WAS THE VOICE OF GOD."
"I HOPE THEY NEVER CALLED HIM THAT. HIS EGO WAS HEALTHY ENOUGH ALREADY."
"I MEAN THAT I COULD USE IT, TOO. I COULD TELL THEM THE AIR IS CLEAN."
"WE'LL BE USING YOUR FATHER'S DATA, TRINARY COMPUTING. HIS SPACE STATION AND MY VAULT WERE IN CONSTANT COMMUNICATION.
"I HAVE QUITE A BIT OF HIM STORED IN MY DATABASE.
"I KNOW HE'D LOVE TO JOIN US."

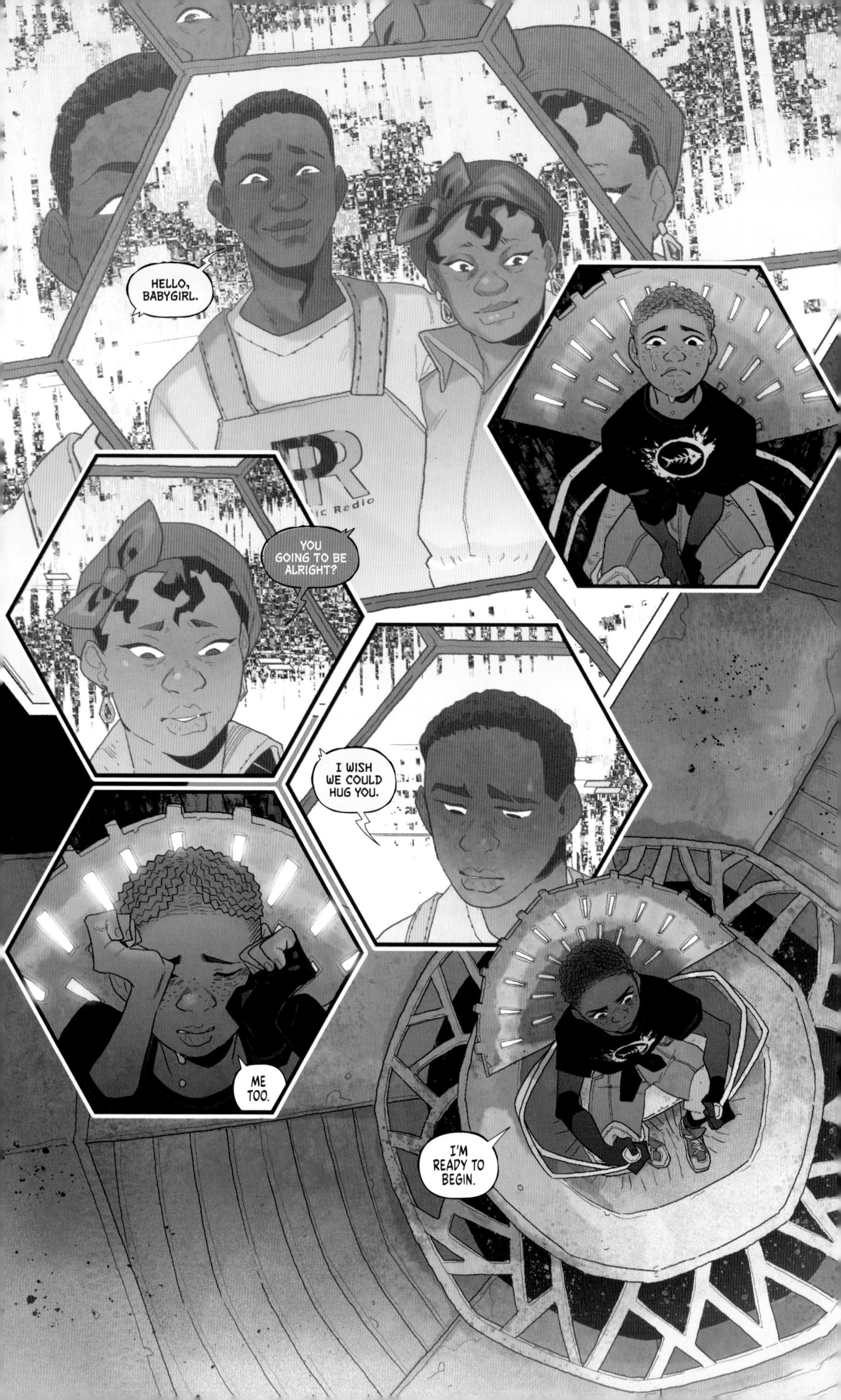
HELLO, BABYGIRL.
YOU GOING TO BE ALRIGHT?
I WISH WE COULD HUG YOU.
ME TOO.
I'M READY TO BEGIN.

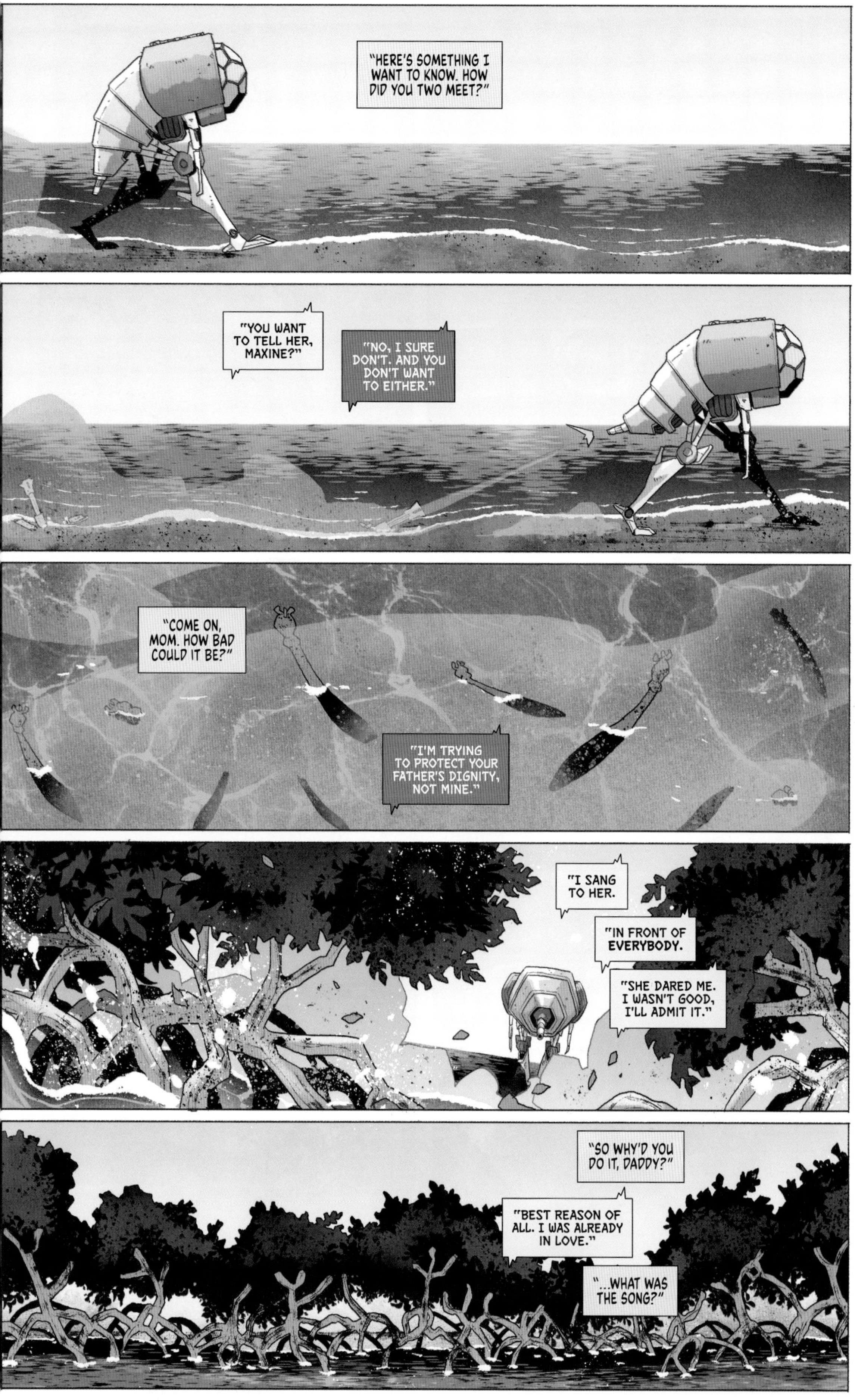
"HERE'S SOMETHING I WANT TO KNOW. HOW DID YOU TWO MEET?"
"YOU WANT TO TELL HER, MAXINE?"
"NO, I SURE DON'T. AND YOU DON'T WANT TO EITHER."
"COME ON, MOM. HOW BAD COULD IT BE?"
"I'M TRYING TO PROTECT YOUR FATHER'S DIGNITY, NOT MINE."
"I SANG TO HER.
"IN FRONT OF **EVERYBODY.**
"SHE DARED ME. I WASN'T GOOD, I'LL ADMIT IT."
"SO WHY'D YOU DO IT, DADDY?"
"BEST REASON OF ALL. I WAS ALREADY IN LOVE."
"...WHAT WAS THE SONG?"

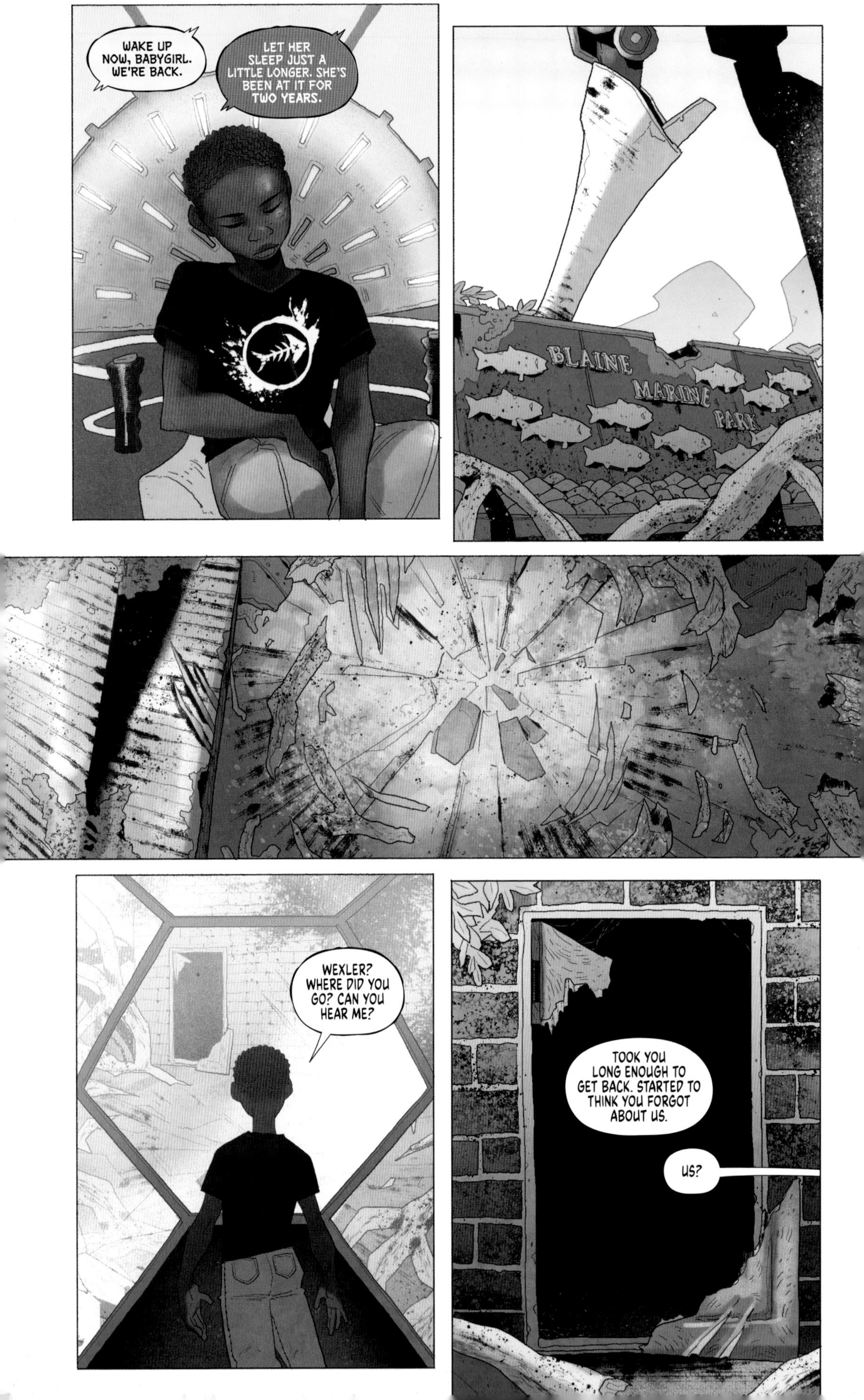
WAKE UP NOW, BABYGIRL. WE'RE BACK.
LET HER SLEEP JUST A LITTLE LONGER. SHE'S BEEN AT IT FOR TWO YEARS.
BLAINE MARINE PARK
WEXLER? WHERE DID YOU GO? CAN YOU HEAR ME?
TOOK YOU LONG ENOUGH TO GET BACK. STARTED TO THINK YOU FORGOT ABOUT US.
US?

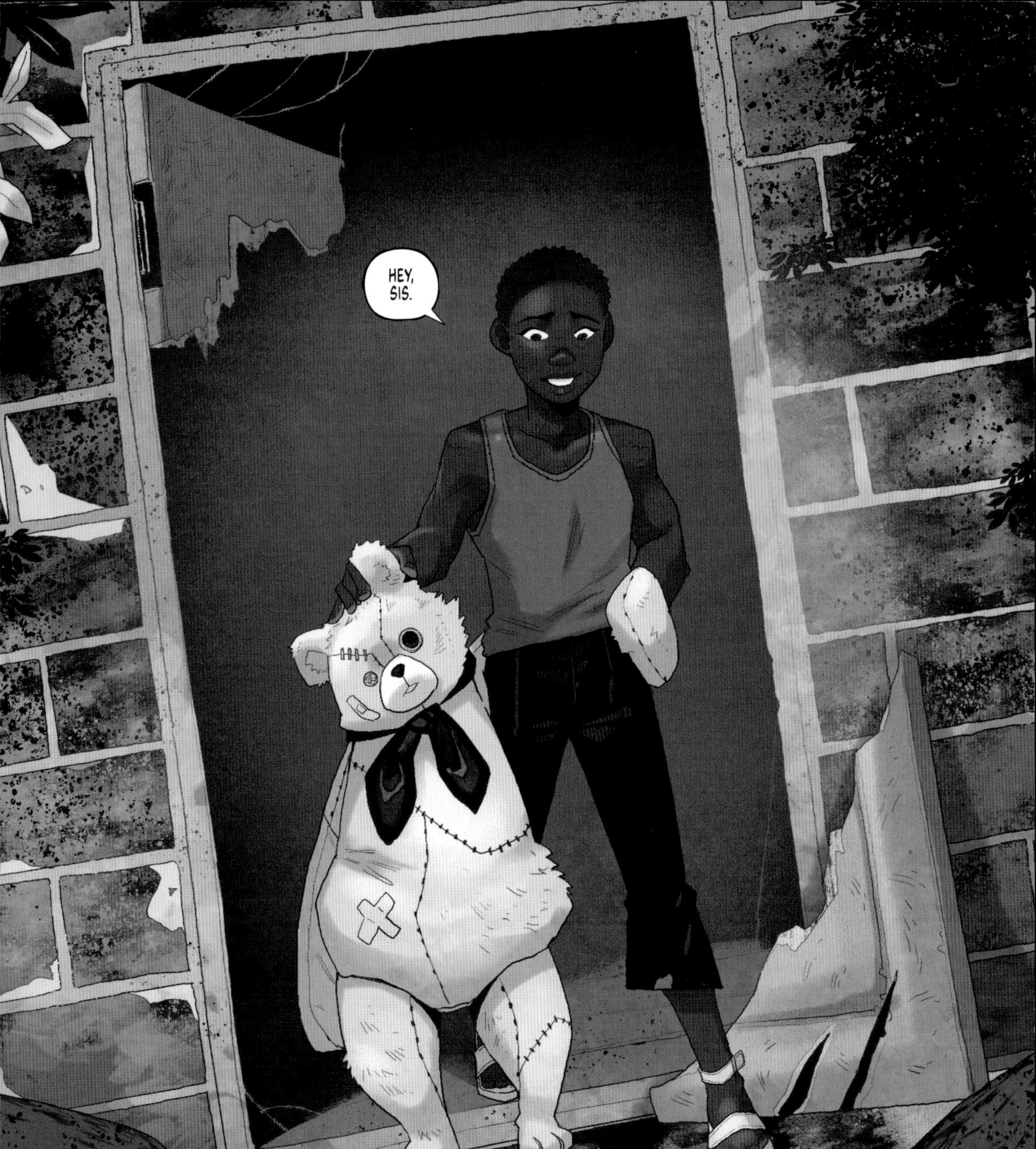
HEY, SIS.

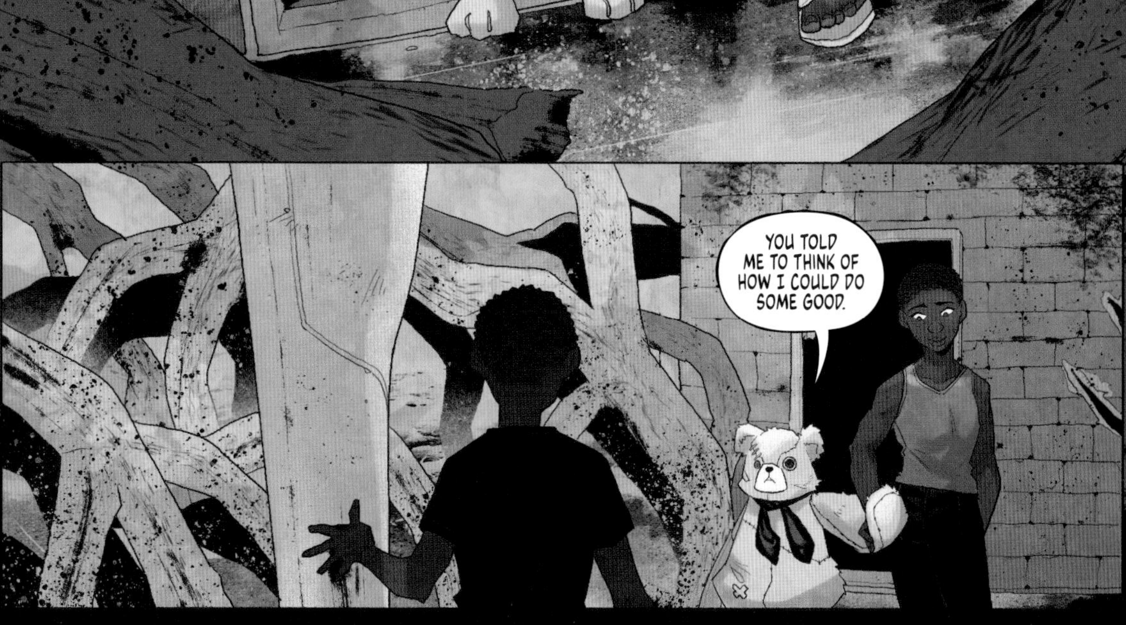
YOU TOLD ME TO THINK OF HOW I COULD DO SOME GOOD.

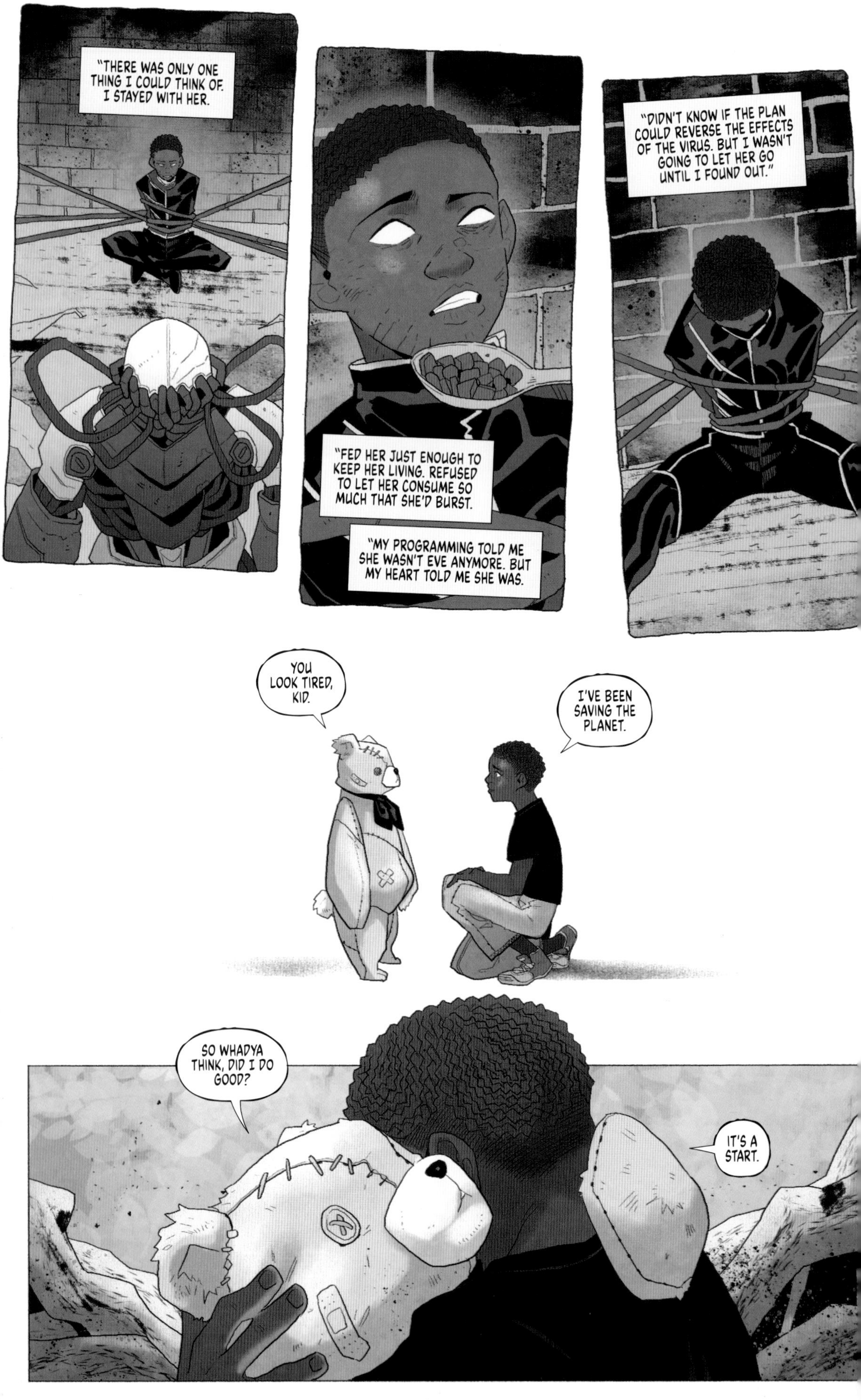
"THERE WAS ONLY ONE THING I COULD THINK OF. I STAYED WITH HER.
"FED HER JUST ENOUGH TO KEEP HER LIVING. REFUSED TO LET HER CONSUME SO MUCH THAT SHE'D BURST.
"MY PROGRAMMING TOLD ME SHE WASN'T EVE ANYMORE. BUT MY HEART TOLD ME SHE WAS.
"DIDN'T KNOW IF THE PLAN COULD REVERSE THE EFFECTS OF THE VIRUS. BUT I WASN'T GOING TO LET HER GO UNTIL I FOUND OUT."
YOU LOOK TIRED, KID.
I'VE BEEN SAVING THE PLANET.
SO WHADYA THINK, DID I DO GOOD?
IT'S A START.

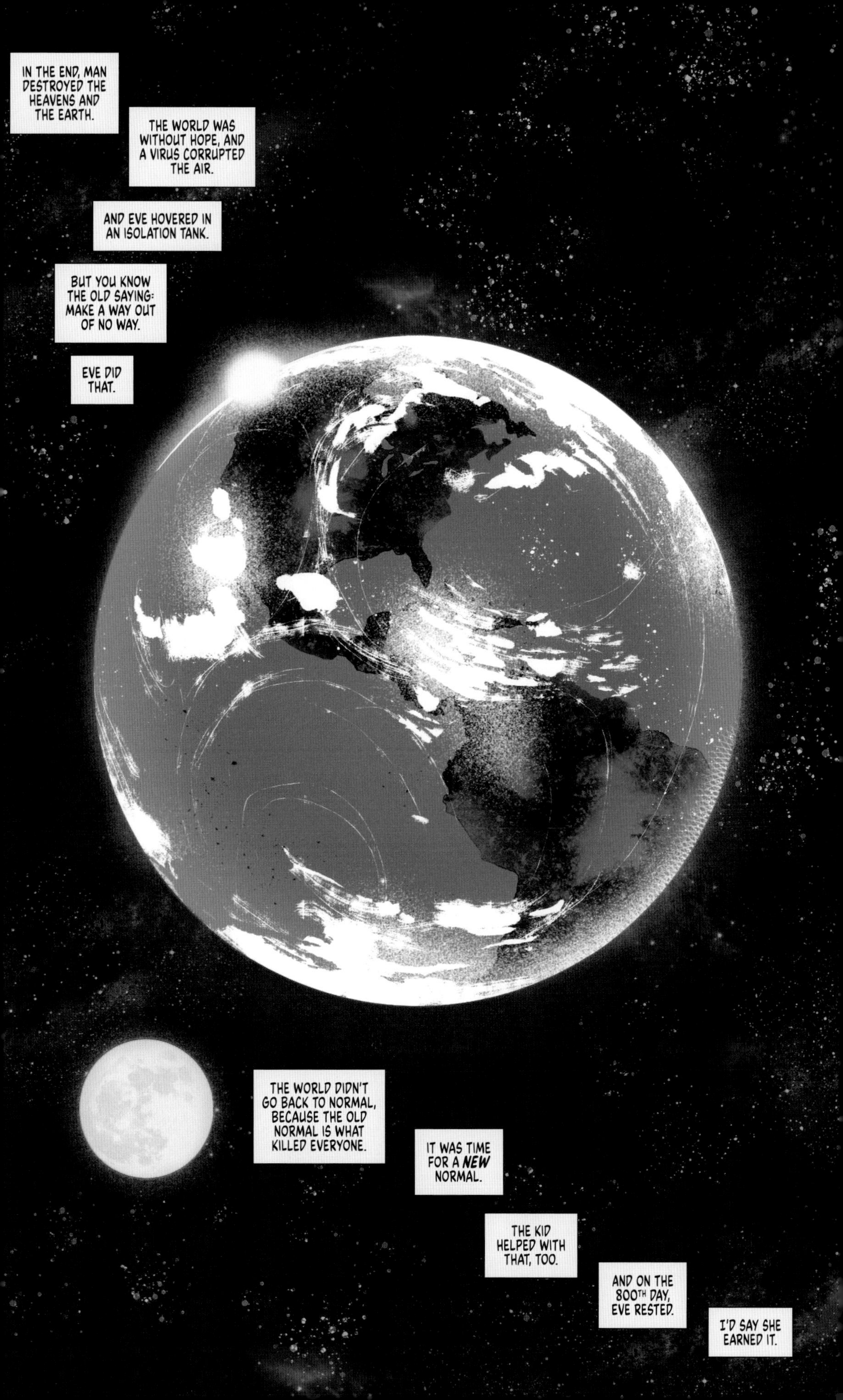
IN THE END, MAN DESTROYED THE HEAVENS AND THE EARTH.
THE WORLD WAS WITHOUT HOPE, AND A VIRUS CORRUPTED THE AIR.
AND EVE HOVERED IN AN ISOLATION TANK.
BUT YOU KNOW THE OLD SAYING: MAKE A WAY OUT OF NO WAY.
EVE DID THAT.
THE WORLD DIDN'T GO BACK TO NORMAL, BECAUSE THE OLD NORMAL IS WHAT KILLED EVERYONE.
IT WAS TIME FOR A ***NEW*** NORMAL.
THE KID HELPED WITH THAT, TOO.
AND ON THE 800TH DAY, EVE RESTED.
I'D SAY SHE EARNED IT.

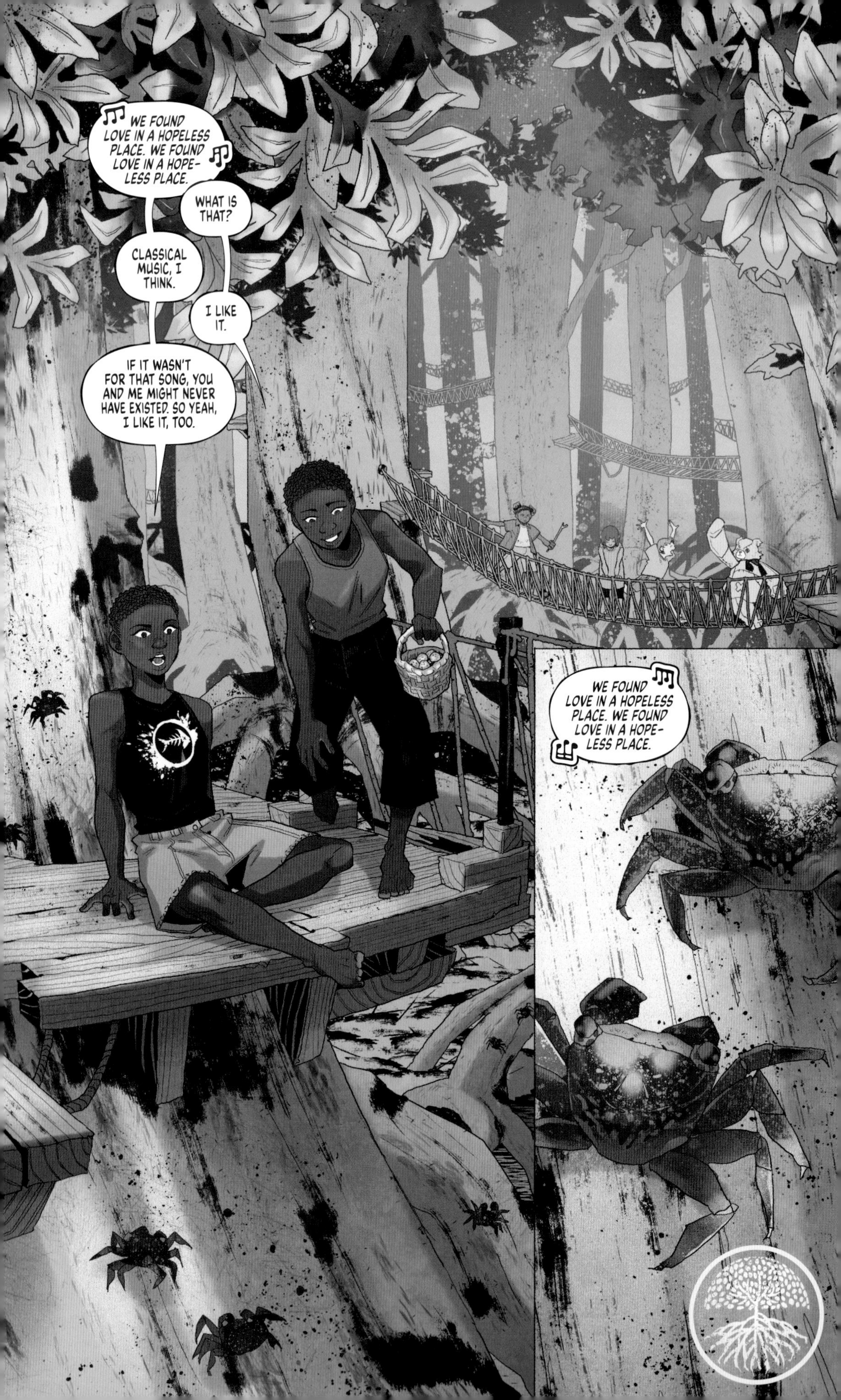
WE FOUND LOVE IN A HOPELESS PLACE. WE FOUND LOVE IN A HOPE-LESS PLACE.
WHAT IS THAT?
CLASSICAL MUSIC, I THINK.
I LIKE IT.
IF IT WASN'T FOR THAT SONG, YOU AND ME MIGHT NEVER HAVE EXISTED. SO YEAH, I LIKE IT, TOO.
WE FOUND LOVE IN A HOPELESS PLACE. WE FOUND LOVE IN A HOPE-LESS PLACE.

I have been trying to get our kids into *Battle of the Planets* for a couple years now. Do you remember that cartoon? (Presuming you were alive.) It was originally called *Science Ninja Team Gatchaman* back in Japan, where it was created. It's about five white teenagers--four boys and one girl--who protect Earth from alien invasions. It was beautifully animated and there were cool vehicles like their primary ship, the Phoenix, which could transform into a fiery phoenix when needed. It's my favorite childhood show. And my kids couldn't give a damn about it. I have tried, but eventually I had to accept that my children were born with awful taste. (It's possible I'm still tender about this issue.)

What meant the most to me, in retrospect, is the fact that all five heroes were kids. There were other cartoons I liked--*Spider-Man, Johnny Quest, Scooby-Doo* and more--but *Battle of the Planets* gave me the biggest thrill. The team fought in space, under the sea, in the air and on land, and the fates of every human life hung in the balance. Oh yes, sign me up please.

In 2017 I created a comic with BOOM! Studios called *Destroyer*. The phenomenal Dietrich Smith was the artist and my co-creator. It's a continuation of Mary Shelley's *Frankenstein*, but wrestling with the issue of police brutality in the modern day. I wrote it because I felt a desire to tackle a political issue that felt current and also, sadly, timeless. A chance to examine structural racism and its corrosive effects on a family. I'm proud of what we accomplished. The graphic novel is taught in colleges and high schools. You should check it out. It's a beast.

When I started dreaming up *Eve*, I again wanted to wrestle with a political--and existential--threat to human life: the climate crisis. I remembered *Battle of the Planets*, those kids fighting to save us all. I wanted to offer that same thrill to readers, and I wanted a girl like Eve to be at its center. Growing up, I'd never seen such a thing.

I want there to be stories about Black characters fighting racism, obviously, since I wrote one. But I don't want Black characters to take center stage only to tackle prejudice. That would suggest the only problem Black folks face, or care about, is racism. It's part of our experience but it damn sure isn't all of it. Sometimes we're just dealing with the hassles of a house with plumbing problems, or having children who won't buy in to our TV show nostalgia farts. Or living on a planet that's being abused by the dominant species.

As a child, I saw myself in Mark, Jason, Princess, Keyop, and Tiny. Those kids saved the planet more times than I can count. I'm geeked that so many of you came on this journey with Eve. In our comic, this bright, funny, brave girl saved the world. In real life, we've got much more work to do.

VICTOR LaVALLE
Bronx, NY; July 16, 2021

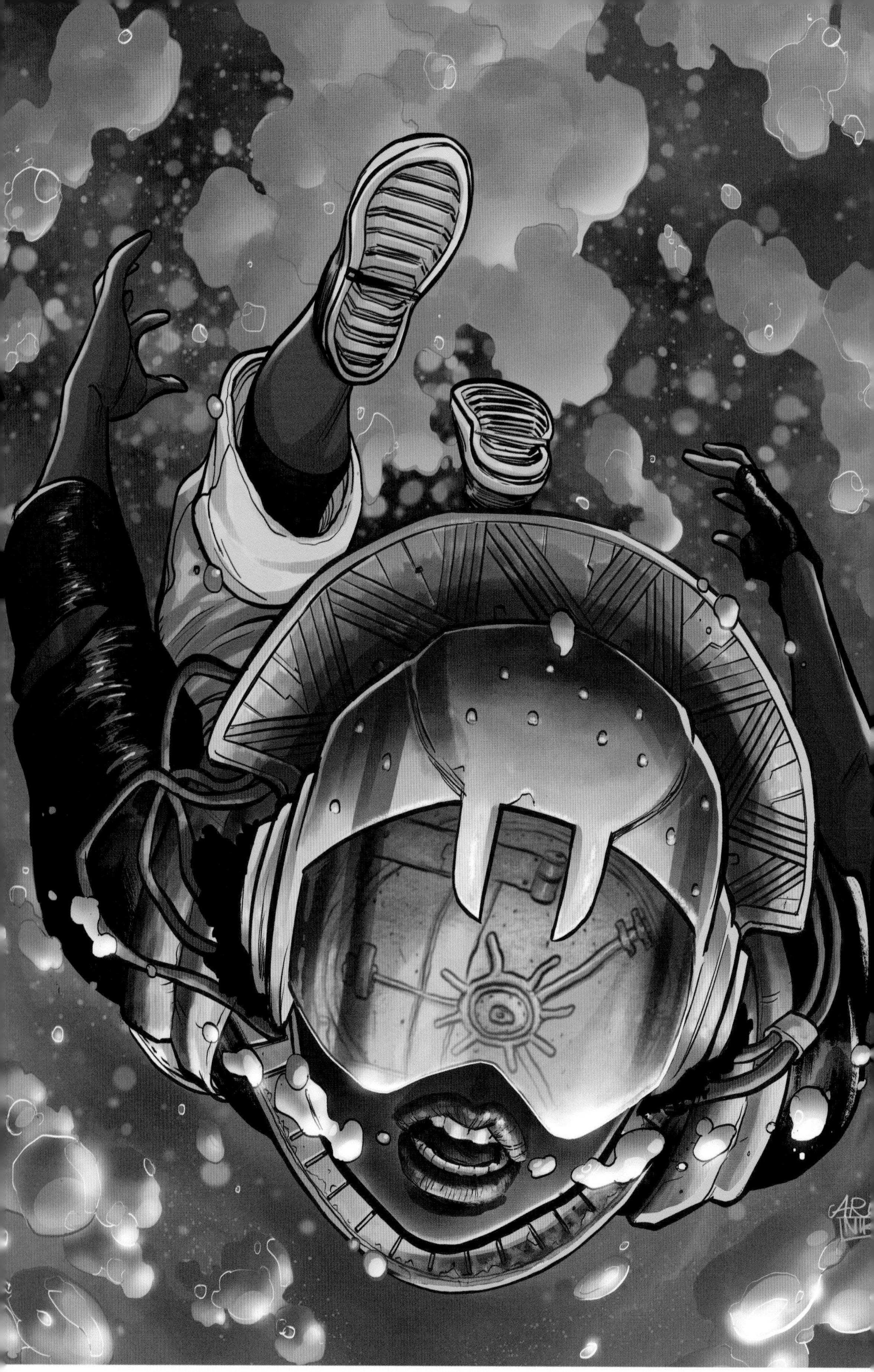

ISSUE #5 COVER BY **ARIO ANINDITO** WITH COLORS BY **NICOLA RIGHI**

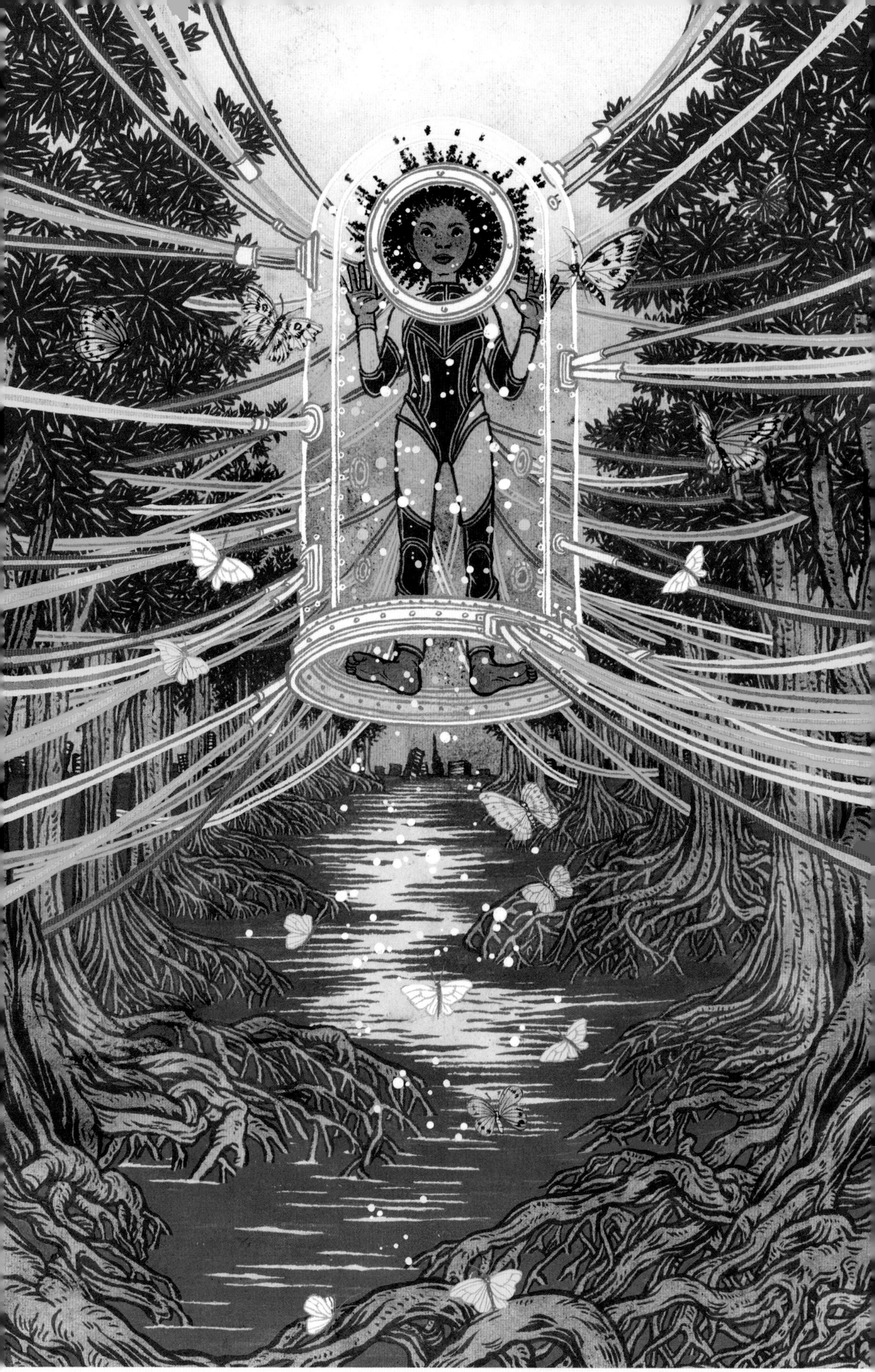

ISSUE #1 COVER BY **YUKO SHIMIZU**

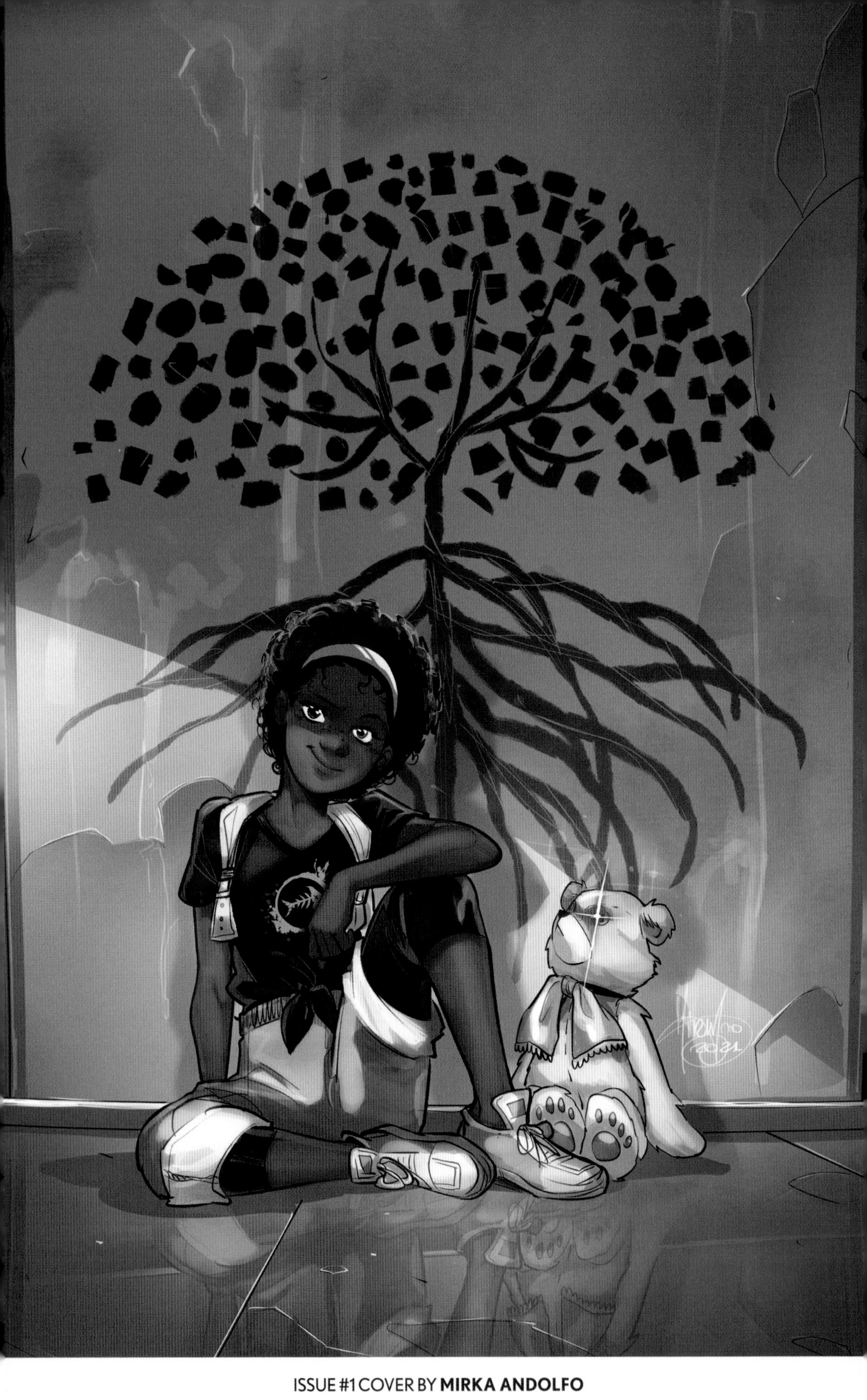

ISSUE #1 COVER BY **MIRKA ANDOLFO**

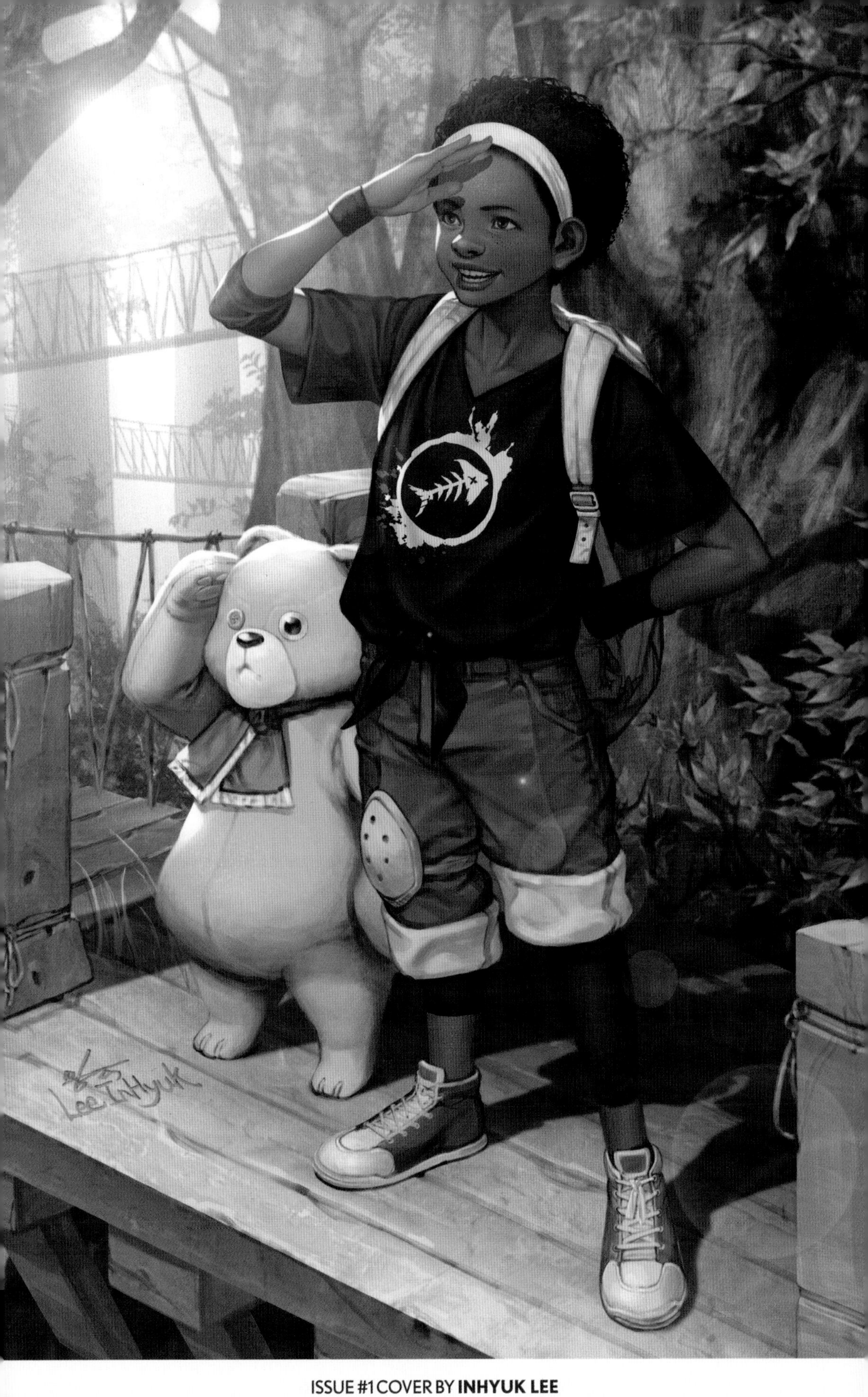
Lee InHyuk

ISSUE #1 COVER BY **INHYUK LEE**

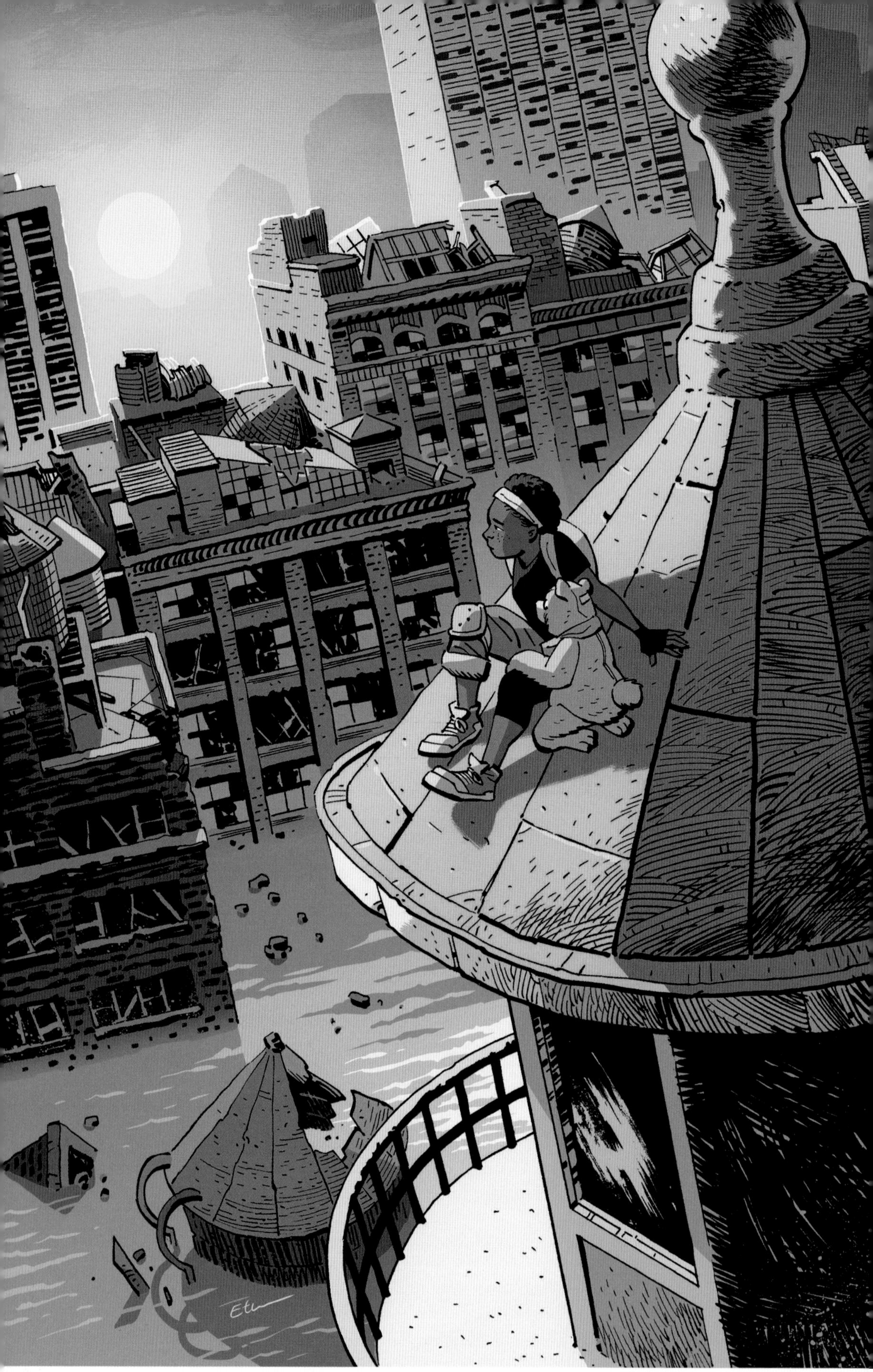

ISSUE #2 COVER BY **ETHAN YOUNG**

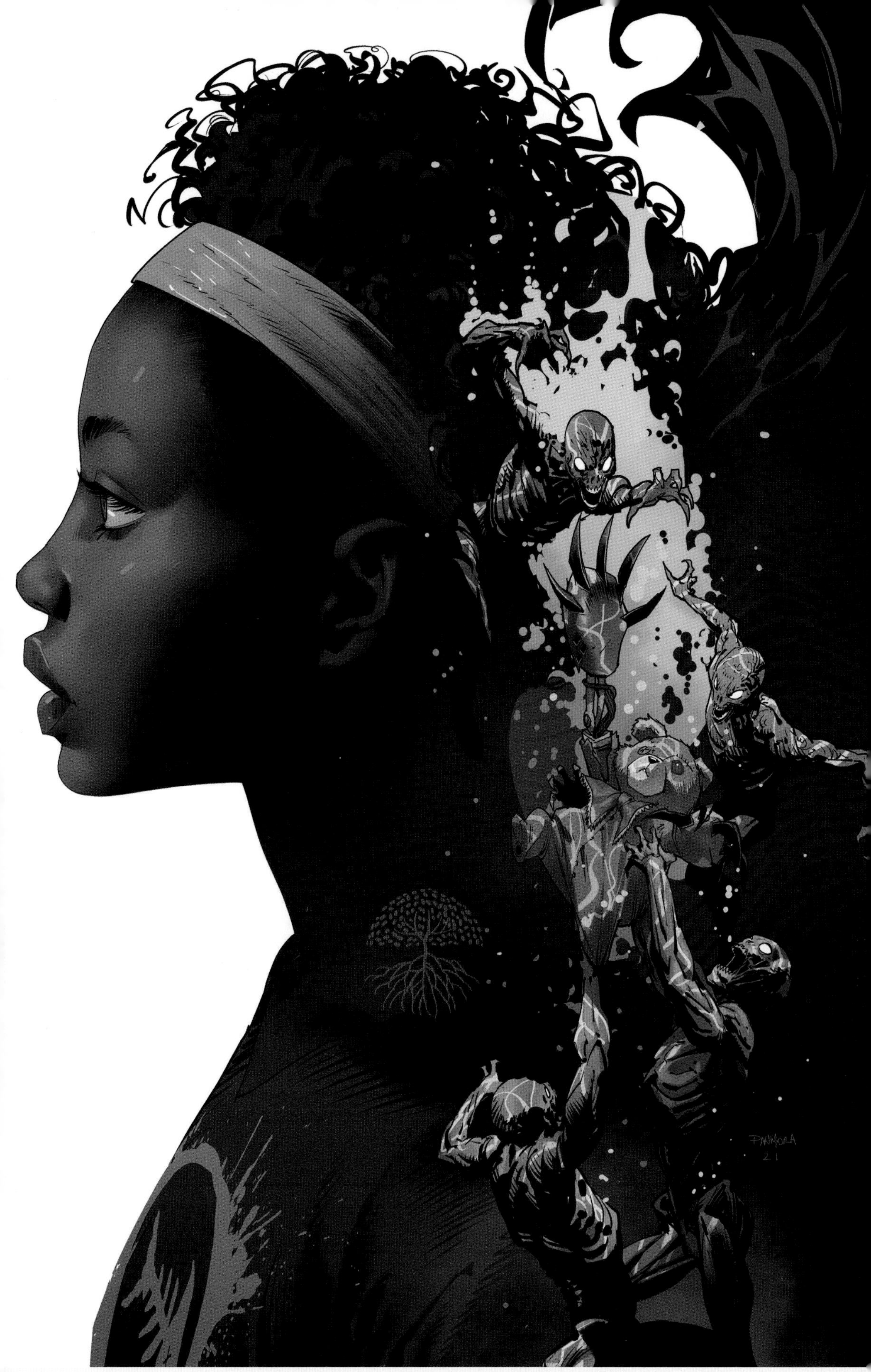
DAN MORA
21

ISSUE #2 COVER BY **DAN MORA**

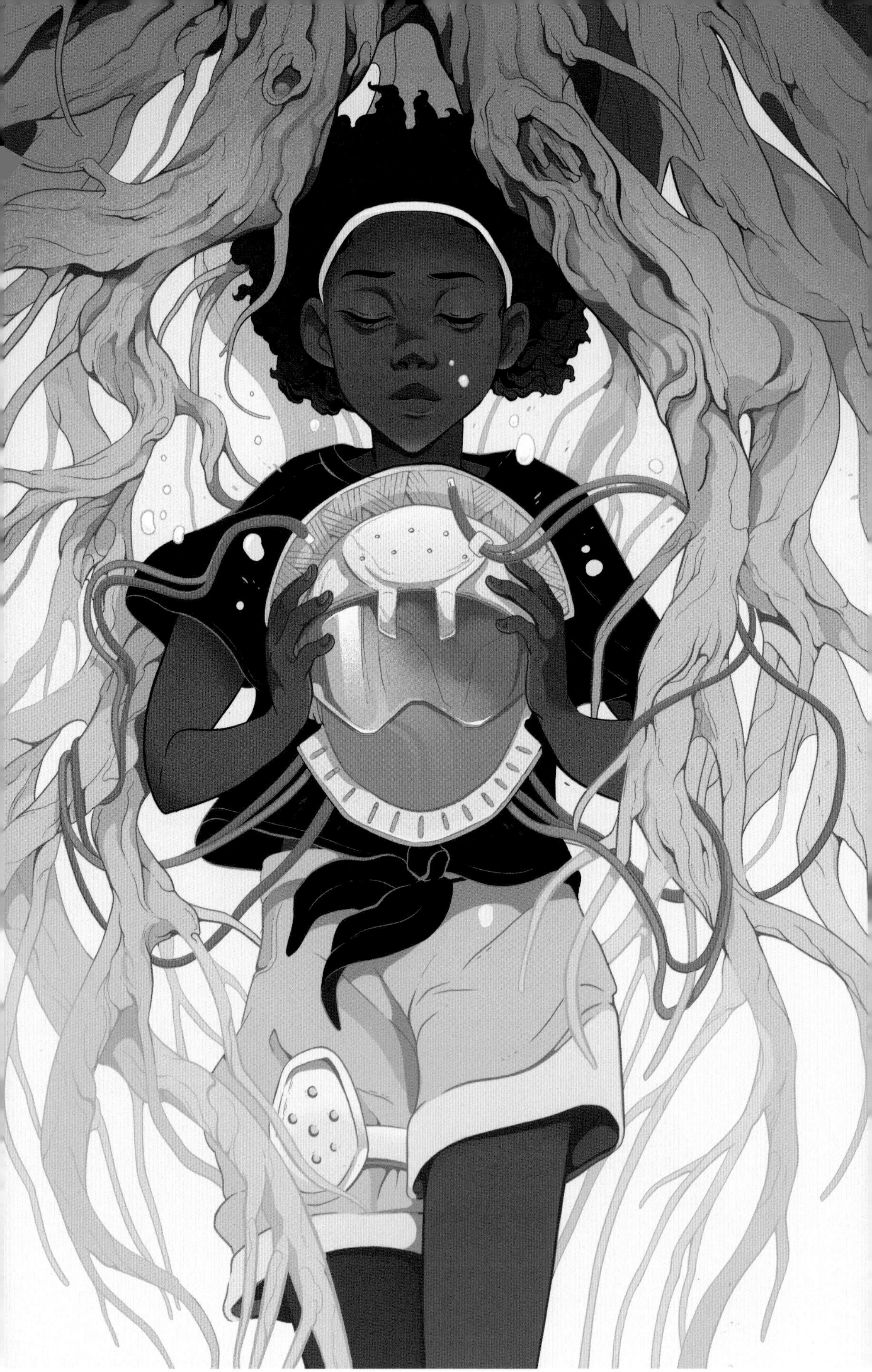

ISSUE #3 COVER BY **DANI PENDERGAST**

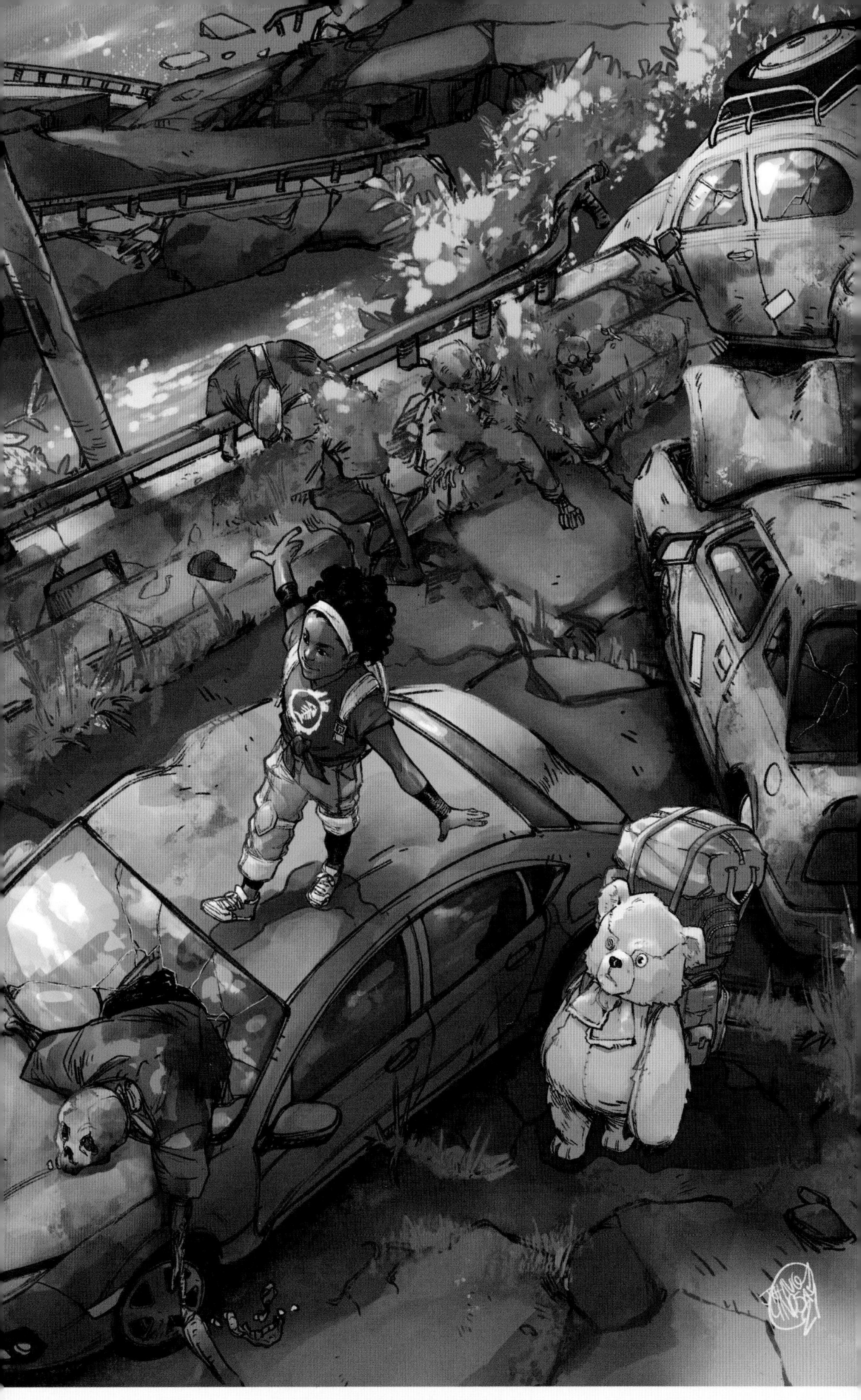

ISSUE #3 COVER BY **JAHNOY LINDSAY**

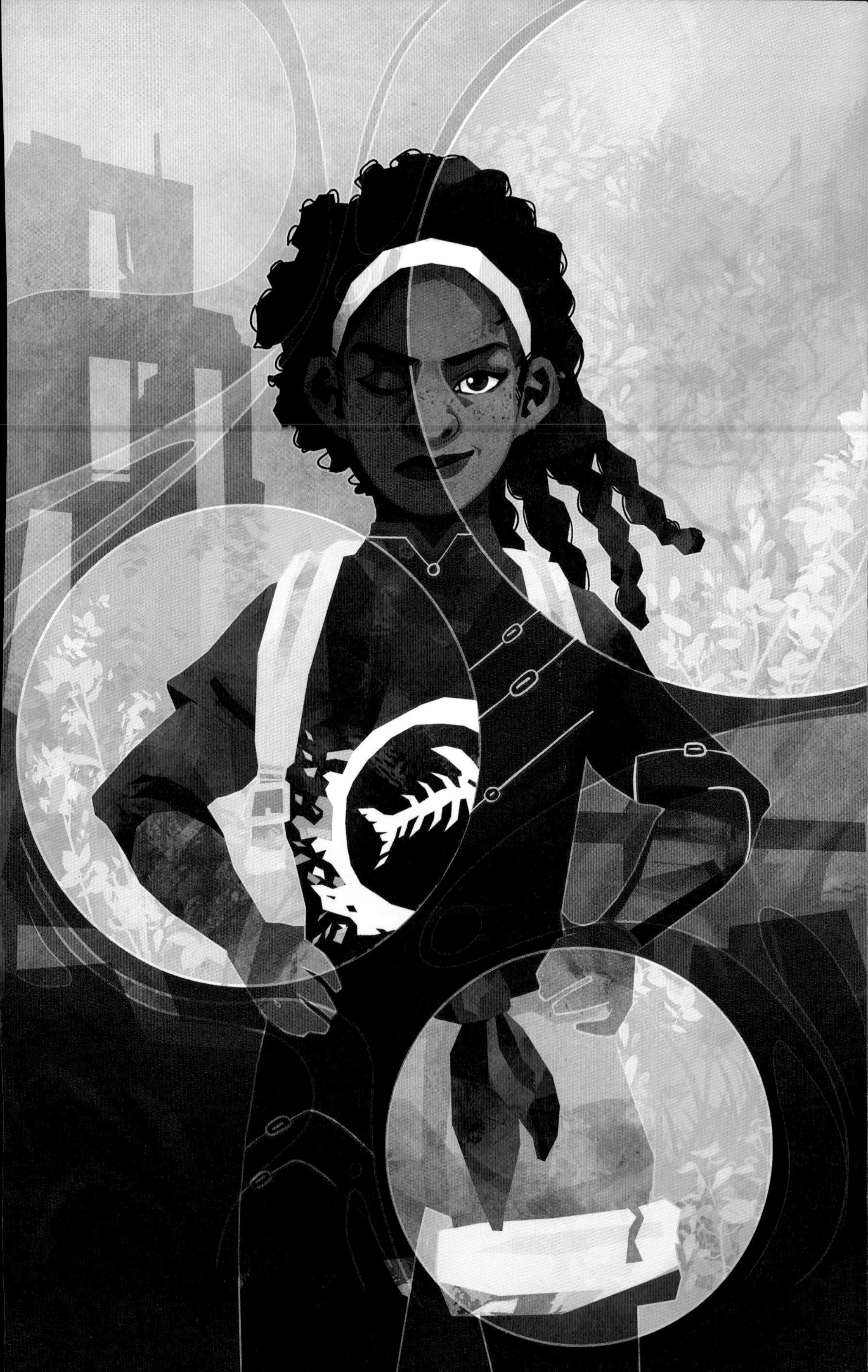

ISSUE #4 COVER BY **MICAELA DAWN**

VICTOR LaVALLE

Victor LaValle is the author of seven works of fiction including *The Ballad of Black Tom*, which was a finalist for a Nebula Award, a Hugo Award, a Bram Stoker Award, and the Theodore Sturgeon Award. His latest novel, *The Changeling*, was released in June 2017. His other books have won the American Book Award, the Shirley Jackson Award, a Guggenheim Fellowship, and the Key to Southeast Queens. LaValle is also the writer of the acclaimed comic book series *Victor LaValle's Destroyer* with BOOM! Studios. He teaches at Columbia University and lives in New York City with his wife and kids.

JO MI-GYEONG

Jo Mi-Gyeong is a comic artist and illustrator based out of Seoul, Korea, best known for her work on *Jim Henson's The Dark Crystal: Age of Resistance* for BOOM! Studios and the original comic book series *Beastlands*.

BRITTANY PEER

Brittany Peer is a colorist based in Oklahoma who loves to bring whimsey and passion to everything she does.

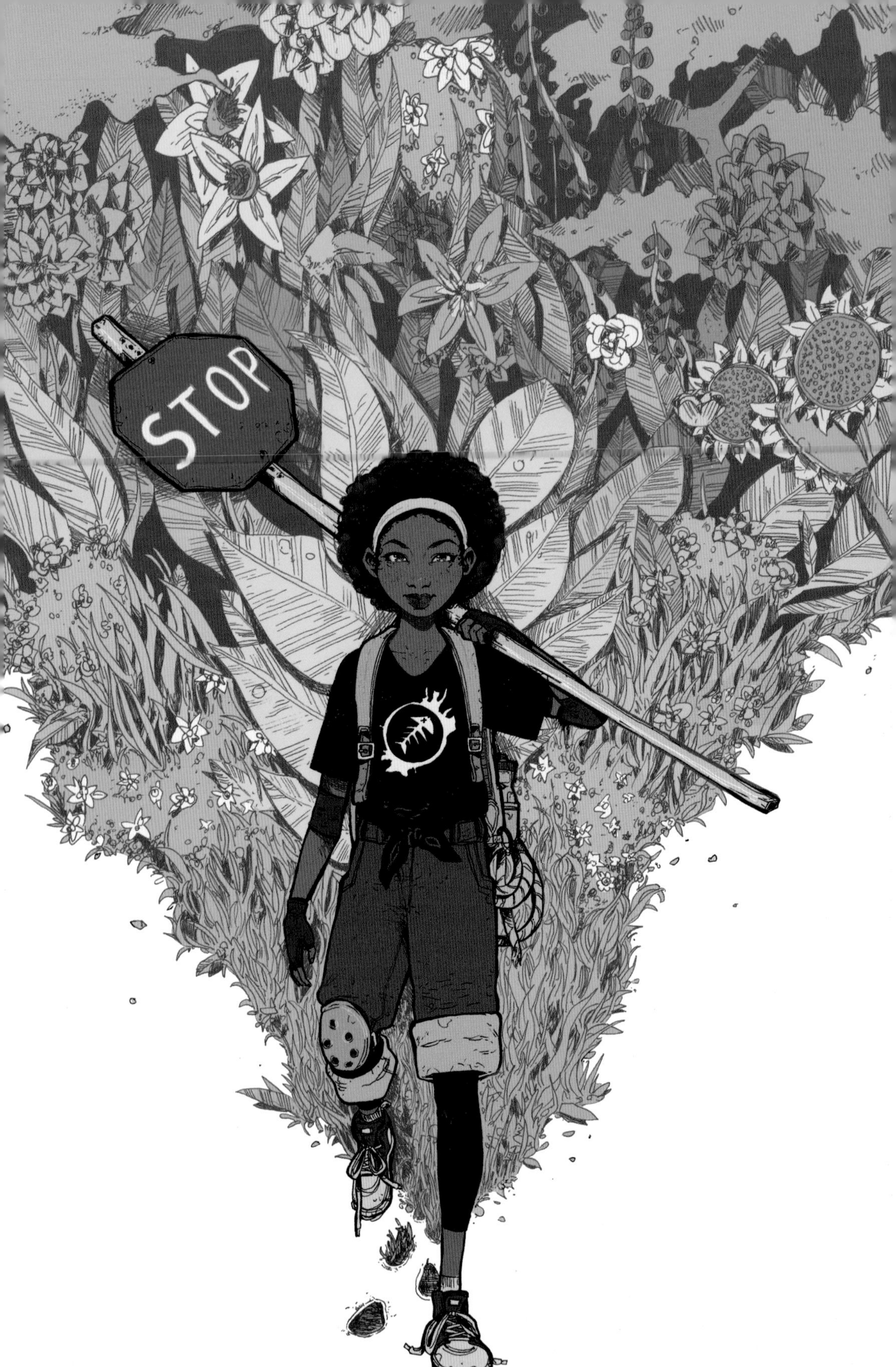
STOP

ISSUE #5 COVER BY **ZOE THOROGOOD**